THE NEW SINGING THEATRE
A Charter for the Music Theatre Movement

THE NEW SINGING THEATRE

A Charter for the Music Theatre Movement

Michael Bawtree

OXFORD UNIVERSITY PRESS

New York

THE BRISTOL PRESS

Bristol

Decorative line drawings by Susan Benson

Library of Congress Cataloguing-in-Publication Data

Bawtree. Michael.
  The new singing theatre: a charter for the music theatre
movement / Michael Bawtree.
  p. cm.
  Includes bibliographical references and index.
  ISBN 0-19-385867-3 (OUP). — ISBN 1-85399-097-3 (Bristol)
  1. Musical theater. I. Title.
ML1700.B24 1991
782.1'4–dc20   90-49620

© 1991 by Michael Bawtree

First published in 1991 by:

Oxford University Press
200 Madison Avenue
New York
NY 10016
USA

The Bristol Press
226 North Street
Bedminster
Bristol BS3 1JD
England

*The Bristol Press is an imprint of
Bristol Classical Press*

*Oxford is a registered trademark of
Oxford University Press*

Printed and bound in Great Britain by
Billing & Sons Ltd, Worcester

CONTENTS

To my colleagues on the Music Theatre Committee of the
International Theatre Institute this book is dedicated

'Perhaps our Music Theatre Committee cannot point to
any great achievements. But I tell you one thing: without
our Committee would be wars.'
Aleksandr Bardini

PREFACE

The refrain of this book is that the medium of singing theatre offers rich opportunities to contemporary artists seeking fresh ways to exercise their art and craft, and to express themselves, their ideas and their imaginings. These opportunities are not obvious, because the kind of singing theatre generally available to us makes scant use of them. We shall see what can bring about a change.

It hardly needs pointing out that a theatre in which people sing, move (dance) and enact roles is not the special preserve of European culture: in almost all other cultures, the only kind of theatre *is* the singing – and moving and acting – theatre. This book is focussed, though, on what could happen in the singing theatre that we have inherited in Europe and the Americas. It does not exclude the idea that the singing theatre of other cultures – including the indigenous culture of the Americas – is also important in its own right, and can serve as a valuable source for our own renewal.

I have been tempted to approach the subject in an objective and distanced way, in the manner adopted by professional observers and critics in every field. How else am I to be believed, unless I appear not to care one way or the other? But it's no good – I do care, because I see opportunities neglected, and timidity enshrined. I am not a professional observer, after all, but something of an activist in the field. It would be devious to pretend otherwise.

New ways of thinking about the singing theatre, new works of singing theatre, and new approaches to education for singing theatre, have for the most part been making their way under the banner of 'Music Theatre'. 'Music Theatre', as I underline in the first chapter, *is* new singing theatre. But there is no question that that phrase 'Music Theatre' has been bewildering people for a long time, and that the puzzlement as to what it 'really is' has been a considerable hindrance to the development of new singing theatre. I have had to confront this confusion at the outset, and will be proposing some definitions. Above all, as I make clear, we must avoid the idea that there is some genre, some esthetic pigeon-hole called 'Music Theatre', into which some works fit and others do not – but which works, and why, people can waste a lot of time discussing.

I have often said that Music Theatre is not so much a genre as a movement; a movement dedicated to breathing new life into the singing theatre. The only criterion for Music Theatre, then, is that it show evidence that its creators and performers are skilled in the arts and crafts of the singing theatre; and that there is freshness and originality in their work. I repeat: Music Theatre *is* 'new singing theatre'.

This, then, is a charter, a manifesto, a guide, a manual, for Music Theatre. It is not a survey of what is now being done, though it will make reference to various initiatives and people. Nor is it a history of what has been done in the past: history will concern us, but only insofar as it can serve as a source of ideas for us, in our own time. The book is written for anyone who loves the singing theatre and would like to know more of tomorrow's possibilities; for those educators who know that change must begin with them; for the producers, artist managements, administrators and granting agencies who sense that something is in the wind and want to know more; and above all for the young artists of the singing theatre – composers, writers, singer-actors and designers – whose gifts we have no right to warp and diminish.

I am grateful to the scores of artists from many countries, and to the hundreds of artist-students, whose hard work, ideas and responses provided the practical experience that stands behind these words.

M.B.
Brisco, Canada
– Florence
– Helsinki
– London.
1987-90

PART 1

DEFINITIONS, ORIGINS AND THE WAY THINGS ARE

Chapter One

MUSIC THEATRE IS NEW SINGING THEATRE

Since the late 1940s a handful of pioneers have sought to bring about a renewal of the singing theatre as an art and have referred to their activities and their productions as 'Music Theatre' – a term adopted in English from the German *Musiktheater*. The phrase is also used nowadays as a label for works of a somewhat earlier period; particularly the collaborations of Brecht and Weill between 1927 and 1934. This Brecht-Weill canon – *The Threepenny Opera, The Rise and Fall of the City of Mahagonny* and *Happy End*, along with shorter pieces like *The Little Mahagonny* and *The Seven Deadly Sins* – has become a standard reference point for those seeking examples of Music Theatre. The term had in fact been bandied about as early as the twenties by composers and critics. But Brecht himself, in his writings on his own works and on the singing theatre in general, does not appear to have used it at all; nor did he adopt Wagner's more literary term *Musik-Drama*. Brecht talked rather of 'new opera', or of 'epic opera'.

It was not until 1947 that the term *Musiktheater* began a full and active life in Germany, when Walter Felsenstein founded the Komische Oper amid the ruins of East Berlin. He seems to have used the phrase at first to describe the enterprise itself; his project, he later wrote, was not a third opera theatre for Berlin, nor an equally superfluous second operetta theatre, but 'a new and genuine music theatre'. But soon he was using the word to describe his theatre's 'working principles' – the painstakingly realistic approach to productions of repertory opera and operetta, which became the Komische Oper's trademark. Felsenstein's productions were revolutionary above all for the pains they took: he often rehearsed an opera for as long as six months, and his emphasis on the inter-dependency of music and stage action made vital sense of the collocation *Musiktheater*. Despite the reservations of some critics about such meticulous realism, his work became increasingly better known during the fifties for its 'Musiktheater' approach to repertory opera, and set a standard of integrity and excellence for the younger opera directors of the time.

In 1967 Felsenstein was asked by the International Theatre Institute

2

(based in Paris and operating under the aegis of UNESCO) to prepare plans for the renewal of the Institute's 'Lyric Theatre Committee', which had fallen by the wayside. The result was the Music Theatre Committee, which made its appearance in 1969; and it was perhaps at this moment that the term 'Musiktheater' became launched on its international career. From the guidelines drawn up for the committee by Felsenstein and others, we can see the beginnings of a definition of the term – and also that the English translator still preferred at that time to render it as musical theatre:

> In practical work, the [Music Theatre] Committee will be guided by the conviction that theatrical demands must be satisfied in musical theatre as well as the musical demands. The Committee will always regard and stress musical theatre as being a theatre art form, irrespective of considerable problems specifically connected therewith. Since present-day interpretation is very often unable to do justice to the values inherent in this art form..., the Committee will critically examine the inherited traditions of musical theatre and at the same time take a stand against all commercial tendencies or a routine way of thought. Thus it hopes to bring about a new attitude of artistic consciousness and feeling of responsibility among all those now working in this profession – with the aim of being able better to meet the demands of the audiences of today and the future, so that the musical theatre will again become a vital and indispensable form of human expression.

These ideas (wrapped up in characteristic 'international committee' style) provided a starting-point for the committee's work. But such a close adherence to the post-War aim of renewing the operatic tradition was found after some years to be constricting; there was a danger of the group becoming an 'opera-directors' club'. So in the late seventies the committee widened its area of interest to include 'other important domains like training, creation of new music theatre pieces, extra-European cultures, related genres, interdisciplinary and experimental work'. In an effort to avoid the now opposite danger of vague all-inclusiveness, it was decided to organise the committee's broadening interests along three main lines, of which only the first follows the original direction of the committee's work: renewal of interpretation (re-theatricalisation of opera and related genres); renewal of repertory (creation of new works and new forms of music theatre); renewal of training methods (education of the versatile singer-actor).

The committee (whose English translator, we see, had by now settled for the phrase 'music theatre') has, since that time, brought together Music Theatre specialists from different countries, and promoted Music Theatre festivals, conferences and training programmes throughout Europe and North America (though rarely beyond).

It would be wrong to overestimate the influence of committees on the direction of art, but perhaps it was this committee that was responsible, at the very least, for disseminating the use of the phrase 'Music Theatre' as a label for new approaches to the singing theatre. Thus in 1972 when Boris Pokrovsky, artistic director of the Bolshoi Opera and a founding member of the committee, gathered together a company of singers to present new operas, he named the new enterprise Moskovskiy Kamerniy Muzikalniy Teatr: the Moscow Chamber Music Theatre. Two years later, when British director Colin Graham reorganised Benjamin Britten's English Opera Group, it emerged – for its few strangled years of life – as the English Music Theatre Company. That same year, 1975, saw the launching in New York City of Encompass Music Theatre Company, under its artistic director Nancy Rhodes; and in Toronto of my own company, COMUS Music Theatre of Canada, whose goal was to provide a platform for new Music Theatre 'of all kinds'. Six years later the international Music Theatre Studio Ensemble was established at Banff in the Canadian Rockies, dedicated to preparing young artists for a revitalised singing theatre. In 1984 the US's National Opera Institute was renamed the National Institute for Music Theater. In the same year the American Music Theater Festival was inaugurated in Philadelphia, sub-titled 'Theater that Sings!'

All this (and it is only a selection) would seem pedigree enough for the use of the phrase *Musiktheater* – Music Theatre – to refer to a revitalised singing theatre, which aims among other things to give (in Felsenstein's words) equal weight to 'music' and 'theatre'. It is Music Theatre in this sense which is the subject of my book.

THE PROBLEM OF DEFINITION

Unfortunately, the use of the term 'Music Theatre' – at least in English – is loaded with difficulties.

In the first place, the meaning of the phrase 'Music Theatre' as new singing theatre cannot be readily guessed at by English-speakers who are not aware of the term's history. When they see or hear one familiar art butted up against another familiar art, there is nothing in the construction to give them a clue as to how one relates to the other. The two words are of Greek origin, but the construction is a characteristically Teutonic one: it is the German language that excels in the capacity to smash two words together, and out of them to create the appearance of a new entity. English allows the same process (toothpaste, billboard), but always with a sense of one modifying or explaining the other. Does 'music' qualify 'theatre' – is it a theatre with musical qualities? Or does 'theatre' qualify 'music' – is it a music with theatrical qualities? French cannot cope at all with the illogicality of such a construction, and *Musiktheater* in France has remained *théâtre musical* or more often *théâtre lyrique*. Other romance languages have the same difficulty – although in being unable to assimilate the collocation they miss too, perhaps, the poetic force of the term. One remembers Samuel Johnson's description of a metaphor: 'two heterogeneous objects yoked by violence together'. Although many may be unable to define the phrase, they are liable, I think, to respond emotively to the struggle toward fusion that lies within it.

Secondly, even if the English language can offer a home for such a phrase, it still brings in its train a swarm of niggling questions. The word 'theatre' is slippery in itself; it can refer to an activity, an art, a repertoire or a building. And of course some North Americans, like the Germans, spell it 'theater'. And then how do we write Music Theatre? Is it like that – Music Theatre? Or is it music theatre? Or Music-Theatre? Or Musictheatre? Or Musictheatre? Or, in the USA, Music Theater, etc.? (There are no rules about this, of course. As you see, my own preference is for the English spelling of 'theatre', and for separate words, both capitalised. The capitals seem to give weight to the thing, help to stop it flying apart. My spelling of 'theatre' is sheer force of British-Canadian habit.)

Thirdly, there is nothing in that word 'music' to suggest that the art of singing is a necessary element of Music Theatre. And indeed the singing theatre has no monopoly of 'Music Theatre' as a descriptive term; it has also been adopted by those striving to bring theatrical life to the concert platform. Works by John Cage, Mauricio Kagel, Luciano Berio, R. Murray Schafer and a host of others – works that mobilise musicians as actor-instrumentalists, and play with the theatrical possibilities of the concert hall; that incorporate the work of sculptors, poets, dancers and singers on the concert stage; that set concert works within stage settings, sometimes with complex lighting – this whole liberating movement in concert performance has also been referred to as Music Theatre. In fact one of the very earliest and most celebrated examples of this kind of Music Theatre is *The Soldier's Tale* of Stravinsky (1917), which contains no singing at all – though it does call for a performance group (three actors and a dancer) with musical skills. And in recent years 'Music Theatre' has been forced to spread its woolly umbrella wider still. The phrase has been pressed into service as a voguish alternative to 'multi-media' or 'inter-media' (or Richard Kostelanetz's 'Theatre of Mixed Means'), to describe presentations of almost any kind – as long as they bring together live, taped or electronically generated music (or sound), with some kind of visual effects, whether video, slides, lasers, holograms, or light effects. Such performances may or may not include live performers, who may or may not sing. For all these presentations, most of which move into the theatre from a technological base – and which often generate effects of startling power – let us for heaven's sake keep the perfectly understandable and appropriate names they have acquired: 'multimedia' or 'inter-media'.

Fourthly, Music Theatre sounds much the same in English as 'musical theatre', which has been used for many years to refer to 'the theatre of the musical'; in other words to the world, or the repertoire, of commercial musical comedy on Broadway and in London – as opposed to the world or repertoire of opera. This is why *Musiktheater* could not for long be translated into English as 'musical theatre', and why Music Theatre people working in English keep finding themselves saying irritably, 'No, I mean Mu-ZIK Theatre – quite different from Musi-KAL Theatre.' (In France, of course, this has not been a problem; *théâtre musical* has never referred exclusively to the British-American musical comedy. But it is a further confusion to have to tell a Frenchman that *théâtre musical* cannot be translated 'musical theatre'!)

Finally, traditional opera people who know of Felsenstein's efforts to 'renew' the theatrical element of opera are these days unlikely to argue against his principles, which have become generally accepted – in principle, so to speak. They are therefore liable to claim that *all* good opera – like that with which they are involved, for example – is in fact Music Theatre. 'Of course, theatrical values have been neglected in the past, but now, with bright young directors bringing radical approaches to the old masterpieces, and with increased audiences and super-titles, we have put the past behind us. Three cheers for Music Theatre!' And off they go to rehearse their tenth revival of *Tosca* – without the stars, of course, who will be flying in next week. The conservative who goes through the motions of stealing the radical's trousers has been a familiar archetype for a century. Whether by design or not, the effect in the case of Music Theatre is to create a further blur of our understanding.

This litany of difficulties cannot be wished away; it is a fact that the term 'Music Theatre' is used in several different senses, and that – as with any other term of reference – the more it means the less it means. The resulting muddle is more than just a nuisance; it has had a destructive ripple effect through the entire support system for new singing theatre initiatives, at least in the countries of Western Europe and in North America.

WHY IS IT A PROBLEM?

The definition of 'Music Theatre' is obviously then a problem for the public. As I have already observed, the general audience is more or less clear as to what 'music' is, whatever its style; although some classical concerts will surprise their public by offering a piece with theatrical elements, people will generally experience even this as music. People are also fairly clear as to what 'theatre' is, because the theatre is well established as the place where plays are put on, or as the art of putting on plays; and they know what a play is, even if the play itself tries to confound them. People reckon they know too what a 'musical' or 'musical comedy' is, and what to expect at an 'opera'. Even though we live in a time when visual artists perform, and musicians act, and opera companies present musicals, and musicals take on the form of opera, we cling to the old categories like pairs of glasses, through which the different arts come into focus. Each traditional way of making art – music, visual arts, theatre etc. – has its public. Opera has its own special audience, which tends to experience it as music, as vocal artistry, as spectacle – and as an important social occasion. Whereas the musical appeals to – or is designed to appeal to – a more general audience; it is different from these other theatrical arts in that its generating force is and has always been commercial.

Into this spectrum of artistic offerings comes the occasional piece of 'Music Theatre'. 'What is it?' we wonder. 'Will I enjoy it? Where is it going to happen?' If I like Broadway musicals, I may worry that I will find it too intellectual, too arty, or too operatic. If I like opera I may be afraid that something called Music Theatre will be too avant-garde, or too lacking in the glamour and power that I expect on the stage. If I enjoy the visual arts, old and new, and have even become used to the surprises of performance art with its generally firm discounting of 'acting' as a skill, I may wonder whether I shall find Music Theatre stuffy and self-consciously theatrical. Music Theatre has attracted a smattering of the curious and adventurous from all these publics, but they tend to arrive in a nervous state because of their confusion as to what they might expect – and quite often leave unclear as to what they have experienced.

General awareness of what 'Music Theatre' means could be considerably increased if the public was guided by an understanding press. Unfortunately, the arts departments of almost all newspapers have their territory carefully divided up between music critic, theatre critic and visual arts critic. So, when it comes to feature articles about a forthcoming Music Theatre production, who will be sent to cover it? The music critic? The theatre critic? Or will both throw up their hands, and send some cub reporter to earn a stripe or two? And then, when the show opens, who will review it? If the production tends towards Broadway it will be likely to receive the attentions of the theatre critic. If it can be classed as musically 'serious' or avant-garde, it is the music critic who will go along. And given the pressure these ladies and gentlemen are under, they may not be able to attend at all, or only at the dress rehearsal, or only the first act. The fact is, Music Theatre doesn't yet have a constituency – it possesses few advocates and no identifiable public. Those dedicated to breathing new life into the singing theatre, to bringing it into the mainstream of twentieth-century art, simply have not succeeded in establishing general understanding as to the aims or context of what they are doing.

When Music Theatre – new singing theatre – does manage to attract a large audience, it has nearly always done so in recent years by hanging on to the shirt-tails of one of the traditional arts, or on to the names of some famous practitioners. Philip Glass had already drawn the interest of the concert-going public with his brand of new music, and Robert Wilson had created revolutionary designer-works within the theatrical medium, before they collaborated in *Einstein on the Beach* (1976). But the fact that the production had its American première in the Metropolitan Opera House – a courageous rental if ever there was one – was what gave everyone a handle to it, even for the regular Met audience who wouldn't be caught dead or alive actually going to the piece. Peter Brook's *Carmen* (Paris 1980, New York 1982) was – well, it was Peter Brook; and, of course, it was – after a fashion – *Carmen*. David Freeman's Music Theatre productions in England are carried out under the name of Opera Factory. *The Electrification of the Soviet Union*, Peter Sellars' 1987 production with British composer Nigel Osborne and poet Craig Raine, was commissioned for Glyndebourne. And at the 'straight theatre' end of the singing theatre spectrum, the National Theatre of Great Britain has given weight, acting virtuosity and intelligence to a piece like *Les Misérables* – attended as a musical by some and as a drama by others, but perhaps identified most accurately as a piece of Music Theatre with somewhat indifferent music, and played by actors whose singing is for the most part more noticeable for character and energy than for virtuosity.

Not surprisingly, there is a parallel difficulty on the financial side. It is not easy to attract resources for an activity that many people don't quite understand; anyone who has been involved in raising funds for Music Theatre activities will have come up against the problem. Strangely, corporate funding on a modest scale can sometimes be found, because there are many companies which like to be associated – at least once – with what they are assured is new; they do not in general expect to understand the arts anyway, and are open to persuasion. But government funding agencies are a very different matter. They have their Music Divisions, staffed by officers who are schooled in music, and who deal with opera as a branch of music. They have their Theatre Division officers, who are equally clear as to what theatre is. Musicals, if funded at all, are handled by the theatre department – and then, of course, only if they are being presented by a non-profit company as part of a regular season. But Music Theatre? It is lucky if it manages to find an understanding supporter within the agency; that supporter is generally in the Music Division – though sometimes in 'Explorations', 'New Directions' or the equivalent. Applications for public money for Music Theatre projects are famous for disappearing through the cracks between these departments, and – especially in times of scarcity – are perfect targets for reluctant refusal. 'What is Music Theatre, after all?' they ask, recommending that the file be placed in the reject tray: 'No one seems to be able to tell us – not even the people producing it. It doesn't quite fit anywhere. Pity.'

The United States attempted to solve this problem in 1983 by creating a new department at the National Endowment for the Arts. The discussions as to what the new entity should be called became legendary for their bitterness and political infighting; there was a strong push towards calling it the 'Music Theatre Department'. But in the end they settled on another bifurcation, and gave the new baby the name of 'Opera/Musical Theater' – a hard name to make sense of in conversation without reference to 'slash' or 'oblique stroke'. And still they are left with Music Theatre as a mystery and an outsider.

Even when there is sympathetic support for Music Theatre at government agencies and corporate sponsors – and this certainly exists – there is still a pervasive and quite understandable rule of thumb: public money tends to go first to those needy projects that seem to have a chance of attracting, or at least building, a public. Music Theatre's continued lack of identifiable constituency does not stand it in good stead. The result is that activities dedicated to the renewal of the singing theatre are inadequately funded by both government agencies and private sponsors, and are therefore constantly marginalised at the fringes of the performing arts. (One log-jam appears to be breaking up. On 1 July 1990, the Canada Council's Music and Opera Division set up a Music Theatre Production Fund, earmarked for $250,000 in its first year; a great day for Music Theatre in Canada.)

The confusion and the vagueness surrounding Music Theatre also extend into the very professions that you would expect to be vitally involved in its creation – composers and writers, singers, opera directors, producers; and equally into the educational institutions that might be expected to be busy now developing the Music Theatre artists of the future.

Even when there is enthusiasm and a vision of what could be, there is hesitation, contradiction and muddle – and these are the people who sit on the juries of the granting agencies.

So these multiple confusions compound the difficulties. If the public, and those who are in a position to inform the public, and those who could provide funds, and those who have the professional skills, and those who teach the new professionals – if all are unsure, then Music Theatre will remain an enigma.

The solution, it has been said, is to create works which will command public notice, and so force an understanding of the nature and potential of 'Music Theatre'. True. An art is defined not by abstractions but by its works. True again. Why then has the Music Theatre movement produced so few new pieces that attract attention and that can be added to the long line of masterworks in the performing arts? Why has 'new singing theatre' not taken its place along-side contemporary and modern dance, and the other arts of our time?

There are no doubt many answers to that question. This book attends to some of them, and outlines a programme designed to push aside the obstacles. But I am convinced that one of those obstacles is a simple matter of words, and that a useful start can be made by agreeing on a small but highly necessary list of terms.

TOWARDS DEFINITION

It is astonishing that we do not possess a satisfactory generic term to cover the entire art and activity of the theatre in which actors sing: there is no equivalent to that simple word 'dance', which covers every manifestation of the art of physical movement. How can we refer in a general way to the splendidly motley family of 'sung-acted' theatre: opera, ballad-opera, folk-opera, operetta, musical comedy, musical revue and music theatre pieces – not to mention the riches of other cultures? The closest we come is with the phrase 'lyric stage', which has been used over the centuries to refer to European opera. But it is a borrowing from the Greek via Italy via France, and in English has a solemn, elevated air, somehow conjuring up visions of large diaphanously-dressed ladies strumming cardboard instruments. It is surely unsuitable for covering the whole range of the art in Western culture, and seems comically inappropriate to the products of Asia, Africa or Latin America. I have therefore settled on:

SINGING THEATRE =   The art of theatrical presentation in which one or more of the acting performers sing some or all of their role(s).

We have already explored in some detail the problems of the phrase 'Music Theatre', and seem to have developed a pretty good case for chucking it out altogether. Unfortunately words disappear not on command, but only when no one can find further use for them. There is at present no other formulation at hand for referring to new singing theatre – except, of course, 'new singing theatre'; until such time as this catches on, we will no doubt continue to talk about 'Music Theatre', first doing all we can to rescue it from confusion and ambiguity:

MUSIC THEATRE =   (i) The movement within Western culture's singing theatre which seeks to renew the art of the singing theatre.

                               (ii) Descriptive term for singing theatre works or activities developed within the spirit and general aims of the Music Theatre movement. Hence we say 'a piece of Music Theatre', 'a Music Theatre work', 'a Music Theatre production', or 'a Music Theatre company'.

NEW SINGING THEATRE = A phrase of recent coinage and brilliant in its simplicity: synonymous with 'Music Theatre'.

Having restored the phrase 'Music Theatre' to its original connection with the singing theatre, we are in need, finally, of a word to describe those works that introduce theatrical elements to the concert stage, but which are not (necessarily) anything to do with singers or the singing theatre. It will be argued that this field of activities cannot be separated from Music Theatre proper; there are, of course, pieces like Maxwell Davies' *Eight Songs for A Mad King*, which seem to confirm such a view. But then I hope to have made clear by this time that I am not advocating names for genres or for categories of art, but simply terms to describe activities, or approaches to artistic work. *Eight Songs*, for example, requires a singer – the mad king – who vocalises beyond the normal bounds of operatic style and range; and a group of instrumentalists who share the platform with the singer, playing inside bird cages – which are part of a setting representing the mad king's apartments. The piece can clearly be performed in a concert hall, making use of as many theatrical elements as the resources of the concert stage allow. But it could also be performed in a theatre with full theatrical resources – and it is in this context a piece of Music Theatre.

I do believe – even in this case – that the contexts and aims of Music Theatre and of 'concert-theatricalisation' are different, and that the latter is in no way diminished by being referred to as:

CONCERT THEATRE =   (i) The movement among musicians –
                        instrumentalists, composers, conductors
                        – which seeks to enrich and enliven
                        the performance of concert music
                        by bringing theatrical elements to the
                        concert stage.

                        (ii) Descriptive term for works on the
                        concert stage that make use of theatrical
                        elements. Hence we say 'a piece of
                        Concert Theatre', or 'a Concert Theatre
                        work'.

These are the senses in which these terms will be used in the following pages. But dictionary definitions, by their very succinctness, are useful only to a point. Let us end this beginning, then, with a more extended look at the quintessence of singing theatre – of the central activity that makes singing theatre what it is.

> 'AT THE HEART OF THE SINGING THEATRE, THERE IS A PERFORMER WHO ACTS AND SINGS A ROLE, IN A DRAMATIC PERFORMANCE, WITH MUSICAL SUPPORT, IN A PERFORMANCE AREA, IN FRONT OF AN AUDIENCE.'

This is the singing theatre's primary act: without it, you do not have singing theatre but something else. It is the common factor in every genre of Western singing theatre, from opera to musical revue: and it is the factor in performances within other cultural traditions that would lead us to define these performances as singing theatre. If, then, we are to see the singing theatre freshly as an art and an activity, we must start by looking closely at what is happening in this 'primary act'; who is doing what to whom? And as we look, we must begin to build a basic vocabulary, which can help us to move away from assumptions and pre-conceptions, and to fix our minds on the primary elements of the art. This can lead to statements so simple and obvious as to seem almost childish. But it is no harm; simple words for fresh thinking.

'A PERFORMER WHO ACTS AND SINGS A ROLE'

A dancer dances. An actor acts. A singer sings. A player plays. But in the singing theatre's 'primary act', the performer must, at the least, be able both to act *and* sing – which is why we talk of the 'singer-actor' or the 'singer-actress'. This double-barrelled formulation is a little awkward, but is useful enough to have made its way in the world. The word 'performer' is less specific, but this can sometimes make it more valuable to us: it neither spells out nor limits the skills required. More useful still, it works for both sexes: we do not, after all, have to talk about the 'performer' and the 'performess'.

By 'acting a role' we mean that the performer behaves as if he or she were somebody else – namely, a character in the dramatic performance.

By 'singing a role' we mean that when the character expresses thoughts, feelings and reactions in words or sounds, the dramatic performance requires that some or all of those words and sounds be sung on musical pitches and within a rhythmic structure.

Though 'acting' and 'singing' are described here as though they are separate activities, 'singing' is in fact part of the 'acting'; the character being acted is portrayed in the act of uttering thoughts, feelings and re-actions. The singing theatre differs from the literary theatre in the musically pitched and rhythmically structured way in which some or all characters utter, some or all of the time.

There is no determining principle as to how many of the character's utterances are sung in the singing theatre; a proportion, large or small, may be spoken. And in a performance in which there is more than one performer, no more than one performer need sing. But if no performer sings any portion of his or her role, then the primary act of singing theatre does not take place.

'IN A DRAMATIC PERFORMANCE...'

In singing theatre, the event in which the performer acts and sings has been constructed according to some organising principle. The most common structure (but by no means a requisite) is that of a time- sequence, within which is acted out a story or incident or dream, involving one or more characters.

Instructions and plans for the preparation of the performance are most often (though not necessarily) conveyed in written form. The instructions and plans may include words (or sounds) to be spoken or sung, music to be played, direction for the action of the performance and descriptions or pictures of scenic requirements.

These sets of instructions and plans – most often in the form of a word-text combined with a musical score, and supplemented with stage directions – are usually composed (meaning 'put together' in its Latin root) by one or more creators, usually in advance of the performance. To be able to create such a set of instructions the creator(s) need knowledge and understanding of a number of arts: dramatic, musical, verbal, vocal and scenic.

There are many ways of 'realising' the work of the creator(s) as a dramatic performance. Very often the work is brought to life through the offices of a stage director, a musical director, a stage designer and other artists. But these mediating artists are not essential to the creation of a performance. What is necessary for the 'primary act' of singing theatre is that the performer operates within the structure of a dramatic performance which requires singing as well as acting. Without that dramatic performance there is no theatre, and therefore no singing theatre.

'WITH MUSICAL SUPPORT...'

Singing in a dramatic performance most often (though not necessarily) requires the performer to have learnt – ahead of the performance – some kind of formal, musical utterance, with prescribed pitch and rhythmic structure. In order to accomplish this, the performer usually requires some form of musical support – if only to provide a starting note.

Minimum musical support, then, is a tuning-fork or equivalent pitch-setter, which can be struck, blown or otherwise played by the performer (or by another performer), as long as this action does not interfere with the requirements of character portrayal within the dramatic performance. Since such an action would often be inappropriate, the support will generally come from elsewhere – from somewhere within the hearing of the performer. And what is in its most elemental form a mere musical support for the performer can become an entire musical environment, a musical continuum that establishes mood and atmosphere, and can call for resources varying from a single instrument to a mighty orchestra. But even in a piece of singing theatre of vast musical scale and complexity, the music must still serve – among other things – to 'support' the performer, making it possible for him or her to utter on the prescribed pitches and within the pre-established rhythmic structure.

'IN A PERFORMANCE AREA, IN FRONT OF AN AUDIENCE...'

The dramatic performance of a piece of singing theatre entails presentation to an audience; and the only primary conditions for a performance area are that it provide sufficient space for the performance, and appropriate space for an audience to 'receive' the performance.

(That word 'audience'; it is not ideal basic language for singing theatre, because it implies a group of people who only 'hear' the performance. But the alternatives are no better: 'spectators' suggests that the performance is only to be seen, while a 'public' suggests that an audience cannot be private. 'Receivers' in its pure sense is the most accurate, but sounds as if they didn't pay for their tickets!)

Sufficient space for the performance will include not only the area in which the performance takes place, but space for whatever musical support may be required; for any technical equipment called for by the performance; for any storage of *matériel* that may need to be on hand during the performance; and for any activity (change of clothes etc.) that may need to be carried out by the performer(s) during the performance and out of the view and hearing of the audience.

And the audience space? To be appropriate, it will be configured in such a way that the audience can 'receive' the total performance aurally and visually, and with whatever other senses the performance's reception requires. Total visual reception is a function of light, distance and unobstructed view. Total aural reception is a function of the acoustic properties of the space, and of the spatial relationship between three locations – the performance space, the audience space and the space allocated to the musical support.

So much for words, and for definitions.

Chapter Two

SILVER SPOON: THE SINGING THEATRE'S INHERITANCE

Music, words and stage action can be allied on a stage in many different mixes and balances; and since its emergence around 1600 as a distinct artistic activity, the singing theatre in Europe has played with a variety of these possibilities, and developed formal conventions for various types of presentation. These conventions have changed and evolved. But those of us who work in today's new singing theatre – the Music Theatre movement – believe that its potential for expressing the human condition has barely begun to be realised; that there are many obstacles which have stood – and still stand – in the way of its developing freely. One of the most persistent of these results from the manner of singing theatre's birth.

All art, of course, has been produced in response to – or as a reflection of – social, political and economic situations, and by artists who are themselves a product of their times; it is not only the art of the singing theatre that reflects the conditions of its making. But the singing theatre, born out of a determination to affect – to dazzle – courtly Renaissance audiences with a powerful and more or less unified multi-sensory experience, began life only as a by-product of exceptional wealth, and its primary reasons for existing were for the display of that wealth. It was an art born with the proverbial silver spoon in its mouth. Only wealth and power could have brought together the multitude of artists necessary for the first forays into singing theatre; only wealth and power had good reason to do so.

In the late sixteenth century, as the universal church splintered and its power declined, the independent power of kings and princes grew, and the medieval polarity between sacred and profane, religious and secular, solemnity and fun, began to shift to new ground. The artists of the Middle Ages had celebrated the glory of God: the artists of the late Renaissance began to serve the glory of the monarch, of the leader, of the secular power; and nowhere more magnificently than in the court spectacle, which brought together music, singing, dancing and scenery in a festal drama that affirmed the prince as the bringer of order, peace, justice and happiness. The costs were vast; but 'magnificence' was considered a moral virtue, extolled by Aristotle as 'liberality of expendi-

16

ture combined with good taste'. The prince paid the bills. The good taste was generally supplied by the artists he engaged.

The new seriousness, then, was not about the next world, but about this one. What once was God's glory was now the prince's. What once was irreligious behaviour or blasphemy now became *lèse-majesté*, or even treason. Attending the spectacle, and applauding both its magnificence and its message, signified the courtier's acceptance of the prince's rule, and also the prince's acceptance of the courtier.

These princely origins of the 'serious' singing theatre established for it a certain lavishness of tradition; and when it emerged from its role as a court spectacle, moving on – under the guidance of humanist artists and some of the more enlightened Italian princes – from direct political allegory to tragic tales of gods and heroes, the magnificence and the solemnity moved with it. *Opera seria* in the early seventeenth century was becoming a form of artistic expression, but attendance at it continued to be mysteriously bound up with confirmation of the prevailing social order. Sustained dignity of style in gesture and utterance on stage remained an emblem of the dignity of the court: so that even when it might have seemed pompous and absurd, there was no possibility of mockery. It was not only because it was tragic that operatic tragedy was no laughing matter.

There was also at the heart of Italian *opera seria*, from its very beginnings, a bizarre and even criminal artifice; the hero's role was invariably sung by a castrated male. The practice had begun in the church choir, where talented boys of eleven or twelve were put to the knife under who knows what wicked pressure of force or suasion from their priest. But the sacrifice for God now became a sacrifice for the prince, and for possible fame and wealth: at the centre of the *opera seria* was a freak, a damaged person, a fine, upstanding man who sang soprano and – everyone knew – had no balls. Eunuchs, like cuckolds, were a staple butt of humour in the old comedies. But the cruelty of jokes about eunuchs are as nothing compared with the savagery of good taste in *opera seria*.

So – just as there are no jokes at coronation ceremonies – the sustained and ceremonial dignity of the operatic stage, with its fluting hero, excluded humour: high political seriousness shaped for it an esthetic that insisted on formal purity, and an unquestioning acceptance of the established order.

Fun, of course, will have its way. Republican Venice was the first Italian city to build public opera-houses – the Teatro San Cassiano was erected in 1637, and by 1678 there were no less than ten others. And it was in Venice, where ticket sales were a factor, that the comics of the *commedia dell'arte* were at first allowed to appear at various moments in the opera, even barging into solemn scenes to cheer them up. Later their presence was restricted to the final scene of each act of a serious opera. Later still they appeared between the acts, in 'intermezzi', which became highly popular in themselves, and were soon expanded with extra songs, to evolve into what became known as *opera buffa*. Meanwhile Naples was developing its own version of operatic fun, and there, in 1709, the first full-evening *opera comica* was presented, an entertainment which – like the Venetian 'intermezzi' – combined song and speech. In its early form the Neapolitan *opera comica* was satirical, relying on topical humour, and with several characters speaking in dialect. But soon it followed the taste of the century and moved towards the 'pathetic' – the sentimental, as we should say. There were, by the way, no castrati in Italian comic opera.

The light-hearted end of the singing theatre spectrum was often able to have fun at the expense of the serious end: the solemn histrionics of serious opera invited parody – and nowhere more than in England, where in the early seventeen hundreds, people of pragmatic British common-sense and un-voguish views looked at the antics of London's newly imported Italian opera companies with huge merriment. *The Beggar's Opera* (1728), by John Gay, was one manifestation of the laughter. With its none too subtle political satire it took the English capital by storm, and is credited with having put Handel – at least temporarily – out of the serious opera business. Gay's opera, with its anti-authoritarian spirit, went on to exert extraordinary influence on the singing theatre, not only in Britain and America (as one of the progenitors of Gilbert and Sullivan and later of the American musical comedy) but even in France, Germany and Austria. During the century, in spite of the efforts of Gluck in Vienna and Paris, the *opera seria* languished further everywhere as democratic sentiment grew; and not long after the French Revolution it was finally put out to pasture in the Elysian fields, castrati and all. It was the *opéra comique* which then became the vehicle for serious artistic statement; and Paris, the capital of libertarian thought and action, was soon recognised everywhere as the new leader of the singing theatre. The events that followed profoundly affected the course of 'opera', and are of critical importance to our understanding of the singing theatre of today.

French society in the years after 1789 went through a series of cataclysmic changes; from the Reign of Terror to the Directoire, from the Directoire to Napoleon's Empire and its vast military campaigns. After Napoleon's final defeat in 1815, in a society that had lost first one tired old heart and then its enlarged replacement, the survivors of the old aristocracy confronted the parvenu and imitation nobility of Napoleon's Empire – as though in a mirror, in a crisis of authenticity. The way was open for wealth to supplant pedigree as a criterion of acceptability. Meanwhile the central power continued to shift. The Bourbon Louis XVIII was crowned king – until July of 1830, when he was replaced by 'Citizen King' Louis-Philippe.

In that same tumultuous year the fever of Romanticism, which had hit England and Germany thirty years earlier, was finally caught by the artists of the French capital – the generation which had been brought up in a world of vaulting Napoleonic excitement and ambition, and for whom life seemed now empty of grand possibilities. Romanticism's emphasis on the rights of an individual in defiance of the world, and on the primacy of passion over social obligation; its yearning for an impossible ideal, and its love of flamboyant style and extravagant gesture – all found a natural outlet in the theatre, where the French had suddenly discovered Shakespeare, and where for a dozen years or so the shapeless historical dramas of the elder Dumas held fashionable sway. But at the opera-house, with its capacity for tearing a passion to tatters through the new power of music, this same Romanticism came to stay, with the lyrical tenor as its sensitive hero wrestling with love, horror and despair. And just as self-preoccupation has a hard time knowing when to stop, so Romanticism in opera evolved, perhaps inevitably, into 'melodramatic' exaggeration.

It was this clash of hugely-felt (or hugely-displayed) emotions, these romantic vistas, this illicit but longed-for primacy of passion, and these vast choruses of well-controlled and reactive peasants or gypsies or warriors, which ravished a new middle-class audience committed to a very unromantic life of getting and spending. This was a new kind of seriousness, in which once again the spoken word had no significant place. The virtuoso singer was even more in demand than in the days of *opera seria* – and even more idolised, because of the power of the new popular press, and because he or she had the task of personifying the passionate, misunderstood, yearning and despairing romantic hero or heroine. The composer obliged by writing arias in which the heights of emotion were matched by the ostentation of vocal display. The Opera had become 'grand'. And what we now refer to derogatorily as 'operatic' had been born: 'monumental scenery, empty emphases, blustering heroics, artificial emotions and language', as Arnold Hauser describes it.[1]

This expansion of the emotional spectrum of opera developed hand in hand with the expansion of the physical scale of the actual operatic work that was created and presented. Mozart in the 1780s was still writing his royally commissioned operas for an intimate court theatre, and for the classical symphonic orchestra evolved by Haydn and consisting of between 35 and 40 players. But the post- Revolutionary age called for larger effects and therefore for larger forces. As the powerful and dramatic brass and percussion increased in numbers and variety, the quieter strings and winds had to be augmented exponentially to balance them. Bigger noise from the orchestra pit needed to be matched by larger choruses and by fuller and more penetrating solo voices. The orchestra had already begun to expand in the early years of the nineteenth century, as symphonic developments found their way back to the opera. Berlioz was one of the first composers whose dramatic – and romantic – imagination demanded gigantic resources, which in the 1830s and 40s he was rarely able to command (he conceived one piece for 450 musicians). But by the 1890s symphonic and even some operatic music was regularly calling for more than 100 players – nearly three times the number for which Mozart wrote.

The expanding scale of the stage presentation meant in turn that there was a larger hole to fill at the end of the auditorium. Although spectacular theatrical effects had been commonplace in Italy since the beginning of the seventeenth century, the nineteenth was – at least in the major centres such as Paris and Vienna, Rome, Milan, Naples and Venice – the century of sheer 'authentic' size, with its vast painted backdrops, its meticulously realistic, three-dimensional trees and crags, its fully constructed city streets and squares. The army of singers on the stage was matched by the army of craftsmen, artists and stagehands required to build, paint and manoeuvre the scenery.

The impression on the eyes and ears of an audience of those days must have been powerful indeed. But the total effect of such presentations and the houses in which they played reflected a passion for size which found expression in many areas of nineteenth-century commercial enterprise. New materials and production methods, and dramatic increases in the power of steam, combined with the dynamism of accumulated capital to make it a century in which for the first time many Olympian projects had become achievable: railways thousands of miles long, tall buildings, iron bridges and iron ships, massive locks and seaways. Size was a testament to power and success, to man's triumphant progress and his mastery over nature.

Was the galloping elephantiasis of the operatic form simply a result of the bourgeois aspiration for romantic grandeur? Only indirectly; it stemmed above all from a change in the administrative structure of opera, a change which came about as part of the shift of power from princes and aristocrats to the rapidly rising middle class. Opera, like every other major enterprise, had become commercial.

WOOING A NEW AUDIENCE

The support of a public audience had been part of the financial equation in Venice from very early days, as we have seen, but towards the end of the eighteenth century court patronage everywhere was feeling the economic pinch. As early as 1768, the administration of the Royal and Imperial Opera in Vienna was taken away from court officials and turned over to a commercial manager, who, assisted by a subsidy from the Emperor, ran the opera theatre at his own financial risk. After the Napoleonic Wars, Milan's La Scala and the San Carlo Opera in Naples were both under the management of one Domenico Barbaja – an entrepreneur who had started out as a waiter, ran a circus for a while, and had then made a fortune managing the gambling saloon attached to La Scala. In 1821 Barbaja was hired to manage the opera in Vienna, where he introduced the Italian system of regular subscriptions, and over the next nine years, assisted by a fixed subsidy from the court but standing the risk himself, succeeded in turning a considerable personal profit.

In Paris, Napoleon had reorganised the management of all three state theatres – including the Opera – in 1807, placing them under the supreme control of an Inspector of Theatres, subsidising them with the help of a tax imposed on all other forms of entertainment, and requiring their staffs to make good any losses incurred. The restoration of the Bourbon monarchy brought few changes to this arrangement. But the rising costs caused by the inflationary economy of post-Napoleonic Europe made it increasingly impossible to make the Opera's ends meet, even with handsome subventions. The July Revolution which brought in the 'Citizen King' also signalled radical change at the Opera; in 1831 a commercial manager, Louis Véron, was appointed, given a subsidy – which was to diminish year by year – and charged to manage the Opera for six years 'at his own risk and fortune'. This direction put commercial profit – and therefore the need to attract an audience – for the first time at the top of the Paris agenda.

It was Véron who rooted out the last vestiges of *opera seria*, and introduced Meyerbeer to the new and burgeoning Parisian public. Meyerbeer's *Robert le Diable*, premièred in 1831, set the tone for a new dynasty of taste; when Véron retired in 1835, he was the butt of artists but rich beyond their power to harm. A 'common man' himself, and ignorant of music, he had managed to take the pulse of the new and largely uneducated rich, and, with the marketing expertise since become so familiar to us, had sold them what they suddenly discovered they wanted: singing voices of heroic quality and scale, dramatic situations of heart-rending emotional intensity and fervent democratic idealism, and scenic spectacle of dazzling authenticity and grandeur. The expansion of opera was thus a direct result of its development of commercial objectives – the need to sell to a market. Larger musical, vocal, dramatic and scenic effects = more public interest. More public interest = more tickets sold. More tickets sold = need for more seats. Need for more seats = larger houses. Larger houses = larger stages. Larger stages = larger-scale presentations. Larger-scale presentations = larger musical, vocal and scenic effects. Larger musical, dramatic and scenic effects = more public interest... etc. Opera was on its escalator ride.

The risings of 1848 throughout Europe renewed the hopes of libertarians everywhere (inspiring Wagner, who backed the rebels in Dresden and had to flee to Switzerland, to set down his dreams for a 'democratic' renewal of opera). In France, Louis-Philippe abdicated. But within the year Louis-Napoleon, nephew of Bonaparte, had been elected President, and in 1852, after an almost bloodless *coup d'état*, he proclaimed the Second Napoleonic Empire. Democracy and intellectual freedom had been defeated by the forces of reaction, with the support of the new and wealthy middle classes – for whom revolution was now less attractive and important than the consolidation of their political strength and their thrusting need for social recognition. In their pursuit of these aims, opera – now both 'serious' once again, and 'grand' into the bargain – confirmed its role as a vehicle of social power and acceptance. In Hauser's perceptive words:

> The bourgeois culture of the July monarchy and the Second Empire, which was a parvenu culture,... looked for the monumental and the imposing in the theatre and exaggerated the appearance of greatness, the more so as it lacked true spiritual greatness itself. There are, in fact, two different impulses which drive society to ceremonial, grandiose and pretentious forms; on the one hand, it may be impelled to seek for grandeur because that is in line with its natural way of life, or the rage for the colossal may be due to a need to compensate for a more or less painfully felt weakness. The baroque of the seventeenth century corresponded to the grand proportions in which the court and aristocracy of the period naturally breathed and moved. The pseudo-baroque of the nineteenth century corresponded to the ambitions with which the risen bourgeoisie was trying to fill out these proportions...Nothing satisfied these needs more perfectly and more readily than the concerted ensemble of this opera, the organisation of the means at its disposal – the gigantic orchestra, the enormous stage and the huge choir – into a whole, which was intended only to impress, overwhelm and subjugate the audience.[2]

And nothing more effectively expresses this gigantism, this false grandeur, and the serious lengths to which the France of Napoleon III went to set the seal on its authenticity, than the Paris Opera House, le Palais Garnier (begun in 1861, opened in 1875), in which the vast illusionistic stage vies for pride of place with the palatial trickery of the foyer and auditorium.

Garnier well understood both his time and its people. He received the commission for the Opera House as the result of a competition – in which the Empress herself had submitted one of the 171 entries. Summoned to the Tuileries, Garnier showed the Empress his winning model, and she was revolted by it: 'What is this? This is not a style: it isn't Louis XIV, it isn't Louis XV, it isn't Louis XVI'. To which Garnier replied, 'Madame, it is Napoleon III – and you complain?'

Garnier commented extensively on his own building, and his comments are illuminating. The spectacle, he wrote, 'is not to be enacted on the stage alone; theatre involves all encounters, all actions. The spectators themselves are actors'. And he described in detail how he had fashioned his architecture with these ideas in mind.

> The Opera was the entire society of the Second Empire. There were, of course, distinctions between different categories of people – those who paid more and those who paid less – and the part of each in the ritual was clearly assessed and defined. If you came by carriage or on foot, there was a sequence prepared, and a place also for intermingling – even though this might be at a distance. Even the act of lining up for tickets was considered as part of the ceremony…In the main foyer there were mirrors set into the columns so that women might glance at themselves and make last-minute adjustments to their dress or expressions, before entering the hall. Here was a climax to the architecture. Here society disported itself in its splendour; people saw and were seen as they passed in procession up the stairs…The lesser members of society watched from on high…[3]

Napoleonic overreaching, nostalgia for Bourbon legitimacy, and middle-class desire for princely status to complement its wealth, were all given rein in this extraordinary building, where Second Empire society was provided with the opportunity to enact itself. These various elements of France's complex psyche combine in a classic monument to fakery.

RISE AND FALL...

What Garnier had so brilliantly captured in stone in L'Opéra de Paris was a mood, an attitude which since early in the century had begun to spread from Paris through all Europe. The middle classes flocked in increasing numbers to the grand spectacles designed to entertain, uplift and impress them, and at which being seen was as important as to see. A large opera theatre had become as essential to the reception of the latest production as a cinema was to be in the 1920s; with this difference, that the construction of a large theatre was more than a practical necessity – it was an impractical necessity, a vast expenditure of funds that could in nearly every case be amassed only by recourse to the public purse, and then only by appealing to royal or national pride.

England's middle class, the first to be emancipated, had begun to put pressure on the seating capacity of London's theatres as early as the eighteenth century (Christopher Wren's Drury Lane Theatre, built in 1674 to seat 1,200, is thought to have had a capacity of 2,000 by the time it burned down in 1792), and its short-lived replacement (which burned in 1809) held more than 3,600 people. But the post-Revolutionary grand opera of Paris provided a new impetus, and the capitals and great cities of Europe, as well as in the Americas, strove to house the new works in neo-baroque theatres as sumptuous as each nation could afford. The nineteenth-century building program was astonishing, as this partial list shows:

> The Hof und Nationaltheater, Munich, 1818 (burnt 1823, re-opened 1825)
> Bolshoy Petrovsky, Moscow, 1825 (burnt 1853, re-opened 1856)
> Teatro Taco, Havana, 1837
> Royal Opera House, Dresden, 1841
> Madrid's Teatro Real, 1850
> Brussels' present Théâtre de la Monnaie, 1856
> Colon Theatre, Buenos Aires, 1857
> London's present Covent Garden Theatre, 1858
> St. Petersburg's Maryinsky Theatre, 1860
> Die Oper am Ring, Vienna, 1869
> Stadttheater, Hamburg, 1874
> Royal Theatre, Copenhagen, 1874
> The Costanzi Theatre, Rome, 1880
> Prague's National Theatre, 1882 (burnt two months later and re-opened 1883)
> Metropolitan Opera, New York, 1883
> Budapest State Opera House, 1884
> Zurich Opera House, 1891
> Berlin's Oper am Königplatz, planned 1896 (completed 1924)
> Royal Opera House, Stockholm, 1898
> Norwegian State Opera House, Oslo, 1900

With the exception of New York's old Metropolitan, which was replaced in 1966 by its larger namesake, every theatre building listed here (some renamed, and some extensively renovated – or rebuilt after bomb damage in the Second World War) is a working theatre today.

These vaunting houses, designed in the Italian configuration with picture frame stage, orchestra pit between stage and audience, and tiers of boxes, were equipped with stage machinery as complex as could be afforded and procured. But, as anyone knows who has been involved with theatre-building, the cost of construction is at least finite, whereas the costs of theatre maintenance and operation march off, ever-expanding, into the future. Some of these theatres were run simply as road-houses, enabling the city to receive visiting companies from the great operatic centres. This, though not cheap, was and is the cheapest way to operate a large theatre building. But many others became the homes of resident artistic companies on the Parisian model, with musical director and staff, orchestra, chorus, *corps de ballet* and soloists, scenic designers, builders and painters, costumiers, seamstresses, stage hands... and so on. The vast theatre building, and the vast company of artists and craftsmen – this was the instrument on which grand opera was written to be played.

In the smaller capitals the opera-house also served as the home of operetta – France's other major nineteenth-century contribution to the art of the singing theatre. It was Offenbach who perfected the genre. He made out of the material of the old *opéra comique* a new, fast-paced entertainment that was perfectly suited to its middle-class audience in their lighter mood – satirising government corruption and the sexual mores of the rich and privileged, but with a tolerance that made it acceptable even to the Emperor. Its heyday was the Second Empire: with the final collapse of the monarchy in 1870, the conniving, frantic and fantastic world of operetta lost its point, and retained its popularity not as a grinning, demonic image of the present, but as a symbol of a golden age gone by. In Vienna, the Viennese version of operetta continued playing this role up to the Second World War and beyond.

Meanwhile the art of grand opera, it need hardly be said, did not stand still. By 1840 Wagner and Verdi were already launched on their careers as composers, each in his own way exploring the power and the delicacy of the mighty combination that Paris had put together. Wagner rejected the style, conventions and content of French grand opera, and was continually at war with music directors and opera house intendants everywhere. But he in no way rejected the size of the operation – in fact he conceived and executed his own mythic dramas on a truly titanic scale, requiring a yet further expansion of orchestral forces, and eventually his own ideal theatre. Verdi brought his Italian love of melodic line, vocal display and passionate theatricality to the genre; and Bizet, Tchaikovsky, Mussorgsky, Mascagni, Puccini, Leoncavallo, Debussy, Strauss and others, went on adding masterpieces to the repertoire up to the First World War, and even after it. The pseudo-baroque opera palaces continued to resound with the surgings of this massive romantic art-form.

If we have to choose a high symbolic point in this triumphal progress of grand opera, it must surely be the presentation of *Aida* in 1871, on the occasion of the opening of the Suez Canal. This commercial and military waterway, cut through 103 miles of desert by Egyptian labourers toiling for pennies a day, was one of the extraordinary achievements of the century; not only a feat of engineering but a tribute to the immense power and reach of European capital and its capacity to mobilise cheap labour. And nothing was more fitting, to celebrate its opening, than the commissioning from Verdi of an opera for which no expense was to be spared.

The opening was delayed because the monumental scenery being designed in the Opera's workshops was caught in the Siege of Paris, enabling Verdi to make further revisions, and also to have six trumpets especially designed and constructed for the production. The Khedive invited crowned heads and celebrities from all over Europe, and they came in swarms, lured by free tickets to *Aida*, and, of course, free accommodation during their stay. When he invited them on a day's picnic cruise from Cairo to the head of the Canal, the party filled no less than sixty-nine vessels. Small wonder that the ruler bankrupted himself.

Aida rolled on to the stage less than a hundred years after *The Marriage of Figaro*. It still remains perhaps the grandest of grand operas, in which Verdi sought to marry the exotic splendour of the East with the massive and complex organisation of Western musical drama, and using the new network of communication by rail, ship and cable to make the event possible. The première production stands almost as an emblem of opera's power in society, its capacity to dazzle and stupefy finally acting itself out on the stage of the world.

But high points are high points. There were to be many other triumphs to follow, but slowly – and even swiftly, after the shattering of Europe between 1914 and 1918 and the collapse of dynasties in Germany, Russia, Austria and Italy – the opera-houses of the capitals and great cities became emblematic not of social and economic triumph in the present but of a departed glory. With the audience's nostalgia for the ersatz but persuasive grandeur of the Victorian period, and with the financial and political straits of so many European countries in the twenties and thirties, the sheer capacity to bring the old masterpieces to the stage was a sign that all was not lost, that the routines of High Art were still capable of renewal. With this 'fixing' of the repertoire, and with economics necessitating minimal rehearsal and the repeated reuse of scenic designs from past productions, the emphasis on vocal virtuosity became still more marked – more important than the drama, more sought after and more cherished than success in the over-all integration of artistic forces. Through the power of the voice the great soloist kept alive the middle-class need for heroes, and its belief, in a world of swiftly accelerating democratic demands and economic decline, for the grand, the noble, the aristocratic passions of an idealised past. If ever an art appeared to have reached a state of advanced decadence, it was opera at the outbreak of the Second World War.

In 1989 the opera company of L'Opéra de Paris deserted le Palais Garnier where it had performed for over a century, and moved to its new, billion-dollar home at la Bastille. The reasons, we are told, were financial and practical. The old house has less than 2,000 seats, la Bastille seats more than 3,000. Le Palais Garnier, with its vast spaces for the public, but cramped production areas, makes repertory change-overs difficult and expensive; la Bastille, equipped with the latest in stage machinery, can present seven performances a week.

A report in *Le Monde* (16 April 1988) listed the permanent salaried staff of the Paris Opera as 1,156, including 158 musicians, 104 chorus members, 154 dancers, 422 technical staff (including those involved in costume and set construction) and 125 stage hands. The reporter mentions that the average salaries of this army are not excessive, but that the organisation's most illustrious artists (as in all the world's top-flight opera houses) command – and are paid – fees of astronomical size. Seiji Ozawa, we hear, takes home US $65,000 for an evening's conducting. And the 'world-class' singers can command a similar amount: occasionally more. Directors such as Strehler and Chéreau are paid many hundreds of thousands of francs for their services: the opera 'did not hesitate' to offer Robert Wilson 650,000 F (US $410,000) for a production.

Michel Sarazin, in his book *Opéra de Paris, les Mystères de la cathédrâle de l'éphémère*, provides a tally of the materials consumed by the Opera's workshops in 1986: '25 tonnes of steel, thirty-one kilometres of undressed boards, 8000 square metres of plywood, three hectares of cloth of various kinds, 500 kilos of nails, pneumatic clamps; 120,000 bolts; 17 tonnes of paint...'

The cost of the operation? In its final few years at L'Opéra, the total annual budget of the operation (which includes the Corps de Ballet and also the Opéra Comique – now the 'Favart') amounted to between 410,000 and 440,000 million francs (approximately US $280 million). As you would imagine, seat tickets were expensive: the Parisian opera-goer expected to pay a top price of 550 F (US $350) for his seat in the balcony or the orchestra. How much, then, of the total budget was earned at the box-office? Only a quarter; the balance, some $225 million a year, was furnished by State subsidy – the Paris Opera has been swallowing almost a third of France's entire annual state budget for music.

The article went on to ask whether the Paris Opera is in the process of choking itself to death. This might have looked like tendentious journalism at the time, but within less than a year – in January 1989 – the Opera, a few months away from its move to la Bastille, fell spectacularly apart, in a welter of political manoeuvering, personal jealousies, strikes, financial irresponsibility, and artistic conflict. How could it be otherwise? And yet for all the chaos, the government seems to accept without demur that it has a general responsibility to kick along the gigantic football *pour la gloire de la France.*

Why does it do it? Why is 'serious' – and grand – singing theatre still thought to be such a high priority in a government's cultural spending? Why, in the new prosperity of post-War Europe, is the huge machine kept running? Could it be that the 'revival' of opera in the years following the Second World War has been simply one more re-playing of the game of nostalgia, one more attempt to match up to the heroics of the past?

AN INTERNATIONAL PERSPECTIVE

The question of the nostalgic purpose of grand singing theatre takes on a special interest when asked about the socialist countries of Eastern Europe, for whom – one would have thought – the views of Marxist Arnold Hauser, quoted earlier, would have been sound dogma. Far from it. When the Deutsche Staatsoper was re-established in East Berlin in 1945 (housed in another theatre) its first performance was of Gluck's *Orpheus and Eurydice* – one imagines that it was too soon after the collapse of Nazism to kick off with Wagner. However, in 1955 the company returned to its home, now habitable, and opened with *Die Meistersinger.* The re-opening address, by one Johannes R. Becher, was quoted in an official tourist brochure:

> The Staatsoper, a work built by the people, is destined to make available to the people the best creative achievements produced through the centuries in the field of musical culture. It should enrich and deepen the concept 'owned by the people' in the field of musical culture and opera art, and endow it with a new form of exemplary character.

The article went on to describe further extensive renovations undergone by the opera-house in the 1980s, and concluded with remarks by one Manfred Haedler:

> In 1992 the Deutsche Staatsoper will be 250 years old. When it first opened it was…a preserve for the elite of the Prussian court, which Friedrich II described as an 'enchanting magic castle'…Today it bears witness to the cultural endeavours of our country, of the responsibility of socialist society for the values of the past and present, of the activating effect of musical art upon society; in full awareness

of its tradition it places the demands of today at the service of the future. It is people's theatre in the most comprehensive and lofty meaning of the term.

Perhaps I am being unfair to these men; both referred not only to the past but to the shape of things to come. No East German, though, could tell me, in 1988, what had come of the plan to endow opera 'with a new form of exemplary character' – or even what was meant by 'placing the demands of today at the service of the future'. I suspect that all this was no more than windy piety to the idea that revolution should be on the side of change. On a visit to the Dresden Opera in 1988 I was told that the productions on stage had to compete with the restored opera house itself for the people's interest. The public tended to go to performances in order to see the magnificence of the building; during a private conducted tour of the amazing pile I was informed that for such guided tours there was a three-year waiting list.

Traditional opera, then, was preserved in the German Democratic Republic – as in other socialist nations – on the same principle by which Gorky persuaded Lenin not to destroy the palaces of the Romanovs, but to turn them into museums and art galleries: they were part of Russian history and tradition, and now belonged to the people for their pleasure. All of us can be princes as we visit the Hermitage, stroll along the lawns of Tsarskoe Selo – or visit the Bolshoi.

There can be no quarrel with this, and we are thankful that the principle behind Gorky's broad humanity saved some of Eastern Europe's most splendid architecture. But in its preserving – and even its meticulous restoration – of the buildings and apparatus of the operatic tradition, the policy had ramifications which seem to have been less clearly understood. The formal structure of traditional grand opera, with its leading parts and its chorus and orchestra, is a reflection of aristocratic (or would-be aristocratic) society, and obliges the production company to assemble a work force which mirrors that society. Grand airs from the highly paid stars, for example, and resentments from the masses, are part of the tradition because they are natural results of a form that is inequitably constructed, monolithic and resistant to change.

Secondly, the re-creation of the art and tradition of the past needs – and attracts – a particular kind of artist and a special breed of *aficionado*, who find in the certainties of the past, in the anecdotal glories of long-vanished singers and performances, in the minute questions of authenticity of style, a haven out of the storms and shipwrecks of contemporary art. In the countries of the West this function of opera is clear – what otherwise would they do, those tireless polishers of the family silver? But it was even more true in the countries whose governments, for many years of this century, were committed to radical socialism. People there sometimes had, God knows, an even more justifiable need to hark back to the old ways; those who could discuss endlessly the correct way to sing a Mozart aria were in a world untouched by time and politics. It was naive of me, before I visited Moscow in 1986, to have assumed somehow that a socialist country would be shorn of artistic conservatives; and I found myself on the first day, in the Moscow Conservatory, surrounded by silver-polishers defiantly entrenched in the noble Russian musical tradition. As our host, the elderly but restlessly alive Boris Pokrovsky, said with a mischievous dart from his eye: 'This teacher is a conductor – of course, because we are in the Moscow Conservatory. You won't find directors here. It's good in a way, because of course it means that there are no conflicts…the rehearsal we are about to see is of a scene from *The Marriage of Figaro* – I understand that *The Marriage of Figaro* is a speciality of the Conservatory.'

The extraordinary changes of 1989 have upset operatic as well as political hierarchies in Eastern Europe. The Party member whose sealed office I was shown at the Dresden Opera, and who controlled all opera company appointments and movements, is presumably out on his tin ear. But it will be interesting to see whether the new democracies, as they open up to the West and start to construct market economies, will rethink the philosophies and the costs of their operatic traditions.

In post-War and 'capitalist' Western Europe, where there had not been so radical a break with the past, opera's role as the apex of culture has been curiously enough more hotly contested, especially in countries with an active socialist tradition. The social glitter, the connoisseurship, the expense, all suggest that opera is an art which excludes the mass of people, and it has been a struggle – above all perhaps in Great Britain – to justify the expansion of operatic funding. But by the 1980s the struggle appeared to have been won by opera; it had confirmed its place as an expensive but culturally desirable activity, as an international, suprapolitical art in which each nation according to its means must strive to shine. The *Finnish Music Quarterly* (2/86 p. 17) accompanies photographs of the model for Helsinki's new opera-house with these words:

> Slowly but surely Finland is developing into a civilised country…At least by the 1990s Helsinki will finally join the capital cities of the world which can boast a purpose-built opera-house…

In North America, the growth of traditional opera since 1945, and particularly since the mid-1960s, has another impetus: the determination to approach – and reach – the cultural standards of Europe. In the United States, and to a lesser extent in Canada, the opera is the one socially unquestionable art, an art to which prosperous individuals and corporations can give money in return for an unimpeachable credit in the programme. It is enormously expensive to produce and to attend; patronage of the opera, whether as member of the audience or as sponsor, is a guarantee of solid, unradical values. Its product, after all, is generally free of left-wing politics, sexual deviance, bad language, and all but the most tasteful nudity.

Opera in North America is the ideal art for the enjoyment of those who do not believe in North American art, whose cultural outlook remains colonial in the most neutral and objective sense of that word. For the American opera lover, supporter and practitioner, art is something that Europeans invented and perfected, and of which the Americans, with their wonderful energy, and their ceaseless capacity to learn, and the wealth that can attract the world's finest talent, can provide a superb simulacrum. Walking the wide galleries and the spacious stairways of the new Metropolitan Opera House, we can – in our New-World fashion – play once again the roles that Garnier established for nineteenth-century Paris.

And just as New York, Chicago and San Francisco compete – in terms of scale and expense and in the hiring of prestigious talent – on an equal footing with the great houses of Europe, so scores of smaller cities strive in their less opulent way to show that they, too, have become 'civilised'; that they too have their opera, and therefore their opera audience, and therefore their claim to cultural sophistication and social weight.

Both in the East and West, therefore, both in Europe and in North America, it has been as a touchstone of national or civic commitment to sophistication and culture, that the 'serious' singing theatre, the traditional grand opera, has established itself. The fact that it costs so much money, far from being an obstacle, is essential to the role it plays. High expenditure, after all, is a testament to the seriousness of the commitment; if it cost less, its iconic value would decrease. This is the irony which has kept these vast ships afloat.

Chapter Three

OLD BOTTLES, OLD WINE:
THE PROBLEM OF NEW WORKS

There are moments in history when some new form of art, a new way of expressing, seems to catch the tide of ideas and for a while fills the imaginative needs both of artists and of their public. The sudden appearance of Elizabethan theatre in England was one such moment. The first strange, round, wooden theatre building was hammered together in 1576. Nothing like it had ever appeared in England before. By 1614 there were at least eight similar public theatres in London, and hundreds of plays had been written for them, including the works of the world's greatest dramatist – who as a shareholder in his company had retired a wealthy man in 1610. By 1620 the excitement had already faded, the creative movement was beginning to exhaust itself – and in 1642, less than seventy years later, the theatres were closed by order of the Puritans.

All creative artists must wish to be born in the flood of such a time, and to have such a chance. First, a new or renewed vehicle of expression; second, the sudden emergence of brilliant creators and practitioners; third, a new kind of place to house the work; fourth, a national leadership which patronises and even delights in the whole enterprise, and allows some intellectual freedom in its execution; fifth, a flood of new thinking and feeling to be absorbed into the making of art; and finally, a truly general public that embraces the work, and awaits every latest development – talks about it, writes and fights about it, lives and dreams it.

The singing theatre has in fact been rich in moments like this: Venice in the mid-seventeenth century, Naples at the beginning of the eighteenth, Broadway between 1925 and 1960. But the rise of Romantic opera in post-Revolutionary Paris was the most astonishing and meteoric of all, and can be identified by those same marks that distinguished the age of Shakespeare. Once again a new – or at least renewed – vehicle of expression, a steady emergence of creators of brilliance, a flood of new and progressive ideas, the support of the government, the excited interest of a (more or less) general public, and – over fifty years and more – the building of a string of new opera theatres not only in Paris but around the continent, to house the marvel. The emergence of opera as a major form of creative expression in the nineteenth century was of course not confined to Paris. Italy continued to produce composers of genius, and Germany was nurturing the mightiest of them all in the person of Richard Wagner. But Paris – at least until mid-century – was the engine of the renewed and expanded art form. And at the heart of the enterprise lay the ceaseless presentation of new works from French, Italian and German sources – among them most of the operatic masterpieces that we know and venerate today.

It is sometimes discussed whether the creators of the new works, which appear in such periods, have arisen to meet the challenge of the circumstances, or whether the circumstances have grown up as a response to their work. Neither one is the case: the phenomenon occurs as the result of several different agents – historical, social and cultural – coming together at the same time, in the same way that certain conditions in combination can cause a particular plant or animal to flourish. Regardless of which might be the chicken and which the egg, it does seem to make sense to judge these moments – when new work is serving as the principal 'content' of an artistic activity, constantly developing and moving in new directions and followed by an eager public – as high creative points in the development of an art. By the same token we would judge a period in which the central 'content' of the art consists in work revived from the past, as a less creative stage of that art's development. And if we use this yardstick to compare the state of the operatic art around 1990 with the period, say, between 1790 and 1890, we would have to judge that the art of grand opera, now so often richly produced and sung, so broadly spread throughout the First World, and so adept in the business of attracting its audiences, is still in a less creative phase now, a less original phase, than it was in the last century.

No-one can deny or diminish the achievements of those who have built or rebuilt the great world of opera in the last forty-five years, and provided pleasure for so many lovers of 'extended' music and of the soaring human voice. But I can dally no further; it is a great world that many people of creative brilliance have had to pass by – because it has passed them by; a world whose very greatness and grandness and social status and expensiveness, re-created with so much love and effort, make it a heavily unresponsive vehicle of expression for our own times.

Opera in the twentieth century has become so multifarious, its activities in different countries so diverse in the way – and in the amounts – that they are funded, in their social function, in their standards, and in their audiences, that as we approach the subject of opera today, general observations about it become increasingly risky. Comments we may make about the social 'éclat' of opera-going will be responded to by our being told the number of pairs of jeans in the Omaha audience, or the strict democracy of ticket distribution in Dresden. Concern about expensive tickets will be repudiated on the grounds that in Vienna the traditional standing room ('Stehplatz') ticket system still offers inexpensive audience places, or that in Toronto there is always a group of seats kept back for students and senior citizens. And so on. When great efforts are made to enable an art to survive, then any apparent criticism of it will be staunchly resisted. An attack on present operatic modes by someone who may not respond eagerly to what they see and hear is likely simply to arouse a defence from those who like what they see and adore what they hear. Opera is difficult to be impartial about because we all have our vested interests, whether as practitioners or audience. Besides, I have not embarked on this enterprise in order to weave a string of half-truths about opera, but to explore the potential of new work in the singing theatre.

At the same time, I believe it is important to search beneath the infinite variety of local conditions, for the reasons why the staple diet of today's opera everywhere continues to be not new work but great works from the past. Let us look at a handful of these reasons.

1 THE AUDIENCE

An opera audience, like most contemporary audiences for music, will generally be one that is not intimidated by traditional culture; which may in fact find its deepest pleasure in the great works of the past, with their assured values and familiarity.

– The opera audience of today can never have too much of a work it loves, provided that the work does not fall below a mean standard – a standard that varies from place to place according to the degree of familiarity and sophistication on the part of the audience.

– In a world where much of new music has moved beyond the idea of delighting an audience, the opera public, given its own head, will prefer to be delighted with works that it knows, rather than having to rise to the challenge of a new work, often unfamiliar and even forbidding in its musical style.

– The opera audience will be attracted by a celebrated voice. The more celebrated the voice(s), the less the audience will care about which work is to be performed. And vice versa: the less celebrated the voice(s), the more important it is that the work be familiar.

– These rules of thumb can all be bent by the power of publicity and public relations. Extensive (expensive) paid advertising in print and on TV and radio, the placing of supportive feature articles and interviews, the solicitation of public support from 'opinion leaders' of prominence, the development of media events and photo opportunities, are all methods by which an audience can be persuaded to move away from its familiar paths – to buy tickets for a production which would otherwise not attract it. Even the drawing power of a celebrated singer is made up of a confusing blend of talent and clever management.

2 ARTISTS AND REPERTOIRE

Those who have committed their careers to opera – directors, conductors, performing artists, coaches – have done so, in general, because they know and love the traditional repertoire, and feel comfortable in their expertise and their sympathy with the great works. A large opera company that wishes – or is urged – to mount a contemporary (let alone a new) work will often find it hard to put together a creative team with similar expertise and enthusiasm.

– Celebrated voices, and the singers that house them, are usually celebrated for a select number of roles; roles that display their vocal instrument to its best advantage. Good singers who master a dozen roles – or less – from the repertoire will find themselves able to make a handsome living from these roles; jet travel has made such people even more readily available. The assurance of an experienced singer in such pleasurable and profitable roles is not too readily exchanged for the dangers and difficulties of a role in a newly written work. Although there are magnificent exceptions, very many singers feel more comfortable and confident in a repertoire and range of vocal styles for which they have been trained and prepared. As a result, new works often have to be performed with young or second-line singers.

– Behind almost every great singer of opera is a singing teacher, almost always a practising or retired opera singer who has passed on his or her vocal skills to a new generation. Singers more than actors or dancers seem to suffer from such dependency, and teachers often exert astonishing influence over an operatic performer even after a career is well established, because – apart from their knowledge of the voice – they can inspire their pupils with stories of the great singers and productions of their youth, and instil a sense that what was done in glorious times gone by is what must be worked towards now, and in the future. There are, as always, signal exceptions, but the influence of most teachers will concentrate the singer on the traditional repertoire. 'I sink zis part of Zerlina most vait vun more year, until ve see vezer ze voice becomss darker: you vait – I tell you'. It has been said that an Italian teacher who knew little about singing but who had touched the hem of Puccini's garment was made for life.

– The development of a new piece of singing theatre requires a particular assemblage of skills; librettists who know how to work with composers and vice versa; directors who know how to critique the new work and contribute to its development; singers who understand and appreciate the process of working with a living composer and librettist on a new work. Very few of these skills can be found in the traditional opera companies, who if they take on a new work often find themselves at sea.

– The initial choice of composers and librettists, and their subsequent guidance, is a very particular skill which few opera producers have a feel for.

– Music has changed in many fundamental ways since the days of the Romantic expansion, and particularly since Schoenberg's move away from 'tonicality' (as Dutch composer Peter Schat describes it – a word more accurate than 'tonality') before the First World War. The grand, even grandiose, forms of nineteenth-century music, whether symphonic or operatic, seem often inappropriate to new work – large scale in itself has a good deal less generic attraction. And 'atonical' music – or even modern 'tonical' music – is much harder for singers and orchestras to learn and get right, and harder for audiences to appreciate.

– Opera seasons have to be put together and cast two or three years in advance, because of the need to contract singers who are in demand. A new work is hard to cast so far ahead because it has often not been finished (sometimes barely begun), and the singers cannot first try out the role before deciding whether it is both vocally suitable and prominent enough to accord with their view (or their manager's view) of what their standing demands. The budgeting of the production is also difficult because until a director has developed a concept for the new work and a designer has developed some designs it is hard to gauge production costs. And the director and designer cannot begin work until the piece is well advanced. If no production plans are made until the work is finished, there will be a gap of five to six years between the commissioning of a work and its performance. In this period intendants and general directors can change, financial conditions can deteriorate, and enthusiasm can wane. It is strange how often – on the rare occasions when a large opera house commissions a new work – the work remains on the shelf.

– A repertory opera company that hires artists season by season must assemble a large cast and orchestra for the grand operas it presents in its large theatre, and cannot easily shift in scale from large to medium, or from medium to small scale. New operas, if performed by such companies, therefore need to be on a similar scale. But the new opera may well be neither good nor popular. So a high risk is married to a large investment.

– Because productions of new works in opera-houses are an exception rather than the rule, composers and librettists are not normally part of the regular creative team, and therefore have a hard time gaining the experience necessary for the development of their talent. That is why many composers of new works for opera companies are in fact neophytes, and write unsuccessful works – thus bringing the idea of presenting new works into further disfavour with artists, producers and audience. After one failure a creative team is discarded, and has little likelihood of landing a second chance.

– Though much fuss is engendered in the media by unexpected interpretations and settings of the traditional repertoire, at the heart of every eye-boggling new version is the unchanging work; the music remains in all its period splendour even if we hear it unrolling in a disco, bomb-site, garage, spaceship or video-world (– if the music is in some way 'fixed' or rewritten, of course, things are different; we are in the presence of a new work). Much is made also about nuances in interpretation of character and situation in new productions – and indeed there are always striking illuminations in the work of those few singers who are also natural actors, when guided by a truly theatrical director.

The fact remains that grand opera is modular – anyone who knows the music can be fitted in at very short notice, even in the most original production. 'Grace Bumbry is unfortunately indisposed, and is unable to sing tonight. But as you were approaching our wonderful theatre this evening, a certain person was winging her way to London from Cologne, and even now a Rolls Royce is wafting her to us here in Covent Garden. Ladies and gentlemen, it gives me great pleasure to announce to you that taking Grace Bumbry's place, at very short notice, will be…Josephine Barstow!' Loud applause and excited chatter.

New works of grand opera offer no such advantages. If your star is unable to perform – for any of the various reasons: physical, strategic or emotional – you are sunk.

3 COSTS

Opera has always (or almost always) cost more than it can earn. So all costs must be minimised, the minimum being set as the point below which the integrity and taste of the producers refuses to go, and/or at which audience attraction is at risk. The legacy of nineteenth-century singing theatre is a group of operatic masterpieces which were created on a very large scale, and are therefore very expensive to produce. Yet it is these very operas which are the 'blockbusters' – the favourites of the audience, for which box office sellouts can be almost assured. You will always lose money, but if you present a blockbuster, you are likely to lose less. Less well-known operas are more of a risk. New works are the highest risk.

– A regional opera company that mounts (once or twice a year) a short 'one-off' season of two or three works, with each being performed half a dozen times or less, has all its eggs in those two or three baskets, and rarely has the financial latitude to risk an untried piece unless a special grant is successfully landed for a particular project – in which case it finds itself with the problem described above, lacking the expertise necessary to develop and present a new work.

– The more operas presented in any season, the more opportunities there are to draw audiences in, and to attract them back. Most large operatic roles cannot be performed on consecutive nights anyway, so that the presentation of two operas in repertory, with different soloists but sharing the orchestra and chorus, is a regular practice for short-season opera companies. But of course each additional production represents increased expense – and the more extensive the repertory the greater the costs of scene-shifting, and the larger the requirements for scenery storage.

– Celebrated voices, which as we have seen are another sure method of audience attraction, are expensive for that very reason – singers are aware of their own drawing power. With a traditional production of a 'blockbuster' opera, the singers know their traditional staging, and often simply fly in a few days before the opening, to be massaged into the production with minimal alterations to their usual performance. Conversely, the more original the production approach is, the less the singers' familiarity with traditional stagings can be relied upon – and therefore the longer rehearsal needed, and the greater the cost.

– The more original and striking the design and production approach is, the less the selling power of the 'favourite' work can be relied on – so a special publicity effort has to be mounted to generate excitement. New works will of course need to start from the ground up, and will require the most rehearsal, and therefore cost the most – especially with celebrated singers (if any can be persuaded to join the adventure). Publicity and public relations plans for new works must be more sparkling and persuasive still – with always that nagging fear that the 'brilliant, ground-breaking new work by Biggsville's young musical genius' may turn out to be a turgid and offensive disaster, and cut next year's subscription list in half.

– The more original and striking the production approach, the more chance of success in creating a major artistic/public relations event. And yet the more original and striking the production is, the more expensive it is likely to be – certainly a lot more expensive than pulling old scenery from the warehouse or renting it from another theatre. New works offer good opportunities for striking design. In fact a striking design might do something to redeem a musical failure. But it will also further increase the cost and therefore the risk.

4 REVENUE

Opera, as we have said, has always (or almost always) cost more than it can earn. So earned revenue must be maximised, and unearned revenue must be sought and also maximised.

– The maximum amount of funds that can be generated at the box office is a product of all seat prices multiplied by number of seats at each price multiplied by number of performances. Pricing of seats is a variable – not only in the amount of money to be charged for each seat, but also in the number of seats set aside at each price, and in the kind of deal offered to group bookings. In countries where seat prices are not fixed by the state, opera administrators must charge the most that they can at each seat price – without charging so much as to have an adverse effect on sales. And they must present as many performances as they can without 1) offering far more seats than they can sell, or 2) escalating running costs beyond the expense they believe they can handle.

– Other sources include the selling of programmes and programme advertising, catering, bookshops, special offers of merchandise, broad- cast rights etc. Most of these sources of revenue are designed to offer additional services to the audience, and therefore their profitability is directly linked to the size of the audience at productions. Amounts earned in this way are likely to be a very small percentage of total revenue. Radio rights do not bring in much direct revenue to the company, although they can be enormously useful in spreading knowledge about the company and interest in its activities. (The long tradition of radio broadcasts from the Metropolitan Opera has done much for American opera – and the Company's 'unearned' revenue is dominated by small donations from radio listeners.) Revenue from television rights can represent a handsome addition to a company's revenue, but the size of the payroll for a grand opera makes the broadcaster's expenses so enormous that the practice is a rare one.

– The principal sources of public funding are: national government grants; state, provincial, county or district grants; and city or municipal grants. The funds from these various public bodies may be conveyed directly to the organisation, or may be channelled through a granting agency. In either case, the conditions and size of the grant are never unconnected from socio-political considerations: the granting agency (even if technically an 'arm's length' organisation) may be working within cultural policy guidelines laid down by the government in power, and/or responding to concerns voiced about priorities by the artistic community. Even when granting agencies make their allocations through some form of jury system, such considerations will affect decisions. Opera producers must therefore work in a variety of ways to demonstrate the value of their companies to the general public, whose taxes are being used for mounting lavish productions of predominantly foreign extraction (except in Germany and Italy), and for the payment of enormously high salaries to creative artists – these productions being seen by only a very small percentage of the citizenry. The producer will normally have to make application for public funds year by year, furnishing the grantor with details of programme, policy and budget for the forthcoming season – and also providing details of the work of previous seasons. (Some bodies are now beginning to make commitments two or even three years at a time, making life a great deal easier for producers.)

The principal sources of private sector funding are: private individuals, societies, private foundations, corporations and companies. These moneys can be transferred to the organisation through: straight cash donations; covenanted donations spread over a period of time; endowments from which the organisation may make use of annual interest; donations or sponsorships tied to a specific project or production.

– The producer has the responsibility for developing a plan for the solicitation of funds, and in most Western countries a whole department is given over to the implementation of the plan. If, as is usual in Western

Europe and North America, the company is run by a board made up of volunteer members, these members will normally make their major contribution to the company by providing and soliciting donations. It follows that the majority of board members are chosen for their capacity to provide or solicit such funds; success in this activity is often in turn based on reciprocal relationships with fund-raising board members in other voluntary organisations ('You give me ten G. for the opera and I'll see you get something for your bank-managers' rest-home'). The success of private fund-raising is finally dependent on being able to 'sell' the quality of the company and its productions, and on the success with which support for the company is seen as a matter of community pride.

– Corporation donations and sponsorships are generally seen by corporations as part of their public relations activities, and will provide the company with something in return – usually in the form of advertising (discreet or otherwise), special arrangements at the box office, media events tying the name of the opera company with that of the corporation, the company's name chiselled into the list of patrons in the foyer or gracing a brass plaque on a seat in the front stalls.

THE BALANCING ACT

> Our job is to choose the right pieces, to put them on in the right way, to attract a maximum audience at high prices, and to make absolutely sure that our friends and well-wishers provide the rest of the money we need.[4]

Of all the factors considered above, it is the financial picture that remains the most powerful deterrent to the exploration of new work. The proportion of revenue drawn from each of the sources I have listed varies considerably from country to country. In some states there is a tradition and/or cultural policy by which large public subsidies are granted to opera companies, these subsidies being sometimes linked to statutory low seat prices, and sometimes not. In the United States, where there is no such tradition or cultural policy, the bulk of revenue must be drawn from high seat prices and from donations; and in countries of Western Europe where the Thatcherian climate begins to shift against increased state subsidy, a similar practice is growing whereby box office receipts are maximised through high seat prices, and unearned revenue expanded through the solicitation of private and corporate donations.

The following table shows comparative revenue figures for a number of Western European opera-houses – none of them in fact subsidised so heavily as the Paris Opera, which we have already examined.

Comparative Income 1987/8 (percentages)[5]

	Cov. Gdn	Hamburg	Munich	Vienna	Paris
Box Office receipts	42	26	27	26	17
Sponsorship	10	1	----	1	----
Public Grants	46	73	73	73	83
Other	2				

It is clear that the larger the public subsidy the smaller role financial considerations have to play in the administration of an opera company. But the problem of balancing the budget makes money an over-riding concern for *all* producers of opera. Because the costs of grand opera are high, the amounts that must be raised to pay for the operation are equally high, and the risks are correspondingly great. A bad judgement can cost hundreds of thousands – even millions – of dollars. 'At the Metropolitan Opera, if we do everything right we lose $30 million, and if we make a few mistakes we lose $35 million'.[6]

It cannot, therefore, surprise anyone that an opera producer more interested in presenting new works than in the traditional repertoire would find the tide running resolutely against such an idea. In fact, a producer with such interests would be unlikely to get appointed in the first place; those who lead the opera companies of the world must care deeply about the past, present and future of the well-ensconced operatic tradition.

Nor can it be surprising that when such opera producers get together, they tend to talk a great deal about money. In the United States, where public subsidies are sparse, the pre-occupation is all-absorbing:

> It all boils down to money. Everybody says 'Oh, we're all in this business of art' – no, we are not. We are in the business of money, because you can't do great art without a great deal of money. So we are all doing the best we can with what we have. But if there were anything I would wish for, it would be, for all of us, a money tree that just shook every morning and the money comes raining down and it grows again ready for the next day.[7]

This comment, like the others I have just quoted, was made at a conference that took place in New York on October 22 and 23, 1987. It was sponsored by the Central Opera Service under the title 'Opera at the Crossroads', and took place the very week of the world stock market crisis. Money was clearly on people's minds even more than usual, but it was still extraordinary to observe to what extent it dominated discussions; it had to, because if opera's financial reach doesn't for ever exceed its grasp, how can opera continue to ape heaven?

ATTEMPTED INITIATIVES IN THE OPERA WORLD

It would be wrong – and much more wrong in 1990 than in 1980 – to say that major opera companies never present new work. Some of them do from time to time, and especially when their financial position looks for the moment healthy enough to allow them to take the risks I have described. German houses, where risk is minimised by handsome public subsidy, regularly include newly commissioned pieces – though these seem only rarely to travel beyond their country of origin. The New York City Opera has increased its presentations of new full-scale works in recent years, as has the English National Opera. The Center Opera company of Minneapolis did some extraordinarily innovative work during the sixties and seventies – until the board decided it had had enough. A number of major opera houses have begun to combine in the commissioning of new work, thus spreading the liability across a larger group of risk-takers. Among the artistic directors of houses which pay no more than lip service to the need for new work, there are a few who feel strongly enough about it to force their conservative boards to take a chance or two. Some agencies, without whose funds the companies could not survive, also use their position to put pressure on opera boards. But the granting agencies, distributing tax-payers' money, also recognise that the opera-going public is likely to be somewhat less opera-going when new work is involved: they are aware that they may be forcing the companies into drastic financial straits – so the pressure they exert is rarely intense. The worldly-wise opera company director has been known in fact to turn around and proclaim the need for an additional grant to do anything even faintly modern or risky; it was thus that the Canadian Opera Company solicited a 'special' grant of a million dollars from the Canada Council to produce Britten's *Death In Venice* in 1984 – thus creating a great deal of understandable unrest among Canadian composers. Only three Canadian operas had been performed by the company in the previous twenty-five years. ' – Yes, I know, darlings, but let's face it – does any Canadian composer know anything about composing an opera?'

Granting agencies have also had for many years a policy of underwriting commissions to composers. These grants are usually applied for by the commissioning body and awarded by a jury made up of appropriate professional artists, who are told the total sum of money available and asked to disburse it among the preferred competitors. The commissioning money is applied for by a variety of musical organisations, including symphony orchestras, choirs and chamber groups. But whereas compositions for these will rarely last more than an hour, and will often be in the twenty-minute range, a full-scale opera with soloists, chorus and orchestra might last from one-and-a-half to three-and-a-half hours, with a complex, many-parted score. Since a composer reckons to spend two to three years on the composition of an opera, and since the librettist will receive a quarter to a third of the composer's fee, the composer's fee is proportionately large. If an opera company does take a deep breath and apply for a commissioning grant, the jury with a total budget of, say, $80,000 is faced with awarding more than half of it to one composer, and dividing up the remainder among the best of the more modest projects. It is not surprising that they decide often enough to reject the opera commission, and make smaller awards to more composers.

For a while, opera companies have seen the Composer in Residence as a solution to the problem of producing first-class, new, full-scale operatic work. The Chicago Lyric Opera launched one such programme in 1984 with the help of a private donor, engaging a composer for a year and promising him the resources that he needed to try out his work. The initial results, for all the good intentions involved, were typical of the ineptness of traditional opera people trying to cope with the new. At the end of a year the competent though inexperienced composer had written one forty-minute segment of a work, and had orchestrated it for forty-two players. The composer was given two days with the orchestra and singers he needed. The results – he said so himself – showed that he needed a lot more experience. The two-day venture cost $142,000, if I remember; and it was discovered subsequently that the rights were not available for the work on which the composer had based his libretto: the segment was scrapped and the composer was to start again. The programme, which still survives, has outgrown its teething troubles, but the tale of its beginnings is a cautionary one.

In a valiant attempt to encourage the development of new works, the American organisation Opera America (whose members are the major opera companies of the United States and Canada) made successful application to the Rockefeller Foundation in 1983 for a $5,000,000 grant, spread over five years, to be devoted entirely to a programme entitled *Opera for the Eighties and Beyond*. The money was to be applied for and awarded in the usual way by a jury made up of professionals in the field. As a two-time ('two-timing', my Music Theatre friends would tell me) member of this jury I was able to see at first hand some ten or twelve applications made over a two-year period. Names cannot be named: but it was clear that in some cases applications had been fired off simply because a distant money-bell was ringing – the reflexes of company managers never twitch so fast as when they hear it. 'Hey, there's some money available over at Opera America – add it to your list of grants to apply for.' 'But it's for new work!' 'Is it? Well, what the hell, let's go for it anyway – cook up a project and send it off. At least it will get those new-music weirdos off our back – when we don't get it we can tell them we tried but were given no support.' 'What if we do get it?' 'Hmm – well, we can always rig something. They give some production money too don't they? We'll do it in the foyer on a Sunday afternoon. And maybe I can hit up those oddballs the Fritzheimers for a few extra grand – they don't seem to like Puccini...'

In trying to open up to new work, several companies sought to commission a 'name', a cult figure whose fame would do something to transcend the stigma of a new piece and make life easier for the public relations people on which success and public interest would so much depend. Folk like Robert Wilson and Philip Glass fill this bill with great aplomb, and can command the kind of commissioning fee that suits their media-status. One company, in what looked like a gallant effort to attract a young audience, was commissioning an opera from a member of a rock group: I am not sure whether it ever saw the light of night. The juries I participated in were repeatedly struck by the ironic fact that the Rockefeller money was available only to Opera America members – to the group of singing theatre people temperamentally least interested and professionally least expert in the development of new work.

Some of the larger companies around the world, sensibly recognising the risks and problems I have already enumerated, have seen the future of new work to depend on the development of a 'second stage'. In 1975 the Metropolitan Opera presented one season of 'modern' works (including Virgil Thomson's 1934 *Four Saints in Three Acts*) at a small theatre in the bowels of the Vivian Beaumont Theatre, Lincoln Center. In 1985 the Royal Swedish Opera – under the controversial and sadly brief intendantship of Lars af Malmborg – opened up a studio theatre near the main house, in which new works were presented on a shoe-string budget, using members of the company. London's 'Opera Factory', which began life in Zurich, received vital seed-money from the English National Opera. In the mid-1980s the Canadian Opera Company renovated an old warehouse to become a second stage, and launched a programme for composers in residence, working in collaboration with the Company's Opera Ensemble of young singers.

Of these initiatives only Opera Factory – built round the energies and idiosyncrasies of one highly talented man, David Freeman – has so far gone on to astonish and draw the public, and to lead a full life in its collaborative arrangement with the London Sinfonietta; and even in this case their novel style of performance (novel to the singing theatre, I mean) is perhaps more significant than their actual commitment to new work. The Met's 'Mini-Met' venture was not repeated owing to lack of funds – too many millions needed to feed the hungry warhorses in the main stable. The Canadian Opera Company's second stage has so far been more useful to them as a rehearsal area than as a theatre. Although

Stockholm still attempts from time to time to mount small works, its separate small theatre lasted no more than two years, in part (I was told)
because the vast majority of company singers would do everything to
avoid the lot of being cast in such unheroic moulds, and in part because
the powerful Swedish unions felt that if there was any money to spare it
should go not to new enterprises but to increasing their salaries. (Stockholm, you may remember, was the place where union crews in 1988
dimmed the lights and lowered the curtain before Hell's trap-door had
opened for Don Giovanni – the performance went a minute or two past
eleven o' clock and they had been told that if this happened they would
not be paid extra.) The experience was enough to propel distinguished
Finnish director Ralf Långbacka into early retirement from theatre and
all its works

A potentially promising development sponsored by an opera company is now under way in the American Midwest, where Minnesota has
given birth to the 'New Music-Theater Ensemble' (note the hyphen!)
This performance group, under the direction of Ben Krywosz (architect
of 'Opera for the Eighties and Beyond' America scheme) evolved in the
late seventies out of training workshops run by Wesley Balk. They believe
in the cardinal importance of honing composer-librettist teams for Music
Theatre, and in 1989 the first fruits of the process were emerging, with
plans to take both their works and their developmental process to other
North American cities. But there are good reasons why this initiative took
place in Minnesota, with its record as a progenitor of new opera since
1964. There are few other traditional opera companies that can build on
any past experience of the new.

The problem with the vast majority of large opera companies setting
up second stages is that their priority is always the first stage; so complex
and so expensive is the main enterprise that any other initiative must be
seen as an extra, to be ventured on when times and funds allow. Grand
'ooppera' (as they spell it so charmingly in Finnish) still remains, for all
the fantasy underlying its continued existence, the measure of singing
theatre's reality and true seriousness.

THE INFORMAL ALTERNATIVE

There is another seed-bed of new singing theatre that should be mentioned: the arts festival. In the years since the Second World War, spring
and summer festivals of all sizes through Europe and North America
have been sponsors for much 'experimental' art, including non-commercial works of singing theatre – of all sizes. Tanglewood had a lively
new-opera policy for a few seasons. Avignon was seen for many years as

the capital of French experiment in the relationship of music to theatre. Glyndebourne as long ago as 1946 was the somewhat reluctant patron for Britten's first small-scale opera, *The Rape of Lucretia* – conceived, written, rehearsed and presented in an eight-month period by a team which became the English Opera Group. Aldeburgh subsequently provided the setting for the remarkable series of Britten operas of all sizes and shapes that began with *Albert Herring* in 1947. Finland's opera festival at Savonlinna, which dates back to 1912, now regularly presents newly written full-scale operas by Aulis Sallinen and other Finnish composers, and regularly sells out its 2,000 seats for these works. Indeed, one Sallinen opera, *The King Goes Forth To France*, was co-commissioned by Covent Garden and Santa Fé; it went forth in due time to both these houses, there to divide the critics and irritate the Toscaphiles – but then, as Sallinen explained to me, '*The King* is not an opera – it is Music Theatre'! Other festivals, including London, Edinburgh and Bath in the UK, Santa Fé, St Louis and Brooklyn in the USA, and Spoleto on both sides of the Atlantic, all have a tradition of producing new works of singing theatre. And there are now even festival centres that concentrate specifically on new singing theatre, including the Musiktheater Biennale in Munich, the annual Music Theater Workshop (leaning strongly towards Broadway) at the Eugene O'Neill Center in Connecticut, and the annual American Music Theater Festival based in Philadelphia (see p. 205).

Many festivals build the bulk of their programmes by bringing in works chosen from the repertoire of other organisations, national or worldwide. Edinburgh, for example, selects many of its offerings from the repertoire of other organisations, choosing them according to a theme or set of preferences on the part of the artistic director, who travels the world in search of the best and the most appropriate. Edinburgh also generates its own productions, and many major festivals do the same, combining guest imports with original presentations.

Festivals by their very 'one-off' nature are in fact in a good position to risk expending funds on new and unconventional works. People who attend them are in holiday mood and in general more prepared to try something out of the mainstream; if they don't work out – well, better luck next summer. Festivals have little chance of exerting their influence on the infrastructures of art. But new pieces of singing theatre first seen at festivals do sometimes feed back into the regular seasons of permanent companies, or are brought to other centres for a (usually) limited run following success at a festival. And just occasionally – as with the English Opera Group at Glyndebourne – the initial sponsorship of a festival has succeeded in engendering a way of thinking, a style or a revolution, that becomes enshrined in something more permanent.

My own experience of this process was at Canada's Shakespeare Festival in Stratford, Ontario. In 1971 the late and splendid Jean Gascon, then the Festival's Artistic Director, wanted to set up a 'Third Stage' season, and asked me to plan and produce it for the Festival, with Raffi Armenian as our Music Director. We developed a policy of concentrating (though not exclusively) on new Canadian works of singing theatre. The scale was modest, with a maximum cast of twelve and orchestra of fourteen. In four seasons we commissioned only one opera, *Exiles* by Raymond Pannell (in which the conductor-less orchestra of seven read their multi-coloured score on changing slides projected on to a screen: a sure recipe for nightmares). But we also produced: 1) the first (and still, as far as I know, the only) stage performance of R. Murray Schafer's gripping *Patria II: Requiems for a Party Girl*; 2) the first professional performance of Charles Wilson's less gripping *Everyman*; 3) and the first English version of Gabriel Charpentier's whimsical and Cocteau-esque *Orphée II*. We also presented Maureen Forrester in Menotti's *The Medium* – not Canadian, nor even a work of profundity, but exciting theatre and a superb vehicle for a great Canadian contralto.

When Lord Harewood was invited by the Ontario Arts Council in 1971 to tour Canada and review the state of opera in the nation, he wrote a gloomy report, but noted that the one light in the gloom was the Third Stage programme at Stratford, Ontario. 'Present thinking has...produced an exciting scheme...Canada's present operatic situation urgently requires experiment of some sort...Stratford should provide exactly the right milieu' (*Opera in Canada*, 1972, p. 32).

In spite of this encouragement, the initiative only survived by one year the take-over of Stratford by forces which I referred to at the time as the Visigoths: 'the man that hath no music in himself...' But that short-lived Stratford Third Stage series was still, indirectly, the progenitor of the first Canadian Music Theatre company; and it triggered an attitude of thinking in my own professional life which has led along highways and byways, spry ways and shy ways, to the writing of this book.

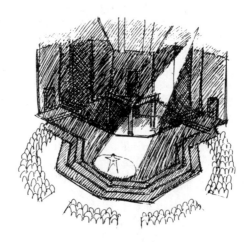

Chapter Four

MODELS AND FORERUNNERS

There are places scattered through the Western world where, despite the daunting problems we have been considering, the operatic system is moving slowly, with its audience, in the direction of change. But it is still – even in houses that are taking some bold steps towards the present – a world dominated by the primary need to re-create the works of the past.

This primary need drives other needs. What it requires of singers shapes the way singers are trained, and the way they plan their lives and careers. What it requires in space and facilities places a heavy burden of bricks and mortar, equipment, security, maintenance, and light and heating costs on every resident opera company. What it requires in technical lavishness and complexity calls for large teams not only of singers and instrumentalists but also of musical staff, stagehands, electricians, carpenters, painters, props-makers, costumiers – all of whom establish vested interests that are hard to dislodge and from time to time throw opera-houses into labour chaos. What it requires in size of audience necessitates intensive and expensive publicity and public relations.

Opera's yearly need for large sums of money to support all this infrastructure forces it in Western countries into the arms of government, of corporations, of the wealthy and powerful – and so into a social role, a display role. And in countries where the state has served as the only patron the opera is one shop-window that always remains stocked: a proof that all is still going well, that the socialist system can maintain high culture. East and West, the opera has represented incontrovertible prestige for governments, and in the West for corporations and individuals also; these prestigious attachments festoon the opera and have the effect of shackling even the most progressive houses to the status quo.

To those of us concerned with the development of new singing theatre, then, this whole interlocking and immensely well entrenched operatic system seems to present an insuperable obstacle. It cannot be blown up. So, difficult as the idea may be, our only course it seems is to leave the whole edifice aside and to contemplate the singing theatre without its traditional home. Taking a last look at that turreted palace with its scurrying, bickering retainers and clients, we turn away down a new road, impelled by the excitement of the pioneer, and carrying with us only a simplicity of intention – and our rambling definition:

At the heart of the singing theatre, there is a performer who acts and sings a role, in a dramatic performance, with musical support, in a performance area, in front of an audience.

But as the high Cs grow fainter on the night air we begin to ask ourselves: 'Is anything left without the opera house? Has anyone taken this new road before? If not, why not? Are we stupid, or mad?'

In order to give us both heart and ideas for the road, it will be helpful to drop our examination of the singing theatre for a spell, and look instead at the recent evolution of another performing art; one which, at the beginning of our century inherited a tradition as rigid and encrusted as that of opera. The most obvious target for our consideration is the world of dance.

THE EMERGENCE OF NEW DANCE

At the turn of the century Romantic ballet, in a state of decline in Western Europe, was re-born and revitalised in Russia largely through the work of the dancer-choreographer Mikhail Fokine. Fokine was influenced by the slightly older choreographer Alexander Gorsky – who had begun to translate into dance modes the naturalistic approach of Stanislavsky in the art of acting. But Fokine went much further. He questioned the 'tutu' and point-shoes of ballet tradition, and also the elaborate system of mimetic gesture which had developed over centuries and passed for acting. He was convinced that each ballet required its own costuming and even its own balletic style. He also incorporated into his work some of the new freedom of movement that had been brought to the stage by the maverick American dancer Isadora Duncan, who had stunned Russia with her solo performances on her first tour there in 1905.

In 1908 Fokine was engaged by Serge Diaghilev, who was then assembling a group of Russian dancers to be presented in Paris under the name of the Ballets Russes. The company's first appearance in the spring of 1909, which featured Pavlova and the young Nijinsky, took the French capital by storm, and initiated a revival of passionate interest in the ballet. The following year the company appeared in Rome, Berlin and London. Diaghilev's company presented further triumphant seasons in the capitals of Western Europe – and also in Latin America – up until the outbreak of the First World War. They were seen for the first time in North America in 1916 at the New York Metropolitan. But from 1914, cut off from Russia first by the war and then by the Russian Revolution, the 'Russian' period of the Ballets Russes gradually gave way to a more international operation. Diaghilev had already made use of innovative

Russian composers and stage designers (Stravinsky, Benois, Bakst, Kochno). But now he began to draw a clutch of Western European writers, artists, and composers into his workshops, including Cocteau, Chagall, Ravel and Debussy (and later the painters Picasso, John Singer Sargent, Braque, de Chirico, Max Ernst, Miró, Matisse, and Derain; and the composers de Falla, Satie, Richard Strauss, Prokofiev, Respighi, Constant Lambert, Poulenc and Georges Auric).

The Ballets Russes survived the war, and continued to function until their leader's death in 1929. But their effect in Western Europe and North America is still being felt today, through the influence of Diaghilev's leading dancers and choreographers. Serge Lifar, his last male star, was to reinvigorate the Paris Opera Ballet during the 1930s: it was he who introduced the practice of presenting the Ballet in productions of their own, rather than simply as adjuncts to opera productions. Britain's two ballet companies of the thirties, Ballet Rambert and Sadler's Wells, were each founded by former dancers in Diaghilev's company – Marie Rambert and Ninette de Valois. Massine worked all over the world, reproducing the choreography of the great classics of the Ballets Russes repertoire. And George Balanchine's influence in the United States has been incalculable.

While the Russian troupe initiated some reforms of ballet 'from within', exerting pressure on the traditional ballet companies to re-examine their techniques and their creative policies, the very different revolution set in motion by the work of Isadora Duncan was also spreading its influence. Duncan's embodiment of emotional and physical freedom served as the symbol of a new wave of libertarianism, as women sought relief from the bonds of domestic duty, and Freud began to lift the veils from sexual libido and the repressed Unconscious. In her later life she increasingly embraced socio-political solutions in the cause of individual liberty, and Soviet Russia, which viewed the Ballets Russes as a suspect, aristocratic operation, invited her in 1921 to found a school in Moscow. Duncan married a Russian and for a while was happy; but losing her youthful physique and spurned by her native America as a Bolshevik, she descended into alcoholism. She died in 1927 as a result of a famous automobile accident in which she was strangled by her scarf. After her death a number of her pupils started schools in Europe and North America, and interest in her approach to dance survived until the 1950s.

But Duncan was only one of several pioneers who changed the face of dance in the twentieth century; she opened a door for others to bound through. Ruth St Denis, another American, was brought up under the influence of the Frenchman François Delsarte, whose exercises for linking gesture to emotion (almost unnoticed in his own country) had been taken up by America with characteristic enthusiasm and thoroughness. St Denis soon became interested in Egyptian and oriental art and dance, and sought to find ways of expressing these cultures through her work. In 1914 she married Ted Shawn, a former theology student and exhibition ballroom dancer, and this dynamic couple became the progenitors of modern American dance. Their school, Denishawn, founded in Los Angeles in 1915, became famous for its spectacular and exotic dances based on themes from Egypt, Ancient Mexico, American Indian culture, and the Far East. St Denis also invented so-called 'musical visualisation', in which the dance 'enacts' a piece of music, providing a three-dimensional, abstract representation of the music's structure and sequences.

The Denishawn school lasted only until the thirties, but it spawned a new generation of dance pioneers. Martha Graham, and later Doris Humphrey and Charles Weidman, rebelled against the exotic and somewhat formalist entertainments of Denishawn as much as against the rigidities of traditional ballet, and set out each in their own way to develop a kind of dance that would more honestly and searchingly express contemporary life and times. It was Martha Graham who, perhaps more successfully than any other single person, accomplished this superhuman task. 'Modern dance' – the name was coined in 1927 – came to mean dance that was truly of our own century, and truly uncompromised by tradition, by commercialism, or by the need for social acceptance.

Fokine and Nijinsky had both experimented with new dance styles and techniques within ballet in the early 1900s; Nijinsky brought dancers down off their toes, inventing for Stravinsky's *Rite of Spring* in 1913 a heavy peasant step, heels pressed into the ground, which helped to spark the furore surrounding the work's première. But it was Martha Graham less than twenty years later who saw clearly the connection between technique and the spirit of the age. Traditional ballet portrayed human beings escaping from the pull of earth and appearing to fly; it was the apparently realised dream of the Romantic soul. But Graham, a modern American, worked to root her barefoot dancers into the earth, and developed a wide range of floor movements – kneeling, lying, sitting, rolling – which took her dancers a long way from classical technique. In her study of movement she started from first principles, developing the two extremes of contraction and release as the poles of physical expression. Her dances were often built around myth and ritual, from American Indian to Ancient Greek. But she treated her subject matter not as a decorative framework for dance, but in the way that Freud treated myth: as a distillation of elemental human experience. Graham also provided opportunities for American composers; aside from the scores created by her musical director Louis Horst she commissioned ballets from young talents such as Aaron Copland, Samuel Barber, Gian-Carlo Menotti, William Schuman, and Lehman Engel. (The financial rewards were not great: Engel records that he was usually paid fifteen dollars 'outright' for a score – orchestration included!)

Doris Humphrey developed similar dance techniques, although she preferred to see the physical mode of dance as taking place between the surrender to gravity and the struggle to stay upright, with the courage to lose equilibrium as the dynamic principle of action. Some of her works dispensed entirely with music, being danced to poems, or even to the sounds of the dancers' breathing. Charles Weidman, who worked closely with Humphrey, was known for his somewhat lighter touch – he used wit, parody and satire to make his points.

This trio of innovators worked for few rewards, and endured many years of poverty and privation. Humphrey and Weidman both found themselves – like Balanchine, Massine, and later Agnès de Mille and Jerome Robbins – working also in American musical theatre, which was enormously enriched by their contributions. Only Graham remained wholly dedicated to her art in its purest form. But for all their differences of ideology and method, between them they laid the groundwork for the astonishing explosion of American dance that began in the sixties and continues to the present.

One other strand of dance development can be swiftly traced. Rudolph Laban was born in Austro-Hungary, and in 1900 went to study in Paris. From there he moved to Switzerland, where he founded a dance school and choreographed ballets for the Dadaists. Laban, brought up under the influence of the intensely active movement for physical culture that swept Central Europe at the turn of the century, developed what became known as *Ausdrucktanz*, or expressive dance. He was also instrumental in widening the scope of modern dance by introducing it into the areas of education, therapy and recreation. He was particularly active as a theorist of dance and movement, and is now known above all for the system of 'Labanotation' which he devised in order to record choreography.

Laban's most famous pupils were Mary Wigman and Kurt Jooss. Wigman founded her own school at Dresden in 1920, and one of her students, Hanya Holm, went on to set up a Wigman School in New York in 1931. Kurt Jooss founded a company which became known for the strength of its social and political comment, most famously in Jooss' masterpiece *The Green Table* of 1931. Two years later, with the growing dominance of the Nazis in Germany, he moved to England and settled at Dartington Hall in Devon, then newly opened as a centre for contemporary arts education and activity. Here Laban also found refuge in 1938; he was to stay in England for the rest of his life.

This thumbnail sketch omits other significant strands of development – among them the influence of Dalcroze's 'Eurhythmic' methods on Nijinsky during *The Rite of Spring*; the short-lived but active and highly experimental Ballets Suédois (1920-5); the dance experiments of sculptor Oskar Schlemmer during the twenties at the Bauhaus in Weimar; the companies which were formed as successors to Diaghilev's Ballets Russes; and even the esoteric researches into voice and movement which formed part of Austrian Rudolf Steiner's approach to creative education, and which he called 'eurythmy'. But enough has been touched on to give a picture of the extraordinary creative ferment which developed in the art of dance in the twentieth century.

It should be pointed out that the great companies of classical ballet are still very much alive, stimulated and enriched by the developments around them. Companies vary. Most still enforce the strict discipline which we associate with another age, and which can turn dancers into automatons, stunting their capacity for independent thought. Ballet companies attached to opera-houses still tend to be hampered by the association and by the resistant conservatism of their audience. But it is not uncommon now for 'modern' choreographers to work in classical ballet, and for the contemporary ballet-dancer, while still firmly grounded in the technique of the nineteenth century, to extend his/her range of style and skill well beyond classical strictures and modes of expression. Commissions of new ballets are frequent, and the décor and lighting of dance is often a leader in the field of stage design.

And what do we find outside the classical ballet companies? Quite simply, dance has attained infinite flexibility of technique, form, scale, and content. There are dance companies made up of a single dancer, or two, or twelve, or forty-eight. Companies dance not only to orchestras or bands but also to electronic music, or the Japanese koto, or Balinese gamilans, or poetry, or song, or silence, or news headlines, or jazz, or radio noise, or sounds generated (either naturally or electronically) by the dancers themselves. Dancers perform in pubs, in the street, on lawns, in community halls, or in the theatres. There are rich companies and poor companies, political or camp, high-serious or frankly commercial. Dance, in other words, is an open art embracing an extraordinary range of possibilities. In North America it has also become since the sixties the most popular of the live performing arts, attracting capacity audiences for almost all its many manifestations.

The history of dance in the twentieth century could easily be matched by a similar account of developments in the dramatic theatre, where the names of pioneers and innovators – playwrights, directors, performers, theorists – are far too numerous to summarise; drama's movements, counter-movements, reforms and revolutions are the subjects of thousands of books. Drama has in fact kept frantic pace with this frantic century, and with Hamlet's dictum that the purpose of playing 'was, and is, to hold, as 'twere, a mirror up to nature, to show the very age and body of the time his form and pressure'. In the visual arts, where fundamental changes in approach began before the middle of the nineteenth century, an even more full and complex story can be told. Concert music, too, has suffered a tonic C-change, and begun to reach out to other ethnic musics – including jazz – as well as launching into electronic sound generation.

But when we put our picture of dance side by side with the evolution of opera in the twentieth century, it is hard not to come to the conclusion that what happened in dance and the other arts did not come within a mile of happening in the singing theatre. In analysing the advances made by dance, we see that they come under a number of headings:

> Courage, leadership and flair
> Readiness to question tradition
> Concern to serve as a vehicle for the expression of the times
> Concern to involve original artists, including artists from other
>   disciplines, in the creating of new things
> Preparedness to sacrifice personal comforts
> Preparedness to re-consider technique, and to think from first
>   principles
> Interest in other ethnic cultures
> Preparedness to work on many different scales and in a variety
>   of work spaces
> Belief in young talent, and the discernment to recognise it
> Benefit from the support of established artists
> Benefit from subsidies for new work and new approaches

The list does not readily impose itself, does it, over the modern history of opera? It is a list to have handy as we take our new road.

FORAYS IN NEW SINGING THEATRE

I would be mistaken to suggest, of course, that while all this excitement was taking place in other arts, the singing theatre continued to echo with nothing but the arias of another century. Because out of the same events that gave such a decisive push to the development of dance came several efforts to reform the scale, tone and technique of singing theatre.

Diaghilev was all his life a lover and supporter of the opera, and had formed the Ballets Russes company in 1909 as a mere adjunct to his second operatic season in Paris; he had introduced Russian opera to the

French capital the year before, when Chaliapin had made a powerful impression in the first performance of *Boris Godunov* outside Russia. It was in fact something of a surprise and disappointment to Diaghilev that his 1909 opera presentations – featuring Chaliapin once again – received scant notice compared with the rapturous response to his new ballet-dancers. The failure of Chaliapin to establish the reputation of Russian opera in the West was a particular disappointment; Diaghilev was fully aware of the qualities of the Russian bass not only as an extraordinary singer and musician but also as an actor of genius. But Chaliapin was unique among Russian singers. His compatriot colleagues had the limitations of most opera singers everywhere when it came to the combining of theatrical and musical talent.

Although the ballet often travelled alone on subsequent tours, Diaghilev made further efforts on behalf of opera, mounting productions in his Paris and London seasons between 1912 and 1914. In fact 1914 saw an experiment in which Rimsky-Korsakov's opera *Le Coq d'Or* was produced in both capitals with the singers singing from the side of the stage while the dancers enacted the singers' roles. The production was well-received – as a dance with vocal accompaniment.

The justification for concealing the singers, significantly enough, was Diaghilev's impatience with their lamentable acting skills and inappropriate physique: the two regular characteristics of opera that most offended his refined esthetic sense. He was unable to repeat the experiment with this production, because Rimsky-Korsakov's widow forbade it. But Diaghilev never gave up in his efforts to promote the singing theatre. In 1921 he commissioned Stravinsky to write the one-act opera *Mavra*, originally to be presented as a curtain-raiser to Stravinsky's arrangement of Tchaikovsky's *Sleeping Beauty*. *Mavra* was premièred in Paris in 1922, as also was Stravinsky's *Renard*, which the composer described in its original form as an 'Histoire Burlesque Chantée et Jouée', and which was – like *Le Coq d'Or* – performed by dancers, with singers and musicians in the pit. Diaghilev continued to commission operatic works from his composer colleagues, and was also one of the first producers to break away from the standard repertoire by commissioning arrangements of operas by seventeenth- and eighteenth-century composers such as Cimarosa and Pergolesi – of whom he was extremely fond. When he launched the Festival of Monte Carlo in 1924, operas became a regular component of the Festival programmes.

But Diaghilev was never able to effect the same kind of revolution in opera that he had so brilliantly initiated in the dance. He was not, after all, himself a creative artist, merely a magnificent *animateur* of the creative daring of others. In the singing theatre, it seems, he never located the creative spirits who could effect a fundamental change in the art; or perhaps his nostalgic conservatism in opera prevented him from following into the singing theatre the more eclectic and outrageous experiments of colleagues like Cocteau, Milhaud and Satie – experiments which he had himself done much to bring about. The espousal of popular musical styles clearly offended a sensibility that had been refined in the court of the Tsars.

So Cocteau and his colleagues went their own way. Cocteau's *Mariés de la Tour Eiffel*, with its rumbustious score (for megaphones and jazz group) by 'Les Six', was performed in 1921 and was the first of a series of knockabout cabaret-style singing theatre pieces that were to delight and shock the post-War Parisian audiences. For a while there was a remarkable convergence of 'serious' composition and the 'lowbrow' popular music of the period, as reaction set in to the High, massive, mythic, humourless art of Wagner and his successors – an art which idealised *ethnos* and power, and had in some sense sanctified (or at least provided background music for) the terrible slaughter of the War. What was striking about the new development was that it rejected the long-standing High Art patronage of folk music as a pure, pastoral antecedent, and instead accepted the new commercial – and genuinely popular – music as a source and inspiration. The models of grand opera were rejected in favour of a new anarchic nonchalance and rowdiness, and also a new harmonic directness. As can be imagined, the movement had minimal influence on L'Opéra de Paris or on the singers who performed there; hoist in another universe, these astral bodies continued to circle oblivious to time.

The year 1921 saw another development which turned out to be significant in the evolution of singing theatre: a small summer festival was inaugurated in Germany at Donaueschingen, by a group of musicians which included Paul Hindemith. The festival was primarily dedicated to the commissioning and performance of new music, and by 1925 Stravinsky had become an annual visitor, describing it as 'the centre of the musical movement'. Much of the work of the festival was instrumental. It was here, in 1922, that the young Kurt Weill first attracted attention with an early string quartet. Hindemith wrote a series of neo-classical instrumental works for the festival, and many other composers contributed. But it was here too that the new adventurousness of French artists found a platform: 'the Germans not only took the French ideas up; they took them seriously; and they took them to the public'.[8] Ernst Krenek wrote his jazz opera *Sprung über den Schatten* for the 1924 season, and the more famous *Jonny Spielt Auf*, with its black hero, in 1927. Hindemith also wrote large-scale operas in a new idiom, and the genre became known as 'Zeitoper', or 'opera that reflects the times'.

In 1927 the festival, of which Hindemith had by now become the acknowledged presiding spirit, moved to Baden-Baden, and in this new and
more exposed setting began to probe more and more deeply into the
possibilities of new music, and more especially into the social functions
of the art. What, after all, was music for? What ought it to be doing? If it
was to respond to the new and fragile republican democracy of post-War
Germany, or to the ideals of a more radical socialism, how was the question of musical 'seriousness' to be handled? Did 'serious' mean nothing
more than 'bourgeois'? If the uncomplicated common man liked uncomplicated music, how are we to treat the complexities of Schoenberg and
the musical avant-garde?

From questions such as these emerged two new alternative approaches to music. The first was the concept of *Gebrauchsmusik* – usually
translated as 'applied music'. The idea had originated with Satie's *mu-
sique d'ameublement* – 'musical furniture' (which we might think of as a
first and jokey version of the sense-numbing noise we now call 'wallpaper
music'). Milhaud's setting in 1919 of texts from farm and seed catalogues,
Machines Agricoles, was a clearly whimsical, anti-Art gesture, giving
music an easy, functional role as a conveyor for practical information,
and linking it to the repetitive noise and function and visual effect of the
machine. Fascination with the possibilities of music in its association with
machinery continued to develop through the twenties, as we have already
seen – and in film music it found its clearest expression.

A second kind of music to develop in Germany through the late twenties was inspired by the concept of *Gemeinschaftsmusik* – 'music for
amateurs'. In meeting with the leaders of youth organisations at the festival Hindemith heard again and again of their lack of music of high
quality and originality yet simple enough to be performed by young
people and other non-professionals. To answer their needs he wrote
string works which could be played in the 'first position', and simple choruses for schools. Milhaud and others followed his lead, and in 1930 Karl
Orff contributed his *Schulwerk*, the first of many pieces designed primarily for schoolchildren. These works led to the development of the
Lehrstuck, or didactic piece, where 'the performers were meant to learn
as they went, and to learn not only the notes but the technique and pleasure of working together as a collective too'.[9] The Baden-Baden Festival
of 1929 was devoted largely to such works.

'What didn't they try out there?' wrote Heinrich Strobel of Baden-
Baden in his study of Hindemith: 'Film music, mechanical music, potted
opera, radio music, music for young people, for amateurs...'

That first year in Baden-Baden the festival presented four small operas, which included Hindemith's own *Hin und Zurück* ('There and Back' – the second half is the first half played backwards); *Prinzessin auf der Erbse* by Ernst Toch; Milhaud's nine-minute *L'Enlèvement de l'Europe*; and – eventually the most celebrated of the four – the 'Songspiel' *Mahagonny*, with music by Kurt Weill, and words by Bertolt Brecht. With the names of Brecht and Weill we are finally back on familiar 'Music Theatre' territory.

BERTOLT BRECHT AND KURT WEILL

It was Kurt Weill who had proposed the first collaboration with Brecht, having been struck by the quality of the young writer's first published collection of poetry, *Die Hauspostille* (1927), and also no doubt aware of Brecht's connections with the German poet-singer tradition: Brecht had for some years been setting his satirical verses to music and singing them in the bars of Augsburg and Munich. Brecht in his turn was impressed by Weill's courage in turning away from his academic training and towards the coarser, slangier, jazzier world of cabaret style. Willett comments: 'Sharply orchestrated, and free from all mushiness, jazz not only fitted Brecht's conception of a down-to-earth vernacular language but also helped to establish his dramatic points...' After the 'top-heavy' *Zeitopern* of Krenek, Max Brand and Hindemith, this first Brecht-Weill collaboration showed the way in which, 'at a new, low, economical level, the problem of the opera could be tackled more effectively'.[10]

This may be so; but that first *Mahagonny* was a typical example of music-dominant singing theatre – closer in fact to what I have already described as 'concert theatre'. Its texts – apart from the finale, which was especially written for the production – were taken from *Die Hauspostille*; and the work had little in the way of dramatic form or content, consisting of a series of musical numbers with orchestral interludes. The drama lies only in the close-knit character of the word-music material, and the power of its social feeling. As a result, of course, the piece offers a splendidly free hand to directors, who over the years have taken full advantage of its opportunities.

This first encounter between Brecht and the world of serious music prompted him to some new thoughts; for the first time his wirily independent mind began to come to grips with the esthetic and social problems of the singing theatre. The following year the two collaborators were to work together again. Reading the text of *The Beggar's Opera* Brecht decided to write a new version of the piece, bringing its 'popular' style up to date, and – as in the original – dispensing with classically trained singers and using instead the less lyrical but grittier gifts of actors. Weill, continuing his divergence away from the world of 'serious' music, scored the new work – *The Threepenny Opera* – for an eight-piece band.

From this extraordinarily successful creation, which opened in Berlin in August 1928, Brecht continued to draw lessons about the relationship of words to music, of the singer to the song, and of spoken dialogue to music. Reacting against the 'culinary' art of the opera, in which a seamless emotional continuum is woven at the expense of logic and reason, he wrote in the programme:

> Nothing is more revolting than when the actor pretends not to notice that he has left the level of plain speech and started to sing. The three levels – plain speech, heightened speech and singing, must always remain distinct, and in no way should heightened speech represent an intensification of plain speech, or singing of heightened speech...The actor must not only sing but show a man singing.[11]

Brecht here speaks powerfully against the very basis of traditional opera, which is the need to accept that characters do not know – as characters – that singing one's thoughts and feelings is not a natural way to behave. The offensiveness of this convention for Brecht lay in its simple duplicity, in that same willing self-deception which he fought in all aspects of life. Brecht's determination to hammer out a whole new idea of how the actor should approach his craft was in the same vein. If the new socialist man was to be a realist, a pragmatist, a committed, thinking, judging, unsubordinated human being, then the performer must reflect that reality, and play roles without surrendering his/her own critical spirit and commitment. In a famous passage Brecht recommends that the actor should enact a character in the same way that an onlooker might describe to the police what happened in a car accident. He/she would 'play' the various parts in turn, not fully 'becoming' them but simply showing the 'Gestus', the fundamental attitude, mien or 'gest', which characterised each participant in the drama. Thus he/she would stand outside each character, commenting on the character's actions and still retaining his/her own personality and viewpoint as an actor and as a person. This is the basis of what Brecht called the *Verfremdungseffekt*, the 'alienation effect', which has intrigued or baffled thousands of performers and audiences since.

Total rejection of the convention of singing as a 'normal' way of behaving would of course eliminate the very foundation of the singing theatre as defined in the first chapter, restricting us to a theatre of songs. Brecht himself, who always had the courage of his changing convictions, was within two or three years collaborating with Kurt Weill on a larger version of their Songspiel *Mahagonny*: the new work, *The Rise and Fall of the City of Mahagonny*, turned away from the alienation effects of *The Threepenny Opera*, its characters showing no reluctance, and no self-consciousness, about singing their thoughts and feelings. It seems in fact, in a brilliant stroke, to use the 'illusion' of singing theatre as a 'Gestus' revealing the self-deception of the characters. If they could stop singing for a moment perhaps they could see more clearly where their folly was headed.

The new *Mahagonny* opened simultaneously in Leipzig and Frankfurt in March 1930, and the two premières caused a furore, with riots breaking out between its supporters and Nazi partisans – who branded it as degenerate. Ironically there was a sense in which Brecht agreed with the charge, though for different reasons: he was not happy at his move back in the direction of the 'seamless' operatic form. The big *Mahagonny* was first scored for some forty musicians, as well as a stage orchestra of twenty-one, and the music is almost continuous throughout the work. In later works Brecht preferred once again to divide music clearly from dialogue, in the style of *The Threepenny Opera*.

Later that same year, for the published edition of the work, Brecht was to write an essay under the title 'The Modern Theatre is the Epic Theatre', in which he attempts to put some new ideas in order. This is perhaps the twentieth century's most important single contribution to the debate on the renovation of opera, not because of the answers it provides so much as for the questions it raises. Above all it identifies the prime obstacle to change in the singing theatre as the whole 'apparatus' of opera production – everything that makes up what I have already referred to as the 'operatic system'. Brecht's response to traditional opera was not different in kind from his attitude to naturalistic drama: it was a socio-political response. He rejected 'culinary' opera not only on formal esthetic grounds but because his whole being rejected the kind of society for which opera was the supreme artistic experience. The separation of esthetic considerations from socio-political ones is itself, Brecht would say, a 'bourgeois' approach to art – a blind disregard for the means of production.

Brecht saw clearly that artists who wanted opera to join the other arts as a twentieth-century activity were up against the fact that the opera-going public adored opera 'precisely for its backwardness'. In trying to bring new musical ideas and new dramatic approaches to bear in the opera-house, he believed that artists and thinkers were deluding themselves. His comments on this subject need to be quoted in full:

> ...the avant-garde are demanding or supporting innovations which are supposedly going to lead to a renovation of opera; but nobody demands a fundamental discussion of opera (i.e. of its function), and

probably such a discussion would not find much support...

Great apparati like the opera, the stage, the Press, etc., impose their views as it were incognito. For a long time now they have taken the handiwork (music, writing, criticism, etc.) of intellectuals who share in their profits – that is, of men who are economically committed to the prevailing system but are socially near-proletarian – and processed it to make fodder for their public entertainment machine, judging it by their own standards and guiding it into their own channels; meanwhile the intellectuals themselves have gone on supposing that the whole business is concerned only with the presentation of their work, is a secondary process which has no influence over their work but merely wins influence for it. This muddled thinking which overtakes musicians, writers and critics as soon as they consider their own situation has tremendous consequences to which far too little attention is paid. For by imagining that they have got hold of an apparatus which has in fact got hold of them they are supporting an apparatus which is out of their control, which is no longer (as they believe) a means of furthering output but has become an obstacle to output, and specifically to their own output as soon as it follows a new and original course which the apparatus finds awkward or opposed to its own aims. Their output then becomes a matter of delivering the goods. Values evolve which are based on the fodder principle. And this leads to a general habit of judging works of art by their suitability for the apparatus without ever judging the apparatus by its suitability for the work.[12]

Brecht goes on to introduce his concept of 'epic opera', as opposed to 'dramatic opera', and then gets himself impaled on the old and rocky question of whether art should be pleasurable or instructive. The position he takes throughout must be seen in the context of the rapidly unravelling fabric of German society in 1930, and of the need to take a sharply polarised position against the rise of fascism; didacticism was necessary to head off a political monster born of fear and ignorance. But even as I say this, I hear myself trying to squirm out of making a necessary affirmation; that distrust of the operatic system, of Brecht's 'operatic apparatus', is to some extent a radical distrust, and that the changing of opera is liable to be pushed forward by those who have the imagination to consider fundamental change, and the courage and stamina to bring it about.

It was unfortunate for the singing theatre – among many far more cataclysmic tragedies – that within three years the Nazis were to achieve power in Germany. Hindemith's festival, like countless other artistic activities, came to an abrupt end, and the line of operatic development marked out by Brecht was snipped short. What is sadder, and more astonishing, is that in the sixty years that have followed there has been such sparse notice taken of Brecht's thinking about opera. It is not even that there has been controversy; his fundamental point about the apparatus of operatic production has been sidestepped, as we have seen, in both Eastern and Western versions of Europe.

And so we find ourselves once again at the starting place of this chapter and of this book. The resurgence of dance in our century gives us courage, and the scattered efforts on behalf of new singing theatre give us hope, as we set out on our new road, definition in hand and alert for challenges.

PART 2

GOALS AND TRAINING

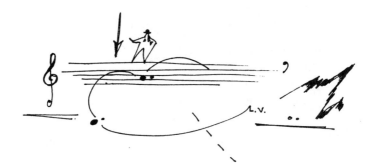

Chapter Five

THE GOAL FOR A NEW SINGING THEATRE

Artists of the singing theatre need a new, shared goal to journey towards
– a vision of what could be. Conjuring this vision is the first job. Without
it our road has no direction, and our decision-making no point of reference.

Central to a vision for any art is the freedom for talented people to
create works, and to share them. A new singing theatre will attract creative people only if it is open to them as an effective vehicle of expression,
and of communication with a public. This freedom and opportunity to
create works includes of course the preparing and performing of them.

Freedom to create works means that there are no *prima facie* restrictions either on the kind of work conceived, or on the content and meaning
of a work. This freedom is social and political in the first instance. In the
second instance it is cultural and esthetic. And in the third instance it is
economic. These freedoms intertwine.

So we need a situation in which talented people with something to
say (express, communicate) have opportunities to say it through the medium of singing theatre, and in which artists can realise their originality
and potential; a context that not only allows but actively encourages creation.

Can singing theatre serve in this way? Can an art which presents one
or more performers who 'act and sing a role in a dramatic performance
with musical support' serve as a vehicle of expression in the twentieth
century? Can we cope with the act of singing-acting without getting
locked into an absurdity? Can we believe, or suspend our disbelief, without a powerful framework of convention and tradition to persuade us or
distract us?

Those of us who plan a new singing theatre don't underestimate the
challenge of singing-acting as a way of representing human reality. But
we point out that the field is open. The last hundred years have established a new perception of 'reality' at almost every level: psychological,
spatial and temporal, semiotic and behavioral, social and economic. The
spectrum of expression from silence to speech to song and back again,
allied with gesture and action, offers to the artists who can make it their
own a multi-levelled language with which to express layers of consciousness, or varying mixes of reason with feeling, or of reality with surreality,

65

or public with private voices. Explorations of the possibilities of the medium have had to be tentative because they have taken place in a context that marginalises them. They have also had to be undertaken by performers who were trained for very different activities, and by composers and writers who are groping in the dark and alone.

Advances can only be made if the artists of the singing theatre are considered not as the servants of a tradition and an industry, apprenticed to the past, but as the primary material – the stuff you start with – the element out of which singing theatre is fashioned.

And what is an 'artist of the singing theatre'? An unsatisfactory term it may be, but for the moment the formula is useful in avoiding a whole host of categories (like 'opera-singer') that serve to muffle our understanding of what we are trying to do. It is a generic term that covers *all* the artists (composers, writers, performers, designers, musicians etc.) whose skills contribute to the making of singing theatre. We can therefore avoid placing these artists in order of seniority or importance, and instead offer them a common identity, a 'citizenship', and so a shared responsibility for the resulting work. Shared responsibility is not lightly undertaken, and can only develop in a context that diminishes 'top-down' authority, in which artists of different primary skills are encouraged to become aware of each others' contribution to the work.

These goals, then – the formation of new singing theatre artists and the provision of freedom and opportunity for work – require the establishment of a new set of principles to guide our activity.

The principles set out below have been developed out of many discussions, and have been used as a basis for the work of many initiators of singing theatre and their colleagues.

PRINCIPLES FOR THE NEW SINGING THEATRE

1 ECONOMY OF MEANS: THE NEW SINGING THEATRE WILL OPERATE ON A MORE ECONOMIC SCALE THAN THAT OF GRAND OPERA.

Implications:

a) The singer need not necessarily develop the size of voice required for large houses and to be heard above large orchestras.

b) The composer and librettist can design their new singing theatre works for smaller houses, smaller orchestras and smaller casts, and be prepared to modify the balance of musical forces for houses without orchestra pits.

c) The designer can apply his/her skills to the particular problems of small houses in relation to singing theatre, including houses without orchestra pits.

2 REPERTOIRE: THE REPERTOIRE OF NEW SINGING THEATRE WILL BE BASED PRIMARILY – THOUGH NOT EXCLUSIVELY – ON THE DEVELOPMENT OF NEW WORK.

Implications:

a) The singer-actor must be familiar with the spectrum of today's music in all its styles, forms, notations etc.

b) The composer and writer must develop the skills they need to create effective works for the new singing theatre.

c) Singer-actors must learn to work not only with directors but with live composers, writers and designers.

3 STRUCTURE AND STYLE: THE NEW SINGING THEATRE WILL OPEN UP ITS RANGE OF STYLISTIC AND FORMAL OPTIONS BEYOND THE CONVENTIONS BOTH OF TRADITIONAL OPERA AND OF COMMERCIAL MUSICAL THEATRE.

These options include:

a) spoken as well as sung text, and various combinations of speech and song;

b) a wide range of possible vocal demands on the singer-actor;

c) breaking away from the format of 'principals and chorus';

d) the choice of different informing styles – realism, expressionism etc. – to suit the material;

e) openness to world music;

f) openness to *all* kinds of thematic material as content for new singing theatre works;

g) use of performance skills such as speech, dance, mime and acrobatics as part of the singer-actor's equipment;

h) a wide range of design options from the barest of stages to full-blown naturalism;

i) the use of appropriate modern technologies as aids to expression of the material.

*4 COLLABORATION: THE NEW SINGING THEATRE WILL
PROVIDE A CONTEXT IN WHICH ITS ARTISTS WITH THEIR
VARIOUS SKILLS CAN WORK IN A CLIMATE OF MUTUAL
UNDERSTANDING AND RESPECT, AND THEREFORE IN TRUE
CO – LABORATION.*

Implications:

> Opportunities must be developed for new singing theatre artists
> (composers, writers, performers, designers, musicians) to nurture
> this understanding and respect, and to develop their collaborative
> skills and experience, in a situation where competitiveness is less im-
> portant than shared responsibility.

*5 TRAINING: CENTRAL TO THE DEVELOPMENT OF NEW
SINGING THEATRE IS THE NEED FOR APPROPRIATE
TRAINING METHODS AND OPPORTUNITIES, TO PROVIDE
ARTISTS WITH THE TOOLS AND EXPERIENCE THEY NEED.*

Training Requirements for Singer-actors

a) performance training programmes will give singer-actors the opportunity to widen the range of their skills as performers, to meet the
demands of movement, speech and acting and other performance
skills, as well as singing;

b) through collaboration with composers, writers and designers,
singer-actors will develop their sense of shared creative responsibility;

c) singer-actors will be given opportunities to become conscious of
the whole range of contemporary art, developing the confidence and
understanding needed to become themselves contemporary artists.

Training Requirements for Composers and Writers

a) composers and writers will become aware of the possibilities opened up for their creative work by having available singer-actors who
can not only sing but also act, move and speak with equal skill and
confidence;

b) composers and writers will be helped to understand the full range
of stylistic and formal possibilities opened up by the new singing
theatre. They will be encouraged to study the history of singing
theatre not merely out of academic interest but in order to establish
their collegiality with composers and librettists of the past, and to
discover initiatives or interrupted developments that might warrant
revival;

c) composers and writers will be encouraged to be alive to the world around them, and to be ready to make use of all kinds of information and material as a basis for new works of singing theatre;

d) they will also be encouraged to think freshly about the 'primary act' of singing theatre, and to find new ways to handle the convention or illusion of singing theatre;

e) composers and writers will be given opportunities to develop their collaborative skills in partnership. For this, writers need a knowledge of both music and the theatre, and composers need to develop their understanding of literature and the theatre. Both need opportunities during training to see their work performed on stage.

Training Requirements for Designers

a) designers will develop specialist skills in the areas of acoustics and configuration for new singing theatre, especially in houses without orchestra pits;

b) they will be given opportunities to learn to read and appreciate music, in order to develop designs related not only to the text and action but also to musical structure, texture, mood and expression;

c) they will also be given opportunities to work not in isolation but in collaboration with other singing theatre artists, and so to develop understanding of the stage as seen and experienced by the performer and the musician as well as the director;

d) they will get the chance, like singer-actors, to fill in the gaps in their formal training.

6 AUDIENCE: THE NEW SINGING THEATRE WILL ALWAYS BE AWARE OF ITS AUDIENCE, AND OF THE NEED TO COMMUNICATE WITH THAT AUDIENCE.

Implications:

a) The language of new singing theatre will normally be in the vernacular.

b) The singer-actor will regard the communication of meaning to be as important as – or even more important than – the production of pleasing sound.

c) Composers will find ways of using twentieth-century musical idiom to serve the needs of the work and without obstructing the audience's participation in the work.

d) Composers and writers will aim to find ways of communicating with an audience without becoming shallow on the one hand or pretentious on the other.

A NEW CONTEXT

It does not take too much creative genius to be able to imagine a 'new singing theatre' system built out of many of the same elements as those that make up the operatic, dramatic or dance production systems, but which operates on the principles we have already outlined. The system will include:

1 A collaborative Music Theatre training approach which begins its work in the high schools or even earlier, and which has its university and conservatory programmes.

2 An association of new singing theatre teachers to share and develop their methods and priorities.

3 A network of small companies across our countries, each of which will have up to six or eight singer-actors, a resident composer and writer, and access to others. The company will be housed in a medium-sized theatre building (or will share it with a drama company) and will present a wide range of new work, from accessible pieces to more challenging ones. Its productions will be transportable, and will frequently be exchanged with those of companies in other towns or cities. It will regularly make television versions of its work in collaboration with local or national networks. It will have close links with the schools, enlivening the Music Theatre training at all levels. And it will take very seriously the responsibility of reflecting the life of its region, joining forces with the best local painters and poets and dancers – as well as composers – in the development of its repertoire.

4 Music Theatre festivals, in which the best work of the individual companies is assembled, both nationally and internationally.

Once such a system is operating it would naturally spawn other activities. Television would not be able to resist the idea of presenting a Music Theatre series. Larger Music Theatre companies could well be established in major centres, and – who knows? – might even begin to experience the same symptoms of elephantiasis that have affected the operatic stage.

This sketch can easily be dismissed as chiffon pie in the sky. But it is hard to find reasons why it could not be realised, unless the fact that it has not yet happened is to be taken as a sign that it cannot and never will. Many leaders of the singing theatre in the last fifteen years have in fact made a habit – in their imaginations – of placing their work within this future context, and the vision has been passed along, to animate the ideas of a new generation of singing theatre artists.

But where do we start? What is the trigger for the change?

My own first impulse in the 1970s, like that of other initiators of Music Theatre, was to begin with actual Music Theatre productions, and therefore to establish a professional singing theatre company. From this beginning, we believed, the other elements of the system could follow. It is instructive to follow the fortunes of a handful of these initiatives.

NEW SINGING THEATRE COMPANIES OF THE 1970s

I have already referred to the year of 1975, when the English Music Theatre Company was set up, while almost simultaneously Encompass Music Theatre was established in New York, and my own company, COMUS Music Theatre Company of Canada, was launched in Toronto. None of these three companies stood the test of time. The leaders of English Music Theatre, which was a company of singer-actors re-fashioned from the English Opera Group, could not persuade their principal granting agency, the Arts Council of Great Britain, that their work merited major grants beyond 1979.

Encompass Music Theatre started life as 'New York's only music theatre company dedicated to presenting new music, lyric theatre and American opera' (notice the unfortunate but inevitable fumbling with definitions). Encompass' goal was to develop a nucleus company of singer-actors, and to enlist American composers and librettists by organising and presenting commissioned works. They also revived older American works, many of which had received only one or two productions before being consigned to the shelf. The company ran each of their productions for a remarkable twenty-four performances; their adventurous programming won accolades and awards, but the combination of financial distress, lost real estate, and the burn-out associated with these problems, led to the suspension of operations in 1982.

COMUS Music Theatre was launched as a production organisation committed to presenting 'all kinds of music theatre'. After receiving initial seed-money from granting agencies in order to develop our plans, we resolved to begin by attempting to make money in a commercial venture; and by setting up a limited partnership with a group of investors we were able to mount a small musical based on the songs of Hollywood song-writer Harry Warren. Though this was an artistic success and well attended (it ran for four months), it failed financially, and thenceforward the organisation moved precariously from project to project, receiving sporadic sympathy and support from some agencies but not others. It was sustained for years – long after I handed it on – only by the strength of its original vision and the self-sacrificing courage and tenacity of its leaders, finally breaking under its debt-load in 1987.

All three companies recognised the need for additional training for its performers, and both English Music Theatre and COMUS incorporated it into their programmes. Because English Music Theatre was immediately launched into a busy round of productions and tours, the training had to be fitted in around rehearsals and performances, but Colin Graham was insistent on the need for it, and his singer-actors were only too happy to take advantage of the opportunity. At COMUS we found that our attempts to mount new and interesting work were always made problematic by the difficulty of finding singers who could act. As a result, supplementary training became more and more a primary activity, at a time when the bug of 'further professional training' had not yet bitten the theatre world outside New York. Courses in Music Theatre were offered to high school students, and summer 'ensemble' training programmes were set up for 'young professional' singer-actors. At the same time it was recognised that composers and writers who could not gain performances for their work needed – at the very least – opportunities to hear and even tape their pieces, and COMUS performed a valuable service in Canada by preparing readings of new works, to which they invited the Canadian Broadcasting Corporation, arts agencies and the ever-sceptical heads of opera companies and arts festivals. On top of this the organisation still managed over the twelve years of its existence to present an important series of Music Theatre premières – every one of them taking place in an atmosphere black with financial crisis.

In the last weeks of COMUS' life, talks were proceeding with the Canadian Opera Company pursuing the idea that COMUS should become the company's 'new work' arm. But the stock market crisis in October 1987 provoked the Opera Company's Board into cancelling all new projects. Once again, a traditional company made clear under pressure that its primary obligation was not to new works of singing theatre. Indeed, why should it be?

The failure of these three companies can be attributed to bad management or a host of other things. But what was clear in all cases was that the companies were seen and treated – even by those who encouraged their activities – as mavericks at the margin of the operatic system. COMUS requested, modestly enough, to be given an annual grant equal to the cost of producing one act of *La Bohème* at the Canadian Opera Company, and promised that with these funds a strong seven-month season of original Music Theatre could be mounted. But COMUS' financial fragility, and its lacklustre box office returns for major productions (there was pathetically little money available for publicity or 'marketing'), were cited as reasons for not giving it generous grant money: thus confirming its instability.

There was a fourth Music Theatre company founded in the same period, to which I have also referred in my first chapter. Boris Pokrovsky founded his Moscow Chamber Music Theatre in 1972, and has managed to steer its fortunes ever since, through several periods in which only his career at the Bolshoi, his unimpeachable reputation, and his Order of Lenin, saved the eccentric little company from quiet extinction. Here, in the land of Tchaikovsky, where the nineteenth- century operatic tradition had long possessed an iconic power, a group of highly trained and competent singer-actors under Pokrovsky's direction was presenting – in repertory – a whole host of new works, spiced with highly original productions of more traditional pieces. In the one week of my stay in Moscow in 1986 I saw: a new Music Theatre version of *The Brothers Karamazov*; *The Rostov Incident*, a seventeenth-century 'nativity opera' sung *a capella*, written by Peter the Great's musical adviser and recently transcribed into modern notation; a double bill of two Chekhov short stories, *The Letter* and *The Wedding*, composed for Music Theatre; a Music Theatre version of a modern novel by V. Rasputin about a deserter from the Heroic War of 1941-5; and one (decidedly dreary) satirical comedy written by the head of the composers' union.

The economic structure supporting the arts in the USSR is clearly worlds away from that of western countries. At the same time, it was hard to understand how Pokrovsky had managed not only to launch but also to sustain his company – until the last day of our stay, when we visited GITIS, the famous conservatory (founded in 1919) in which many of the most distinguished Soviet actors received their grounding. There Pokrovsky runs a five-year Music Theatre course, in which the singer-actor undergoes rigorous training: dramatic and musical instruction are combined in a carefully designed, gradual and exhaustive process. It was from the graduates of this training programme that Pokrovsky was able – at least in recent years – to draw the bulk of his company.

We shall return in our final chapter to the Moscow Chamber Music Theatre. It is an institution that all of us who care about the new singing theatre should know better.

THE PRIMACY OF TRAINING

My one disappointment with Pokrovsky's training programme was that it did not appear to recognise the need for the training of composers and librettists alongside the singer-actor. He was therefore having to collaborate with artists who were trained in a wholly different approach and mode of work. The teaching of opera composition in the USSR is as spotty and sporadic as everywhere else, and equally isolated from the singer-actors.

It is, of course, in response to this traditional division and speciali- sation of labour and skill that the initiators of new singing theatre press so hard for a shared 'citizenship' for its artists, and have realised that the foundation for this must in the first instance be established not in func- tioning production companies, with their tight schedules and production pressures, but in the comparative calm of training situations. They have understood, in other words, that preparation for a collaborative art must itself be collaborative; that if the eventual working model for singing theatre is a collaboration of singing theatre artists of different skills, then that model must be the basis of training.

The history of post-War Music Theatre training has in large measure been the story of how these model training groups have been assembled, and what they have achieved together. My own experience running the Music Theatre studio ensemble at the Banff Centre in Canada seems to insist on having space to itself; I know of no other long-term course any- where that has attempted to bring together the principal artists of the singing theatre – singer-actors, composers, writers and designers – in an integrated programme, and what we did and discovered is surely worth sharing. But it is important first to describe some of the other Music Theatre training initiatives that have been taken since the mid-1970s. Chief among these was a series sponsored by the International Theatre Institute's Music Theatre Committee, whose beginnings I described in Chapter One.

For the Music Theatre Committee of the ITI, the creation of a train- ing meeting or 'encounter' of some kind seemed from early on a natural priority in their work of encouraging Music Theatre. Their first three- week venture took place in Austria in August of 1975, under the artistic direction of Professor Aleksandr Bardini of Poland, Lars af Malmborg of Sweden (former pioneering director of Sweden's National Music Drama School, see pp. 203-4), and Philip Nasta, of the Committee's (now separated) Dance Section. Singers, dancers and actors were invited to apply, and the teachers were described in the brochure as 'experts from all forms of Music Theatre: conductors, producers, composers, singing teachers, mimes and experts in dance and movement'. Fees were kept at a minimum, and the faculty came for no more than their travel and ac- commodation expenses (a practice that was followed through the entire series). There is scant written record of what went on and, with the mix of languages and cultures as well as skills, we can imagine a certain amount of genial chaos, but enough was apparently achieved to 'confirm the contemporary relevance of such an event and justify the organisation of a second such meeting'.

This took place the following August, once again in Austria, and once again under the direction of Bardini and Malmborg. This time the brochure went into more detail about the structure of the encounter:

> The main accent will...be laid on ensemble and improvisatory exercises and collaboration between composer and performer – with the intention of enriching the participants both personally and professionally and of providing them with fresh experience to meet more fully the present and future requirements of theatre.

> The practical work will take place in various forms and in both larger and smaller groups (individual teaching will also be available).

> In addition to the programme there will be opportunities to develop ideas suggested by the participants themselves. It is intended to hold some kind of public demonstration at the end of the working meeting.

There was also a more focussed description of the kind of participant expected:

> Young singers who have completed their studies and have already acquired their first professional experience...young professional dancers and actors who are interested in music theatre as a form of expression and are in possession of a solidly based musicality.

Reading between the lines we can guess that the first year's meeting had been hampered by wide divergences of training level and particularly musical skills, and that the course's directors were now making attempts to rectify this. But once again there is no available written record of how many participants came, or how they got on.

The Austrian connection broke off, and it was 1978 before the next training meeting took place, this time in Breukelen, Holland. More details have survived of this third encounter. The brochure describes the thinking behind it:

> The aim of this meeting...is to share experience and to get impulses from other specialities than one's own, and so to make us all aware how we can enlarge and enrich our artistic capacity. So a great deal of the work could be described as listening, watching, learning and talking man-to-man.

Participants (there were 22 in this year: 8 singers, 4 dancers, 9 actors and 1 composer) were required to bring a piece of work to the meeting. The survey of this material was to be 'decisive for the development of the work during the course...working together in creating Music Theatre.

This will be done above all by improvisation, both movement, theatrical and musical improvisation.' In addition, 'technical training' was to be given according to each participant's wishes and needs.

Malmborg's report on the meeting is worth quoting at some length because it discusses many of the challenges that confront Music Theatre training:

> The important thing: to be absolutely serious, not to cheat for one second, to forget all thoughts of obtaining a visible (or audible!) result in a fortnight...This must be stressed since there could be, of course, a risk of being superficial when entering new artistic fields with artists from other disciplines...As usual, we found the professional level of the participants too uneven and that remains a problem for the future: how to make sure that the participants have reached a decent professionality in their own field. On the other hand they should not be too mature, too fixed in their professional attitude.

The report ends with a series of conclusions:

> 1 There is a lack of music theatre training in the present situation, especially for singers.
>
> 2 The artistic education of different groups of performing artists together should be tried more. Investigations should be made concerning the value of such a common training.
>
> 3 The music theatre institutions all around the world should contribute much more (and more consciously) to the development of new forms, to a new repertory and new ways of working than they actually do. Their conservatism is terrifying.
>
> 4 Joining together speech, singing and dancing does not necessarily result in musical comedy.
>
> 5 Music theatre contains endless non-discovered artistic and human possibilities.

Two years later yet another training encounter was organised, under Bardini's solo direction. The aims:

> To extend limits of the traditional genres and – starting from the singing, acting and moving human being – to stimulate the creative imagination of young artists by providing them with fresh experience so that they can better meet the constantly increasing demands of music theatre.

That year there was greater emphasis on contemporary music, and in addition to a programme of classwork there were two creative projects planned: an 'African project' led by Akim Euba of Nigeria and Roberto Blanco of Cuba, and a Dutch project led by Bernard van den Boogard and Pavel Smok.

The final report tells us that there were 31 participants that year: 4 singers, 7 actors, 15 dancers, 1 actor/director, 2 dancer/choreographers, 1 dramaturge and 1 musician. There was little said of the work done; merely that 'time was too short to come to a "final version" of the musico-dramatic scenes but the experience gained while working on these projects was very worthwhile...'

The Committee's last training encounter in Holland was in 1982. Its stated aims were the same as in 1980, but an introductory letter to the participants gives a flavour of the plans:

> Apart from group and individual lessons some special projects...will be in the centre of our activities...Nancy Rhodes...will work with the participants on fragments of *Oklahoma!*, *Gypsy* and *South Pacific*...Another idea is to work, both musically and scenically, on Hans Werner Henze's musical play *The Miracle Theatre* (*Das Wundertheater*)...if you think that one or the other part is good for your voice range,...feel free to prepare whatever you can achieve ...before we meet. Another important aspect of our gathering will be the Third World aspect, and here we hope to profit from Roberto Blanco's presence as well as from the participation of the Filippino composer Lutgardo Labad...We think that the very different cultural and musical backgrounds of these projects will lead to a lively exchange of contrasting artistic ideas, and, therefore, everybody should participate in each of the projects.

There were 22 participants, this time showing a marked reduction in dancers, and a doubling of singers: 8 singers, 6 actors, 3 dancers, 2 actor/dancers, 1 pianist/composer, 1 oboist/composer, 1 percussionist. The final report was once again laconic:

> The American continent and Asia, this time, provided us with new experiences; by a Filippine workshop and Broadway musical studies as well as by a Cuban musico-dramatic scene. (The music by Leo Brouwer was especially composed for this event.) Apart from this, a great deal of work centered on Henze's music theatre play.

> Time was too short, of course, to come to a 'final version' of all these projects...

One can detect a faint odour of internatspeak in some of these reports. It was important to tread on no toes, to sweep problems under the carpet, to put spokes in no one's wheel, and generally to give ITI and the world the impression that good things had happened.

In this case, though, we have one further angle on events. In August 1982, two months after the last encounter, a special Music Theatre session was held in Royaumont, France, with the financial and

organisational support of France's Ministry of Culture, the French ITI
Centre and the Fondation de Royaumont:

> 16 participants (professional singers – not only from the opera field
> – as well as some musical actors and instrumentalists) from 10 coun-
> tries worked along artistic lines developed by the 'Atélier Lyrique
> du Rhin', Colmar. Two courses: for dramatic improvisation (led by
> Colmar artistic director Pierre Barrat) and for musical improvisa-
> tion (led by the Moroccan composer Ahmed Essyad) preceded each
> day by physical training (given by Mareke Schnitker, Ecole Jacques
> Lecocq) paved the way for building up, in a process of collective cre-
> ation, the structures of a 40-minutes improvisation on an old Aztec
> myth ('The birth of the sun and the moon') and striving for a new
> metaphorical theatre language by using all means of gestural, vocal,
> instrumental and movement expression of the performers' group.

The two courses were compared:

> While the main accent in Breukelen was laid on 'production' (via 4
> contrasting projects providing different sorts of challenge to the par-
> ticipants) the emphasis in Royaumont was more on 'improvisation'
> in many artistic directions. [Breukelen] was structured as a pluridis-
> ciplinary exchange of experiences, [Royaumont] was more focussed
> on the singer's work – but common to both these workshops was the
> modern composer's stimuli as one centre of the course; projects, par-
> ticipants and instructors from the Third World as the other centre,
> as an integral part of these undertakings. The predominant training
> method was: to learn not only from 'lessons' but even more from each
> other, from working together, from meeting people from other cul-
> tural backgrounds, from overpassing the limits of the traditional
> genres which means, altogether, to strengthen the creative imagin-
> ation and the personality of the young artists...

> To sum it up: Breukelen and Royaumont complemented each other
> and – while working with different artistic methods – both con-
> tributed to come a little bit nearer to one of our main goals: to form
> a more polyvalent type of singer-actor that is more and more in de-
> mand on the contemporary stage.

Of course these could not be the only Music Theatre training experiments taking place during these years, but they are the only ones of which
I have access to historical record. The work of Pierre Barrat in his 'Até-
lier du Rhin' had begun as early as 1969. From the beginning he had seen
the need to link together the activities of production, creation and training, and he has realised as clearly as anyone the impossibility of making
advances in the area of new singing theatre without the development of
the total new 'context' of which we have spoken. France has in fact occupied itself at length with the problems of *théâtre musical*, and has been

more open than many countries in its preparedness to experiment. But discussions in the home of classical art have often tended to revolve around the vertiginous problem of 'genre': 'What is Music Theatre?' It is a good question, but one to which I believe we should not stay for an answer – if it means even ten minutes taken away from actually doing something. The writers Marie-Noël Rio and Michel Rostain have performed a remarkable service in charting the difficulties of new *théâtre lyrique* within France's operatic context. Their two books *Aujourd'hui L'Opéra* (Éditions Recherchés, Paris, 1980) and *L'Opéra Mort ou Vif* (Éditions Recherchés, Paris, 1982) have unfortunately no counterpart in English.

And so to Banff. I approach these chapters with some qualms – especially following a slippery compliment paid to me recently in Sweden after I had delivered a pep talk to a Music Theatre workshop: 'It's not usual in Sweden for us to talk about ourselves when we are talking about something important.' But our experiences at Banff are in a sense my qualifications for having anything at all to say about Music Theatre, and it would not make sense to exclude it – not even in deference to Swedish politesse.

Chapter Six

MUSIC THEATRE AT BANFF: BEGINNINGS

Banff, Alberta, is a small town in the heart of Banff National Park, in the Canadian Rockies. The Bow River valley in which it sits was first surveyed in 1883 as the route for the Canadian Pacific Railway; and when hot springs were discovered in the side of a local mountain the CPR decided to build a hotel there to attract summer visitors along their newly completed trans-Canada line. The Banff Springs Hotel was the result; the present massive pile was erected in the 1920s, when it became a summer resort for the wealthy. The town grew up around the hotel, and in the last twenty years has become, winter and summer, one of the most famous tourist attractions in the world.

The name of the town is also known as the site of the Banff Centre. The centre's origins go back to 1933, when a summer school was set up to train theatre amateurs of the province of Alberta. The leaders of this modest initiative soon joined forces with a summer art school, introduced musical studies, and called the new entity the Banff School of Fine Arts. Their summer courses were originally housed in Banff's schools, but in 1948 a permanent site above the town was acquired from the park authorities – leased for a dollar a year – and the present campus was established. Buildings went up slowly as money became available, and by 1976 the school could boast a 900-seat theatre with flyhouse; a 250-seat theatre/concert hall; a visual arts building with spacious studios and a gallery; classrooms, dance studios and practice huts; and accommodation for as many as 600. Students and teachers converged on the place from all over Canada and the United States, and the school concluded each summer's activities with a festival that offered opera, ballet, drama and concerts at a reasonably high standard and low cost. The festival was well attended by tourists – and also by citizens of Calgary, which lay eighty miles away and was in those days starved for cultural activity. In winter the buildings were used to house conferences, and courses in business administration.

The School of Fine Arts, through fees and with the help of private donations, more or less paid its way until the seventies, when under a new president, Dr David Leighton, it was resolved to cut down the numbers of students, apply for government assistance, introduce auditions, and dramatically raise the quality of the school's artistic standards. The institution was reorganised, and under a special act of the provincial legislature became the Banff Centre for Continuing Education, a part of the provincial educational system. The arts segment of the Banff Centre, still its most celebrated division, now became known rather clumsily as the Banff Centre School of Fine Arts.

The school in its extraordinary mountain setting had always been led with a certain visionary fervour; a favourite saying of its first full-time director was 'Make no small dreams; they hold no magic to stir men's blood'. Part of the dream for the school from its early days had been the development of a year-round international conservatory for fine and performing arts, and this now became the prime goal for the new administration. When I was first invited to Banff in the summer of 1977 to direct students in a musical for the festival, it was to discover that these plans were rapidly advancing, and that we summer faculty – from Canada, the United States, Britain and elsewhere – were being encouraged to assist in the development of the new venture. There was money for expansion, promised by a province awash with oil wealth. All that was wanted was ideas. It seemed too good to be true.

The new 'Winter Cycle', as it was soon named, was aimed not at university-age students but at 'young professionals' who had completed their basic training and perhaps even worked some years in their profession. They were to be known therefore not as students but as 'participants'; their teachers would be referred to as 'resource artists'. The maximum stay for a participant would be two winters. The Centre was of course well aware that the costs of such a training, leading to no formal university degree, would prohibit most likely candidates from applying. But a scholarship fund was already in existence, supported by annual private and corporate donations and also by some of the proceeds from the centre's conference business. The plan was to augment this fund, and thus to make it possible for participants – whatever their nationality – to have a very high percentage of their fees and accommodation paid. We can be sure that without such a scheme very few young artists would have been lured into the mountains.

The Centre was keen on providing an interdisciplinary ambience for the new Winter Cycle. Having had some experience in the inter-field I was asked to help develop a philosophical framework for the new plans, and in 1979 – the first year of the seven-month winter programme – I resigned from COMUS and took up a full-time position with the Centre as Arts Planner and Director of Inter Arts.

THE PILOT PROJECT

Music and Visual Arts were the first major programmes to be established, but the plan was to include theatrical activity as well, and much
advice had been sought from all over Canada on what form this should
take. Theatre people pressed for a young company of actors. Opera
people favoured an advanced opera training program. Dance people
wondered whether there was room in Canada for another dance course.
One way or another there was a hole here, and as early as 1978, coming
home on the plane from another beautiful summer in Banff (directing
Brigadoon if I remember), I had a sudden inspiration, and swiftly scribbled out the description of a Music Theatre training programme. I sent
it back to the school and to my delight it was greeted with considerable
interest. At a time when anything was possible, a genuinely new initiative
seemed more attractive than a mountain-girt imitation of something done
better in the cities 'back east', or in Europe. No one, as far as we knew,
had yet perpetrated anything similar anywhere; but President David
Leighton was enough of a 'builder and dreamer' to find this uniqueness
an exciting rather than a daunting prospect.

   And so in the autumn of 1980 a six-week pilot project was set up to
test the new idea. The rationale for the project talked about the growth
of interest in staging musicals and song-and-dance shows, opera's increased interest in acting as well as singing, and the development of
interdisciplinary artwork. The report then continued:

> But the need goes beyond the supplying of candidates for an expan-
> ding job market. The structure of the proposed Music Theatre
> program also developed out of the conviction that composers and
> writers must be brought back into the living theatre to work along-
> side performers; and that visual design must be integrated into the
> creative team. By putting these groups of artists together, and by de-
> veloping an integrated professional program which would combine
> training with research and with original Music Theatre creation, it
> was believed that Banff could even provide a fresh and much needed
> stimulus to the whole theatrical activity of Canada – and beyond.

   We designed the pilot project to simulate the conditions of a full
seven-month winter programme in Music Theatre. In this way we would
be able to test schedules, activity ratios, resource artists, interdisciplinary
methods, space requirements, participant qualifications and staffing
needs. Because of the need to develop data in so many areas, we planned
the project to be highly intensive, with swift changes of focus and rapid
turnover of resource artists. The participants, a total of twenty-five, were
to be accepted under three categories: 'Performance' (singers, dancers,

actors); 'Environment' (designers, lighting designers, costume-makers, props-makers); and 'Sound' (composer/arranger/conductors, writers, sound designer/technicians, stage managers). These overly abstract categories were soon discarded. The final selection of candidates, chosen on the basis of background and references, broke down as follows: 6 singers, 2 dancers, 5 actors, 3 singer-actors, 2 writers, 3 composers, 1 set designer, 1 costume designer, 1 stage manager and 1 lighting designer. Three or four of the group were from the United States, two from Britain, the rest Canadian.

For the pioneers who took part, that first Music Theatre venture in Banff has taken on a certain mythic quality. Resource artists of remarkable distinction – Lehman Engel, Michael Langham, Maureen Forrester, Oren Brown, Michael Colgrass, Susan Benson, Kristin Linklater, Neil Peter Jampolis, Cameron Porteous, Sydney Hodkinson and others – flew in and out of the place like splendid migrating seabirds, while a crew of resident teachers and administrators toiled in the galleys, steering the ship clear of one reef after another. We had made a plan, and a detailed one; but the whole point of a pilot project is to be able to change course in response to the unexpected.

The participants – who paid nothing for their experience – were right to complain from time to time that all was not as it should be: we had a 'forum' every day to find out how people were doing, and sure enough they had problems. This experience, incidentally, taught me the Parkinson-type law that 'complaints expand to fill the time allotted for them'. There were no 'how are you doing?' sessions in later programmes. Instead participants were encouraged to search out the ensemble's directors and if possible bring with them not only their problem but also its solution. Or, in the words of Canadian composer Murray Schafer before one of his workshops with us: 'If you have a problem come and see us. Maybe you are the problem.'

And yet for all the difficulties, the fundamental hypothesis of the project – that composers, writers, designers and performers brought together in a single ensemble was an explosively creative mixture – was triumphantly vindicated. On the last evening of the course a two-and-a-half-hour performance programme was offered to the public. The evening was made up of nine Music Theatre pieces, varying in length from four to twenty minutes. All but one of these pieces had been written, composed, orchestrated, designed and rehearsed during the final weeks of the project. The standard was, of course, uneven, and none of the pieces had been adequately rehearsed. But the sheer profusion and variety of the programme, and the energy and commitment behind it, were what grabbed the public. The celebrated Montreal poet Irving Layton happened to be in the audience, and was stupefied: 'Where the hell does all this talent come from?'

Everyone at the Banff Centre was fully aware of the strains and pressures of the pilot project. We had driven the theatre's technical staff round the bend, and the directors of the (at that time) somewhat conservatively oriented music programme had watched our antics with incomprehension and distrust. The genial head of the school's summer opera division asked in carefully rounded tones: 'What is going to happen to the produced voice?' But the administration continued to stand behind the idea, and early in 1981 I was appointed Artistic Director of a new seven-month winter programme, to be called the 'Banff Music Theatre Studio Ensemble'. It was to offer a one-year course, with a possible second year.

So began an exhilarating six-year adventure.

EARLY DAYS

I now had a mandate to develop a Music Theatre training programme. My pilot project colleagues and I had shown that we could keep a rather haphazardly assembled group of singers, actors, dancers, composer, writers and designers fruitfully occupied for a six-week period, and we had learned a great deal about priorities, training needs, and activity ratios. But a seven-month operation was a very different proposition. There was only our harum-scarum model to fall back on, and no comfortable feeling that other people had been this way before. Everything had to be invented, and we had to be persuasive enough, and honest enough, to earn the trust of those we were bringing with us into the unknown.

To establish this trust, we first needed public credibility. The whole point of the new approach to the singing theatre is that musical and theatrical elements are treated with equal seriousness and professionalism, and if we were going to attract young artists from either quarter our programme had to have the respect of both theatre and music people. Since these two professions have tended for some centuries to stare balefully at one another across a swamp of ignorance, the task would not be easy. And this is where the unimpeachable distinction of our short-term guests during the pilot project was so important to us – not only for their ideas, but for their generous and visible support for the project.

Having worked professionally as a director in both theatre and opera, and having founded a Music Theatre company, I was in the fortunate position of being able to count these people as my friends. If Canada's most beloved classical singer was with us, then suspicious professional musicians could only mutter. If Michael Langham, internationally known director and former leader of the Stratford Shakespeare Festival in Ontario, was behind us, then sceptical theatrical types would have to hold their fire. If Lehman Engel, perhaps the leading authority on the American musical, publicly backed our aims, then the Broadway babies – always a more straightforward lot – would be less intimidated. And if the venerable Oren Brown, voice teacher at the Juilliard School in New York and a famous exponent of the need for healthy use of the singing voice, was able to spend a week with us and even participate enthusiastically in improvisations (I will never forget him as an elk), then crotchety singing teachers could not easily claim that we would tear their prize pupil's larynx to shreds. And similarly, though they could not join us at this time, the private advice and public support of Colin Graham and Steuart Bedford, as the former directors of English Music Theatre, were invaluable.

I was also lucky to have as manager of the new programme a man who had trained as a singer and had experience both as a stage manager and stage director of opera. Music Theatre had not been George Ross's particular interest until now, but once the administration established its chosen direction, George and his assistant Douglas Riley – also trained as a singer – put endless hard work and professional enthusiasm into the project.

Now, anyone who organises professional arts training knows that there are several decisions which must be got right if the plans are going to make sense. With a programme like ours the sensitivity of decision-making was even more acute. The primary decisions, of course, involved the selection of people.

As a theatre person with musical instincts, I first needed to find a musical person with theatrical instincts to be my partner in crime: a composer in fact, with operatic or theatrical experience. There were a number of possible choices in Canada, but no one suitable was also available, and eventually my choice fell on the young British composer Stephen McNeff, whom I had first met in England a couple of years earlier as co-founder (with his Canadian wife Renée) and artistic director of a small and – of course – struggling West Country group called Southwest Music Theatre, which had opened its doors in 1976 and was being forced to close them again in 1980 for lack of funding. Stephen had been with us in the pilot project as a composer- and conductor-in-residence, and his gifts had been evident. He had been resident composer at two British theatres, and had written several Music Theatre pieces, including projects with Adrian Mitchell, Ann Jellicoe, and Cornish poet Charles Causley. He was imaginative, intelligent and witty, with Irish charm and good Welsh horse sense, and his musical predilections seemed to strike the right note for our work: Stravinsky and Britten were his particular interests, but he also appreciated Sondheim and was intrigued by Philip Glass. He was in no way an avant-gardiste but was not prejudiced against good 'new music'. He was offered a full-time position at the centre, and became associate artistic director, and composer-in-residence. From then on he shared fully in all our planning. He was the first of a steady stream of colleagues who were to join us from the United Kingdom.

We now had a cohesive planning team, and our next job was to decide what categories of participant we would invite into the programme, and how many of each. We knew that composers, writers and designers would be part of the ensemble, and decided to accept up to three of each. In the area of performance, though, we made an important new decision. It had been my original proposal that we accept a combination of 'young professional' singers, dancers and actors, and for the pilot project had even developed the idea of accepting precisely five in each category; we would teach the five actors to sing and dance, five dancers to sing and act, and five singers to dance and act. The symmetry of the idea was appealing, but like many symmetries looked best on paper. We were not in a position to choose five from each category; and, more importantly, we found that we needed participants who were not only suited for the programme by virtue of their 'primary skill' (singing, dancing, acting), but who could also bring us some aptitude in their 'secondary' performance skills. And of all these performance skills, the one that could not be taught from scratch – and the one most urgently necessary in the singing theatre – was musicality, and the ability to sing.

It was Colin Graham who in a discussion at ENO had first expressed some doubts about our trying to be all things to all kinds of performer, and we now decided that we would put singing first on our list of desirables. We would continue to take actors and dancers, and would not expect 'bel canto' voice quality from them. But they would have to be able to sing pleasingly and in tune, and to have some musical training. Otherwise the ensemble's ability to perform works of singing theatre would be seriously impaired.

In deciding how many performers we would accept each year, we had to consider first the workloads of the teaching staff who would be giving individual classes. In the first year we eventually accepted fourteen. But when we initiated a second-year programme, inviting six performers back, we reduced the intake of the first year to twelve, thus requiring from our singing and speech teachers, and from our coaches, a total of thirty-six 40-minute individual sessions each week. The number twelve has further advantages, in that it divides into two, three, four and six. Let no-one underestimate the advantages of this in the life of harried schedule-makers.

APPOINTING INSTRUCTORS

With these decisions taken we could proceed to list the teaching staff we would need, and begin our search for them. At Banff only the artistic leaders of programmes are offered full-time faculty positions; our teaching staff would be hired on short-term contracts. This was both an advantage and a problem in acquiring faculty. We could often attract excellent resource artists who were able to take a few weeks' or months' leave of absence from their professional engagements or teaching positions. These tended to be one-time appointments since they were often not free to return. There was thus quite a turnover of resource people, and we had the benefit of many personalities and approaches. But we also needed continuity. The coming and going of movement, voice and speech teachers in the pilot project had particularly disconcerted the participants and taught us that there should be a regular and ongoing programme of instruction available in all these areas. Stephen was also anxious that we put together a reliable team of accompanist-coaches to provide solid musical support.

In the areas of movement and speech we were immensely lucky. Our choice for movement instructor was David McMurray Smith, who had degrees in both dance and theatre, was an accomplished mime, and had danced with Montreal's Ballet Jazz. He also had experience of teaching with Banff's summer dance division. The qualifications were impressive, but nothing could have prepared us for David's idealism, dedication and hard work. He was to be with us for five winters.

For speech we were equally fortunate with our choice of Colin Bernhardt, a former actor at Canada's Stratford, who had begun to teach speech in Toronto some years earlier, and brought a sure instinct and a wide-eyed caring to his work which endeared him to everyone; he was also to stay with us five years. Our first coach accompanists, Kerry McShane and David Boothroyd, were splendidly different, and the two of them could cope with any style of music, sight-read almost anything with ease, work like dogs, and convey unquenchable enthusiasm for the aims of the programme. During periods of heavy activity we would engage a third pianist. One of them was the remarkably fine soloist Glen Montgomery, who later became a loyal and enthusiastic full-time colleague.

It was only in the area of singing voice instruction that we were unable at that time to pick a 'regular' appointee. But we were nearly always able to find, then and later, a first-class teacher who could come for half the winter: they included Jeanette Ogg (a pupil of Oren Brown's) from South Carolina, Philip May from Regina, Noelle Barker and Mollie Petrie from the Guildhall School in London, Maureen Callahan from Australia (and at that time head of the European Opera Studio), Canadian Lois McDonall from English National Opera, and Selena James from Victoria. All these choices were made with care; we had to be sure that our voice teacher was fully aware of our orientation to new work, our catholicity of musical taste, and our determination to put the theatrical and textual elements of singing theatre on a par with the music. We needed someone in this position who could instil courage in timid breasts; who would help performers meet the challenges of modern music (including music by sometimes inexperienced composers) and not encourage them in their inevitable tendency to retreat into 'safe' repertoire; and who also had the patience to teach actors for whom singing was a secondary skill. With all these appointments our luck held.

I approached the area of acting instruction somewhat differently, deciding not to appoint a full-time acting instructor, but instead to invite professional directors, actors, singer-actors or teachers to join us for workshops lasting anything from one to eight weeks. This policy was often contested by those who felt that continuity in acting instruction was as important as in other performance areas, and in subsequent winters the time given to acting instruction became longer and longer. But I still feel comfortable about the instinct behind my reluctance. The teaching of acting is so beset with methodologies, frustrated ex-actors' egos, and the exercise of power over eager victims, that I was determined not to commit us to anyone until I was sure that their talents would provide us with everything we needed, that they would appreciate the particular demands of singing-acting, and above all that they would work in a mutually respectful way with our nucleus of regular staff. We had many wonderful talents joining us for acting workshops: David Freeman, Jean Gascon, Helen Burns, Wesley Balk, Richard Jones, Lee Devin, Charles Hamilton, Leslie Yeo, Bill Glassco, Michael Langham...But none of these could have offered singly what they all offered together.

For the composers and writers, McNeff and I were to be the 'regular' resource, together with the gruff, eccentric presence of writer and teacher Leofwyn Luke, whose powerful sense of musico-dramatic form made a unique contribution in our first winters. And for the design participants we were to appoint a series of resident designers, who would between them cover the complete seven-month period. Cameron Porteous, Peter Wingate, Susan Benson, Richard Willcox, Shawn Kerwin,

Neil Peter Jampolis, Michael Whitfield, Sam Kirkpatrick and John Ferguson made up our design stable over the years; it would be hard to imagine a more powerful and committed line-up.

FINDING PARTICIPANTS

While flying about and interviewing potential resource people we were also beginning to advertise the ensemble programme, and to set up auditions and interviews. We were well aware that the choice of participants was as crucial as the selection of their instructors. They had to have not only the talent, skills and motivation to allow them to get the best out of the programme, but also the character, the psychological stability and stamina, that would enable them to undergo change and to withstand pressure. We needed artists with solid grounding, but with the courage to confront a new and untried situation. We needed in fact, especially in that first year, pioneers like ourselves.

The Banff Centre since I had first come into contact with it had always congratulated itself on the way it balanced artistic and administrative competencies. Its mode, at least in the early eighties, was to give its programme leaders full artistic freedom to plan their programmes, and to support them with the work of a manager who controlled the budget and organised the logistics of the operation. They prided themselves on bringing good business sense to bear without letting it dominate; and in one area in particular they were confident that they had something to offer. This was the field of 'marketing', in which our president was an internationally acknowledged expert.

Orthodox marketing strategy goes like this: if you want to produce something, make sure before you produce it that there is a need for it, and that other people are not producing it already and more cheaply. Identify your 'target market' (the consumers most likely to want to buy your product) and if necessary modify or replace your planned product to suit what you perceive to be their needs. And then, when you create your product, make sure that the target market is fully aware of its existence; focus your marketing efforts on them, and on whatever forces, media or otherwise, will help to convince them to buy. And finally facilitate the distribution of the product to the targeted consumers. That is the way to run a successful business.

The Banff version of this strategy is only slightly different; if you want to offer an arts training course, make sure before you produce it that there are students who need it for their careers as artists, and that it is not already being offered by other schools more cheaply and closer to the main centres. Identify the students who are most likely to be interested in the course, and if necessary modify the proposed course in response to their perceived needs. If you cannot identify a need, don't offer the course. Once you offer the course, make sure that the students you have identified as being suitable for the course know of its existence. Focus your marketing efforts on them, and on their teachers or other influential parties – on whatever will convince them to apply for the course. And finally make sure that any successful candidate for the course is not prevented from attending by lack of funds.

While the process of transferring a profit-motive philosophy to an artistic/educational process never ceased to bother me, all this made eminent sense. But in the area of Music Theatre training we were up against the problem (referred to in Chapter One) that no one quite knew what Music Theatre was, or what was in it for them. Young actors tended to imagine it as a training for musicals, and we were liable to attract their interest if they had a singing voice and wanted to develop it in order to play parts in musical comedy. Classically trained singers were usually groping along the tunnel of their vision towards La Scala, and were not easily convinced that a 'Music Theatre' course (what's that?) would speed them to the goal. Young composers were hard to find, and usually busy grinding out their statutory bassoon sonatas; one young spark told us that anyway 'writing for the voice was totally out of date'. Writers were an even harder bunch to locate and entice.

So began the patient building of an international network of information about Music Theatre and its potential, and about the new programme. Banff was anyway realistic enough about its far-off location to put a great deal of money into the promotion – 'marketing' – of all its new winter programmes, but the Music Theatre Studio Ensemble needed a special effort, and I found myself on aircraft to Vancouver and Victoria, to the Prairies and Toronto and Montreal and Halifax, to New York and Chicago and Los Angeles, to London and even to Paris, making contacts through previous contacts, and working to establish the fact, the goals and the possibilities of our new initiative. I gave talks to composers, writers, designers, producers and agents, to opera and music and drama departments, to conservatories and associations of singing teachers, to deans and principals and professors. A great deal of talking was done, and we were able, I think, to convey to many artists and teachers a sense of our own excitement.

What these people were told was that we were launching a new initiative in the singing theatre, which combined training and the creation of new work; and that while we believed our ensemble work would be of value to young singers if they were aiming at the opera stage or at musical comedy, the long-range goal for which our programme was a preparation was nothing less than the development of a new singing theatre, in which creation was central and not marginal. For this, we believed that the singer-actor must be given opportunities to develop all-round versatility in all performance skills; that young composers must be given a chance to learn something about the theatre, about the human voice, about collaborating with a writer and director; that young writers must become aware of the extraordinary and undeveloped potential of expressing themselves in singing theatre; and that young designers could be a genuine part of the ensemble, not locked away in a design studio but working alongside performers, sharing in the developing ideas of composers and writers, and having a chance to realise their designs for these new works on stage and under the guidance of a professional.

We were well aware, I said, that there was very little evidence at present of a new 'Music Theatre' job market for our graduating students to move into; but that what we offered would deepen and enlarge the skills of any young artists regardless of their future. And beyond this, we were convinced that by offering the experience of the ensemble year after year to a select group of talented people, we would be creating slowly but surely a 'bank' of talented artists who had an idea and an experience in common, and who would eventually provide the leaven for a much-needed and long-overdue change in the structure and goals of the singing theatre.

It must be said that the telling of our vision roused many tired and cynical teachers and practising theatre artists to a fine and eager frenzy, and received a warm welcome wherever there was a spirit of adventure and a frustration with the status quo; and that it fell on stony ground where people felt they had a tradition, or indeed their own lifework, to defend; where the priorities and over-arching hegemony of the operatic system were accepted without question or complaint. I was twice scheduled to speak at the Opera School of the University of Toronto. The first time not a soul turned up. A year later eight people bustled in and my spirits rose, until I found that they were there for a rehearsal and had mistaken the room number. I stood with my back against the door anyway, and gave them a five-minute harangue.

One of our most reliable sources of participants, curiously enough, was Banff itself. The summer programmes still continued, and included both an opera and a musical theatre (i.e. musical comedy) course, both of which had for many years attracted students from all over North America and occasionally beyond. I had even led the summer musical theatre course since 1978, and so was in a position to steer likely candidates towards the winter Music Theatre Studio Ensemble. And some of the opera students also found their way in our direction.

As the years went by, our own resource artists, coming from many parts of the world and then returning home almost always flushed with enthusiasm, were perhaps the most powerful agents of all in the promotion of the ensemble and the discovery of promising participants. The Voice Department of the Guildhall School of Music, under Noelle Barker, made it almost a practice to send their talented students to us, and it was gratifying to give a talk there once to a crowd of thirty or forty, including the Principal. Fie, fie, Toronto!

Through much strenuous effort of this kind we generated fifty or sixty applications for that first year, and were able to choose a likely bunch, mostly Canadians but with a few also from America and Britain. Soon we would have to think about a second year, about how it should be structured and staffed. But for now the challenges of the first year were quite enough.

And so, in the middle of September, 1981, our first ensemble arrived in the Rockies; and after a few days and nights which (following a curious but pleasant school policy) they had to spend walking in the mountains and sleeping under canvas or in alpine huts, we assembled for the first time in our largest studio. We sat in a single, wide circle: participants, resource artists and management staff. There were some thirty-two of us. The autumn sun beamed in, filtered through pine-trees and dappling the bright floor. We began.

Chapter Seven

MUSIC THEATRE AT BANFF: TRAINING

All education for the artist has to grope towards, if not actually strike, a balance between classroom training and the kind of training which comes from actually making art. Classroom training, simply described, works by unravelling the composite of technical skills needed by the artist, and practising these skills in isolation from one another. A month can be spent on attacking a problem of breathing, or on handling a bow or a brush or an errant little finger, or on sketching feet, or on the phrasing of a speech or a sonata – a month, or a lifetime, indeed. In the oriental artistic tradition the practising of isolated skills becomes one with spiritual training, and knows no end. 'Learning by doing', on the other hand, is exactly what it says: the student goes through the actual process of making the art, and then has both process and result subjected to some kind of critique, from which a lesson of experience is drawn. Somewhere between these two processes comes what is often these days referred to as 'project' work, or 'workshopping'; parameters are set up that reproduce the conditions of full performance in some but not all respects.

Collaborative arts, in which the artist works as a member of a group, pose an additional set of challenges in training. Not only must the artist develop individual skills, but those skills must be fitted into a larger pattern; and one component of his/her individual skill is the very skill of how to fit into the collaborative artwork.

Decisions as to how much time is to be spent in the classroom, and how much in the preparation of some kind of performance, will depend both on what is being taught, and on the degree of skill and readiness on the part of the student. Even mature artists may be learning a new skill or approach, or trying to rid themselves of tiresome habits. New ways have to be mastered before they are applied in creative work.

The Banff Centre's tradition had always been that of 'learning by doing'; its practice since the beginning was to bring in the best artist-teachers it could find and then to put a group of students into their care during the preparation of a performance or other kind of finished artwork. Classroom training of course took place, but it was to a greater or lesser extent feeding into the final product. The support system for stage performances – the planning and building and painting of stage designs, the stagework, sound and lighting, and so forth – was also set up as a learning experience for young stage technicians and designers, in just the same way 'learning by doing'.

Within the confines of a summer course lasting four to six weeks this was no doubt the most practical policy. But the raising of standards at Banff in the seventies brought with it an increased emphasis on the importance of classroom training and workshops, and in the theatrical arts (ballet, drama, opera, musical theatre) the co-ordination of classroom time with production time became the essential juggling trick for course leaders. The summer festival, for which so many students prepared performances, was often accused of having become the tail wagging the less showy dog of classwork. It was pointed out that many students, however keen they were to perform, were simply not ready to meet a paying public in a fully produced show, and that putting a superficial performance polish on their raw skills was even harmful to them. And so during the eighties the practice gradually developed of expanding the programme of 'free admission' workshops, and limiting the experience of full festival performance to only the most advanced students. 'Master Classes' of young or not so young professionals were assembled in opera, drama and ballet. Less advanced classes of dancers and actors were dropped; and the summer musical theatre programme, which had always catered to a generally more junior clientele and could not make the switch effectively, was eventually abolished – to the indignation of the local public, for whom it had been for twenty-five years the highlight of an otherwise somewhat esoteric playbill.

But in 1981 these changes were just beginning, with orthodoxies not yet frozen, and we in the Music Theatre Studio Ensemble were left free to decide just how the components of our programme were to be balanced. This was just as well, because the simple activity ratio, of classroom training versus training through full or workshop production, was only one of the judgements we had to make.

An integrated Music Theatre training programme, built around the two poles of skill training and the creation of new work – and so designed for composers, writers and designers as well as performers – must always be a multiple balancing act; in fact the difficulty of pulling off all these balancing tricks in such a complex four-ring circus is probably why long-term programmes of this kind have not been undertaken. Consider:

– Singers must be helped to develop their acting, movement and speech skills – without letting them lose ground vocally in the process. They must be helped to feel comfortable with the demands of contemporary works of all styles – but must not lose the legato line and the vocal condition necessary for the classical repertoire. Dancers must be exposed to a whole spectrum of new skills, and yet maintain their physical condition. And attention must be paid to the needs of all performers as individuals – but also as members of a group of performers.

– A context must be created in which instructors can operate with understanding of and support for each other's discipline – and yet each of them must be given enough class time for them to feel they can make a satisfactory contribution of their own.

– Composers and writers have to be given enough basic information and stimulus for them to be able to tackle the writing of a good Music Theatre piece – but also enough time to write it.

– Designers must be given the chance and the basic resources to design Music Theatre pieces and to execute these designs – but also enough time to improve themselves as designers and as artists. And the decision to mount new Music Theatre pieces must always be weighed by their value as training vehicles for all ensemble members.

– And for all these artists, membership of the total ensemble must be made a practical reality; the programme must find ways of interconnecting the work of performers, composers, writers, designers, not only in performances but also in the process of training – while still giving everyone the time and opportunity to develop strongly in the area of their own speciality.

At Banff the particular nature of the Winter Cycle, which I had helped to put on the road, laid even further demands on our participants. One of the unique features of the seven-month experience was to be its emphasis on interdisciplinary activity. We therefore had to try and make it possible for ensemble members to take advantage of the opportunities provided at the Banff School to undertake inter-disciplinary projects with artists in the Music and Visual Arts programmes, while taking care that the focus and energies of ensemble members did not become weakened or diffused. I cannot pretend that we were as successful in this last aim as others would like us to have been. But our ensemble was in no way deprived thereby of interdisciplinary activity, because our whole programme was already just that.

The balancing acts I have described are at the heart of training for the singing theatre. Before tackling them in more detail, let me clarify the schedule at Banff, and also the structure of the Banff Music Theatre Studio Ensemble. We began, of course, with only one year's intake of participants, and the structure and training schedule outlined here deals only with this first-year programme. A second-year programme was instituted the following winter, but its activities were for the most part separate, and so will be separately outlined (see pp. 112-14).

THE SCHEDULE AT BANFF

The Banff Winter Cycle is made up of two terms, each approximately thirteen weeks long:

1. Fall Term: mid-September to mid-December.

2. Spring Term: first week of January to first week of April.

With a mountain expedition starting off the year, and two half-term breaks, it is practical in fact to consider each term as a twelve-week period.

THE ENSEMBLE

This was the name given to the total group of participants, first- and eventually second-year, in the Music Theatre training programme: Performers, Composers, Writers and Designers – and also other categories which from time to time we included, such as Stage Managers, Accompanists and Directors. This Ensemble broke down into twelve Performers, six male, six female (the number of performers increased to a total of eighteen when six were invited back for a second year); three Composers and three Writers; and four Designers.

The other categories which we occasionally accepted into the programme became members of one or other of these groups, with the exception of two Stage Managers, for whom a separate specialist group was twice established. (Mention should also be made briefly here of our interest in offering technical trainees – being trained by the theatre staff of the Centre – a kind of associate membership of the Ensemble, with the invitation to participate in our Ensemble exercises and to observe classes. The experiment, designed to close the gap between 'technical' and 'artistic' ways of thinking, was regrettably discontinued after two years – for technical reasons.)

It will be clear from this list that in spite of the apparently free-wheeling nature of our approach, we attached a definite label to each participant we accepted. This is by no means to say that we were suspicious of candidates with multiple gifts – in fact the nature of the programme made it immediately attractive to multi-talented people, and we encouraged them to exercise their gifts. But whatever multiple gifts they might possess, we asked them to decide on which of their skills they were going to concentrate their attention while with the ensemble, and therefore what their home base was going to be. Such a policy might seem unnecessarily rigid, but there were two reasons for it. In the first place, specialist training in the different groups often took place simultaneously, so that it was not possible to be a fully operative member of more than one group. Secondly, creatures who flit from group to group as the spirit moves are unsettling to regular group members, and can easily fall into all the unpleasing characteristics of tourists: never satisfied because never focused, an alien presence wherever they go, and warping the everyday activity of local populations. I long ago developed the maxim – in regard to inter-artistic activity – that you cannot build a bridge without firm ground on either side. The groups needed a sense of home within their own specialist group in order to have the confidence to make links with others.

Let us now look more closely at the questions of balance as they affected each specialist group at Banff – and as they might operate within any integrated singing theatre training programme.

PERFORMERS

Since the group of twelve first-year performers was not merely a class but a performing ensemble, we were caught up with questions of balance in the very selection process. We determined early on that we would aim for an even mix of six men and six women, not only offering equal opportunities to each sex but also enabling us to present a balance of male and female voices for our composers to write for and our audience to listen to. We could well have tried to go further, insisting on a strict break-down of soprano, alto, tenor and bass. But we contented ourselves with ensuring that there were high and low voices among both the men and the women. With our concentration on new works we were not convinced that voices had to be herded into the various pens prescribed for them by Renaissance Italy.

Made up of a mixture of trained singers, trained actors, and the occasional trained dancer, the performing group was the only one in which the instrument of expression was simply the body and its voice. Since good bodily and vocal condition requires daily work, the schedule of training for performers is always intense.

This is also the group in which the balance of activity between classroom and production is the most crucial. The way this balance is struck will always depend – as I mentioned earlier – on the state of the student at the outset. At Banff we were accepting a group of performers, with an average age of 27, who had already completed their specialist training (and often had professional experience). Singers had perhaps been through a university music or opera programme, or through a school or conservatory of music. Actors had attended a university drama department or a professional theatre school. Dancers had studied at a dance school or with a company. In all these training experiences they had developed their 'primary' skills with more or less success, but their secondary performance skills had been neglected.

Singers had spent years refining their vocal instrument, as well as having a certain amount of exposure to music history and theory; but their acting training had generally consisted of two hours a week of improvisation for a term or two, followed by work on scenes from the operatic repertoire. They had never studied dramatic masters such as Shakespeare or Chekhov, and had little sensitivity for literature. They had perhaps learnt a little fencing. Their movement training had often been limited to an hour or two a week of folk and period dancing in their last year. Their sight-reading of music was often not nearly as good as it should have been. And they had never had a speech class in their lives.

Actors had a similar history, but in reverse. Their training was in general much more comprehensive than the singers'; they had received extensive training not only in acting but in speech, stage fighting and acrobatics, in dramatic styles and in stage movement. But their musical education had been limited to a handful of singing lessons, often as one of a group. They could rarely read music, and had little knowledge of musical or vocal style. If they sang well – and they sometimes did – this was not the result of their work in acting school.

Dancers were perhaps the least rounded of all. Subjected to many hours a day of rigorous dance training, they had rarely been offered singing, speech or acting classes, and knew little of music history or theory. Even the dance training they had received often had the effect of limiting rather than freeing their physical movement; one can nearly always tell when an actor is a former dancer.

This picture of the separated traditions of performance training is of course a generalised one, and there were always cases where the exception stood out, testifying to the rule. Many of the candidates we accepted had in fact already begun to reject the pattern of their own training. They were actors who had started remedying their own musical deficiencies by studying privately with a singing teacher; or trained singers who had enrolled in an actors' training studio, or in dance classes, because of their interest in being rounded performers. But the rule was there – in auditioning candidates over a six-year period in North America and Europe, we found again and again that young performers' formal training fitted into a pattern of uneven development. The result was a professional singer who was an amateur actor – or the reverse. And because one of Music Theatre's cardinal principles is its need for versatile singer-actors with comprehensive skills, it follows that our work for this particular age group was to a considerable extent remedial – filling the gaps in earlier specialised study.

The growing awareness of this state of affairs led us to make several adjustments to the programme over the six years, particularly in the relationship of classroom training to performance. For our first term we programmed a full production (or evening of short productions) every six weeks (i.e. four over the winter), as well as a series of 'cabarets'. Since Stephen McNeff and I had both come to the programme from the practical world of theatre, this seemed a reasonable schedule for us; we were perhaps more comfortable with the roar of the greasepaint and smell of the crowd, than with the niceties of training. But it soon became evident that nothing much could be done in a three-week training period, and that moving immediately into a hectic round of part-learning and rehearsal meant that our performers were unable to bring what had been learned into the performance. So in later winters we abandoned the idea of a first mid-term production, and eventually even reduced our Christmas production to an in-house acting workshop – a move that made me wonder whether the balance had begun to swing too much the other way.

Lists and charts do not make easy reading, and the schedules on this and the following pages can be skipped over without damage to the general argument. But for the sake of those with professional interest in such things I have outlined the two primary balances – the 'activity ratios' – that were established for first-year performers after three years of operation:

BALANCE 1: CLASSROOM TRAINING/TRAINING THROUGH PERFORMANCE

First Term:

8 weeks full-time classroom training

4 weeks rehearsal and performance with reduced classroom training

Second Term:

3 weeks full-time classroom training period

3 weeks rehearsal and performance with reduced classroom training

6 weeks of music preparation, rehearsal and performance with reduced classroom training

BALANCE 2: SPECIALISED INDIVIDUAL TRAINING/ SPECIALISED GROUP TRAINING

Training for performers was made up of the standard principal elements
of movement, acting, speech and voice. The time allotted to each, indi-
cated here in hours per week, varied according to whether the ensemble
was in 'full' or 'reduced' training period.

In full training period	*In reduced training period*
GROUP	
Movement * 9 hours 20m p/w	6 hours 40m p/w
Acting * 13 hours p/w	------
INDIVIDUAL	
Singing 1 hr 20m p/w	1 hr 20m p/w
Speech 1 hr 20m p/w	1 hr 20m p/w
Movement	Special classes as required

* 'Movement' includes body conditioning, dance, acrobatics and stage
combat.
* 'Acting' includes mime and maskwork.

COMPOSERS AND WRITERS

While there was often some novelty involved in singers, actors and
dancers working closely alongside one another, this was nothing compared to the strangeness for composers and writers when they first came
together in a single group.

Because we were concerned to invite fully trained composers into
the programme, we often had to accept along with their compositional
flair and/or competence a fair amount of inexperience in working with
writers. Composers normally study and work either alone or among other
musicians; and if ours had written song settings or even Music Theatre
works, we found that they had most often chosen their texts from pub-

lished literature – or written their own. In fact most of them had already started muttering what I have found to be the perpetual moan of serious composers everywhere: 'Can't find a librettist'. Now they found themselves in a room with two or three writers, with the prospect of collaborating in the next months on projects for which their training had in general not remotely prepared them.

Writers were in even stranger territory. Of all our 'specialists' they were, as I have already mentioned, the hardest group to locate and assemble, and so were generally a mixed bag in themselves: a graduate of a university writing programme, a novelist or poet game for a new experience, a dramatist with musical interests, a journalist with nobler aspirations – in fact not specialists at all. Some of them may have penned the words to a few songs, but none of them had ever 'studied' the writing of words for music. The composers did at least have the comfort of a shared professional language; the writers did not, and the less musically literate found themselves at first intimidated by music and musicians.

How grand it would have been to have been able to muster a group already trained in some of the basic skills of singing theatre! And yet there was also something valuable in the inexperience of most of our composers and writers, provided they had talent. If we could not build on their previous training, at least there was very little mis-training to have to shove out of the way, and we could introduce them to a set of ideas without fighting rearguard battles with convention and tradition.

What we tried to insist on in accepting these creators into the ensemble was that they had not only talent but a record of achievement; that they had at least once – and preferably many more times – experienced the confidence that comes from having actually finished something. We were not in the business of setting up hoops for them to lumber through, but of simply helping them get started on the new road, giving them the equipment they needed for the trip and being available to them when they needed direction. We expected the initiative and drive to come from them.

The training programme for a creators' group such as this is clearly not easy to predetermine, dependent as it is on the particular needs of each annual intake. McNeff and I began in 1981, in our breezy way, by planning a series of informal meetings in the early weeks, in which we would introduce some of the ideas behind the programme, and describe the potential of new singing theatre. We would play recordings of a variety of twentieth-century Music Theatre/operatic pieces, from Sondheim to Britten. We would look at what Verdi did with Shakespeare's *Othello*. We would plunge back into the beginnings of opera for an hour or two, and admire Monteverdi, and ponder the uncertain beginnings of opera in England. We would lead discussions, and encourage the participants to lead others on subjects of interest and relevance. And meanwhile we would encourage them to start talking about projects, and to form themselves into pairs.

In addition to the group meetings and discussions, we planned individual sessions for each composer and writer. As composer-in-residence McNeff would be 'tutor' to the composers. If we had one of our writer resource artists in residence he/she would perform the same function for the writers: if not, I would take it on myself. As projects were developed they would be presented to the total group, and then extra sessions (with either McNeff or myself or our writer-in-residence) would be arranged as needed.

As with the performers, the amount of time spent in 'classroom' training has finally to be dependent on the degree of expertise which the participants bring to the programme. For some, our easy and somewhat makeshift sessions were all that was needed to spur them into action. But as winters came and went, we became aware that the composers' and writers' group needed more, much more. And so at the same time as we lengthened to eight weeks the preliminary training session for performers, we also extended and made a lot richer and more detailed the initial 'training' weeks with composers and writers (being also able sometimes to make use of the services of a second-year composer or writer as an extra resource). By the final weeks of this eight-week period, some Music Theatre pieces would be in development, and much of the remainder of the winter would be spent in writing these pieces, preparing them for performance, having them performed and 'critiquing' the result.

It will be evident that with the composers' and writers' group the initial training period, while long enough to be of substance, had also to be short enough to allow time for the creation of works, since these were planned as the high point of the ensemble's work together. In the first term, of course, no participant composer-writer team would expect their work to be performed, except possibly in a cabaret or with a group of songs written for the ensemble performers; the première productions presented during this period were therefore commissioned in advance, either from members of our home team of resource artists or from elsewhere.

It was in the middle of the second term that the new works of our participants were performed, in a four-day event that eventually became known as the 'Music Theatre Minifest'. This schedule allowed approximately eight weeks (including the Christmas break) between the end of the initial training period and the day we needed the finished manuscripts for rehearsal. We shall examine this process in more detail in the following chapter, but obvious as it may be, I should make clear right away that the pieces were not expected to be full-length. Our composer-writer teams were advised to shape their projects to all the resources available, including time. Better a five-minute masterpiece than a bogged-down Ring Cycle.

The hardest task of all in administering this group of the ensemble was of course the matching of collaborators – marriage brokering must be a hit-and-miss profession at the best of times.

We had our failures because writers suddenly were not able to write at all, or could not write fast enough, or well enough; or once or twice turned out to be people whom no one could truck with. Sometimes the collaborators could not agree on their subject matter – or the composer was the untruckable one. And sometimes, of course, the numbers were simply not even, and I or a performer or one of our short-term 'resident writer' resource artists – or Steve himself if it was a composer we were missing – would step into the breach. It was unusual that things fell smoothly into place, and towards the end of our six-year operation we began searching for 'pre-formed' partnerships; but they turned out to be as rare as animals with two heads, and for much the same reason. The difficulties of this kind of collaboration are legendary, and our experience amplified the legend; but one way or another, one year after another, a raft of pieces continued to emerge from the vortex.

The balances of the composers' and writers' group therefore looked something like this:

BALANCE 1: CLASSROOM TRAINING/TRAINING THROUGH PERFORMANCE

First Term:

8 weeks of seminars and study projects. Development of idea for major Music Theatre piece

4 weeks to finalise text and begin composition, with weekly group meetings

(work continues through 2 ½ week holiday break)

Second Term:

1 ½ weeks of final work on score and text of Music Theatre piece

4 ½ weeks for discussion with directors and designers, orchestration, rehearsal process, alteration of piece in rehearsal, performance

6 weeks for critique of piece and production. Work on changes if necessary, and preparation of final version. Development of new

ideas for Music Theatre pieces to be continued after programme ends – perhaps for following year's ensemble

BALANCE 2: SPECIALISED INDIVIDUAL TRAINING/ SPECIALISED GROUP TRAINING

The process of writing and composing dictated that the dominant rhythm of activity swung between creative work done privately (singly or in pairs), and group meetings in which the creative work ws shared and discussed and new information fed in. Individual 'tutorials' (or discussion and critiquing of projects at various stages) were arranged on an ad hoc basis, at the request either of tutor or of participant. The balance between group and individual training would therefore vary from one participant to another, and the schedule might look like this:

8 weeks initial training period:

GROUP: Meetings 4 x 2 hrs = 8 hrs p/w

INDIVIDUAL: Tutorials 1 x 2 hrs. Thereafter scheduled as requested

Remainder of winter:

GROUP: Meetings (average) 1 x 2 hrs = 2 hrs p/w

INDIVIDUAL: As requested

DESIGNERS

The stage designers who came to the Music Theatre Studio Ensemble were for the most part recent graduates of stage design programmes at universities or theatre schools. Some had had professional experience as assistant designers, or props makers, or costumiers. And one or two came to us from other areas of the visual arts, often bringing with them a freshness of imagination which made up for their ignorance of the basics of stage design. Application for the course required the submission of a portfolio of work done (sketches and slides); and the selection was made with the help of at least one of the designers who were to be in residence for the coming year. These resident designers were also instrumental in steering young designers towards the programme.

Though we felt that with our busy production schedule we could offer a valuable experience for up to four participant designers, we were rarely able to find that number of talented and qualified young artists who were available to join us; so that the design group generally consisted of no more than two or three. The small number made it possible to offer a highly individual course of study for each participant, tailored to the needs of each. The difference between group and individual work is obviously less significant in so tight a group.

However, the rhythm of the ensemble's work as a whole was clearly reflected in the shape of the designers' programme. The first eight weeks was primarily a training period, in which they undertook projects (separately or together) under the guidance of the designer-in-residence, who geared the work to what he/she felt to be the needs or weaknesses of each participant. This period also included a certain amount of necessary reestablishing of the designers' sense of themselves as artists – a sense that can sometimes be lost in the technology-rich world of modern stage design. Often the resident designer would accompany them on sketching expeditions in the mountains, or to life drawing classes in the Visual Arts building – where they were also introduced to some of the interesting work being undertaken by painters, sculptors, fibre artists, photographers, video artists and ceramicists. This exposure often led to some highly original use of materials in the theatre.

Meanwhile they would be attending the meetings of the composers and writers, and absorbing the ideas and ways of thinking and working that were being discussed there. As projects developed they would respond with a visual concept in sketch or model form, which might later expand into some kind of performance. And as the 'Christmas' production approached – usually designed by the designer-in-residence – they would serve as his/her assistants. This would also be the period in which composers and writers were developing their pieces for the following term, and the designers participated in these preparations, offering visual and staging ideas as the works progressed.

The high point of the designers' creative activity was of course the Minifest, which occasionally offered as many as six or seven short pieces of Music Theatre. Each designer would be given the design responsibility for two or three of these, and would collaborate – under the supervision of the resident designer – over the developing of a modular stage concept within which the various production designs would have to fit.

The final production of the winter, generally the largest of the year, would find the designers once again serving as assistants to the resident designer.

Clearly the balance between the designers' group and individual training cannot be summarised at all in terms of hours, and it would be specious to attempt it. The balance between classroom and production training also swung easily and often as it followed the running year:

*BALANCE 1 and 2: CLASSROOM TRAINING/TRAINING
THROUGH PRODUCTION AND GROUP TRAINING/INDIVIDUAL
TRAINING*

First Term:

First 8 weeks: Individual and group training, with study projects. Attendance at composers' and writers' seminars. Individual 'remedial' classes in areas not covered by previous training. Life and landscape drawing and painting. *Also* assistance with end-of-term production designs

Last 4 weeks: Assistance on execution of designs for end-of-term production. Participation in development of composers' and writers' new Music Theatre pieces

Second Term

First 6 weeks: Collaborative planning of overall design concept for Minifest. Design of individual Music Theatre pieces, and execution of design

Second 6 weeks: Assistance on design execution for final production

ENSEMBLE ACTIVITY AND WORKSHOPS

These programmes of specialised work and training with their different swings and balances, must themselves be balanced against another activity: the work of the ensemble as a total group. It is evident that a programme that claims to 'integrate' the training of singer-actors, composers, writers and designers must do more than bring the various specialists together at the beginning and end of the affair. Music Theatre pieces which are created by the composers and writers, designed by the designers, and performed by the performers, are naturally the high integrating point of such collaborative work – the 'result', you could say. But the training programme itself must be designed to take continuous advantage of the presence of parallel specialists – each of whose specialities is after all only a part of the whole.

   The first necessity in such a programme is to establish the principle that all classes – except individual classes in certain circumstances – are open for all ensemble members to observe. There must be no closed doors. We have already seen that the designers sat in on the formal meetings of composers and writers; composers and writers also joined in on sessions in the designers' studio. But it was of equal importance that designers, composers and writers all spend time sitting in on singing and acting and dance classes, both in order to be exposed (some of them for the first time) to the principles of performance skill, and also to get to know the characteristics and potential of the performers they would be writing and designing for. The early morning body conditioning class (obligatory for performers) was open to all ensemble members – as well as resource artists – not only to observe but to participate in. Designers were encouraged to sit in on dance classes and sketch – later pasting up the results on the wall outside their studio to share them with the rest of the ensemble.

Sometimes involvement across the specialist disciplines went further than observation and auditing. Designers and writers were offered a number of sessions with our accompanist coaches, to initiate or improve their ability to sight-read music, and also to understand its language and structure by listening and analysis. In fact, thanks to the extraordinary spirit of generosity and service on the part of our resource artists, many individual classes and tutorials were offered to almost anyone who asked for them. Charles Causley, who served three times as our writer-in-residence, made it clear at the beginning of each visit that he was happy to read and discuss any piece of writing which anyone wanted to share with him, and many of us (including myself) took advantage of his kindness and discerning critical spirit. Nearly all our singing teachers found themselves giving voice classes to interested composers, writers and designers. And all members of the ensemble could ask for their own individual speech classes from Colin Bernhardt, whose classes went well beyond elocution.

These 'cross-over' classes did not always involve the teaching staff. On many occasions our singers gave voice classes or piano lessons to fellow participants – sometimes in exchange for help with acting projects. Composers also gave instrumental lessons, and helped to notate songs that performers had written. These arrangements were informal and private, but they contributed to the climate of collaboration and interchange. In a world in which specialisation requires us to turn our subsidiary talents into mere hobbies, this climate encouraged us to take all our gifts seriously; exploring them, even if they were unlikely to be our livelihood, helped to make or keep us whole.

The keystone of all these over-arching activities was the ensemble workshop, referred to in our early days as 'labs'. Let me conclude this explication of the training elements of the Banff programme with a discussion of this, one of its most important elements.

I should first pay tribute to the source for what has become almost a trademark of integrated singing theatre training. In 1980 a three-week national Choreographer's Workshop was held at Banff under the direction of Robert Cohan of the London Contemporary Dance Theatre. For this workshop, modelled on others given elsewhere, six choreographers were supplied with the services of a total of twenty-four dancers, six composers and an assortment of instrumentalists. Every morning each choreographer would collaborate with a different composer on a dance project, to be based on a title given to the team by Cohan. The dancers were divided up among the choreographers according to their requests – within the limits of the total number. And every evening a group of six dances would be performed. This would be followed by a discussion, led by Cohan, of each performance in turn.

Invited to watch the process at work, and able to talk about it with all the participants, I began to realise that this was an activity which might well be adapted to the singing theatre. The composers of this workshop, who were by no means neophytes but established professional artists, began in a panic, faced by what seemed to be the sheer impossibility of writing several minutes of music to order – to a deadline a few hours away. Their first efforts tended to reflect this nervousness, restricted to few instruments, and making liberal use of improvisatory or random techniques: 'percussion and flute' became a familiar sound. But all of them reported on how the experience changed them. As the days went by, each challenging them afresh, they found themselves developing methods to deal with the demands of the project, and above all found themselves *learning to trust their first impulse*. They wrote without filtering the work through their rational processes – because there was no time. I thought a lot about this, and discussed it with my colleagues.

Does quick mean dirty? There used to be a well-known expression around Tin Pan Alley: 'D'you wannit good, or d'you wannit Toosday?': speed of composition can often mean sloppy and ill-considered work. But does it have to be so? As Constant Lambert observed, 'one cannot add to one's musical stature by taking thought'. We are reliably told that Handel wrote *Messiah* in twenty-four days, that Mozart — while at work on *The Magic Flute* and his *Requiem* — dashed off *La Clemenza di Tito* in three weeks, and that Gershwin, in a somewhat different idiom, took the same time to compose *Rhapsody in Blue*. These are unusual feats by unusual men. But it is interesting and perhaps more relevant to know that the young Benjamin Britten's pressured composition of music for the documentary films produced by the General Post Office was always valued by him in later life. As a writer of film music he was required to complete his scores at short notice, and to rigid specifications – 17 seconds of music here, 11.5 there. His manuscript had to be not only delivered punctually but legible and error-free in order to waste no time in the studio. And the impetus for the music came not from his own life but from the rhythmic and dramatic requirements of the image he was given. It is not the way he would have wanted to continue his career, but he enjoyed the challenges, and referred to the experience as his period of 'professionalisation'.

As an antidote to the leisured anguish of tenured academic composers, this idea of 'professionalisation' seemed to have much to commend it, and as early as the 1980 pilot project we incorporated the basic idea of Cohan's workshop into our Music Theatre training – but with one major difference. His workshop was specifically designed to give young choreographers, or dancers who were beginning to move towards choreography, an opportunity to try out their ideas and their methods of work. The dancers and composers and instrumentalists were there at the service of choreography, and any benefit that accrued to them was really a bonus. In our integrated programme there was no such pecking order; the needs of all the various specialists of the ensemble were considered to be of equal importance. This commitment to equality of importance in fact became a cardinal principle of day-to-day management throughout our programme, and the stuff of yet another balancing act – we had to ensure that at no time did one group feel that they were simply being 'used', or, if this did become a need for a specific project, that it was clearly billed as such, one group assisting another.

And so began the ensemble workshop. In 1980, and in the first weeks of every Banff Music Theatre Ensemble programme that was to follow, the afternoon and evening of one day would be periodically set aside. The entire ensemble would meet together after lunch, and would be divided into three or four groups in each of which we would try to place a composer, a designer and a writer, as well as three or four performers. Then we would give to each group the same working title, carefully chosen to be either ambiguous or simple enough to offer alternative approaches (e.g. 'Silence', 'Spare Parts', 'Circle'). The task was straightforward, though not easy; each group was to produce a piece of Music Theatre based on the title, and be ready to present it that evening to the rest of the ensemble. Each was given a room to work in, and an hour or so in the performance space that was to be used for the presentations. There were few other rules – apart from requesting that groups did not compare notes with one another. It looks and is a tall order, but over the years since then, at Banff and many other places where such workshops have been held, there has never been a group unable to present a piece at the end of the day.

Four or five minutes long, and occasionally stretching to as much as ten, the pieces are for the most part strikingly different from one another, in spite of the common title. More astonishingly, many of the pieces show considerable dramatic power and insight, and in a few cases have become the basis for more extended works.

Central to the process, of course, is the discussion that follows the presentations. It took many sessions for us to get the tone of this right; it can so easily become a mere judging process – are the pieces bad, or good? But we soon realised that there must be no question of placing any kind of critical value on what was shown.

First, the exercise was designed to introduce the participants to one another within a creative context, and help to build a sense of ensemble: A group of participant students, coming together from many different backgrounds and often with no previous acquaintance, need to work together in order to develop cohesion as an ensemble. But productions, which are often the key to developing this spirit, will normally come much later in a training programme. Workshops fill the gap; nothing is more effective for the swift perception of one another's strengths and weaknesses – in character, imagination and talent – than this collective task.

Secondly the exercise was to introduce the principle of collaboration: no rules are imposed about how the group is to manage itself; no leaders are appointed. Hence each group has to decide for itself how it is going to function, and finds itself facing primordial socio-political problems concerning leadership and government. An easy way out is for the group to choose a leader to make the decisions; even easier for them is not to appoint anyone at all but simply to allow the most dominant personality to have his/her way. In practice, an exhausting but more satisfying democracy generally prevails, in which tiresome people have to be heard out, pet ideas have to be given up in the need for agreed decisions, and dominant personalities find themselves having to hold back. A perfect recipe for mediocrity, you may say – cut off the budding Wagners. But the development of mutual trust and respect soon leads to a generous recognition of the gifts of others.

And finally the exercise should develop a sense of shared creative responsibility. Although composers, writers and designers are used to facing the blank page – the empty space, which they must fill with ideas and action – performers become accustomed to having basic materials supplied: 'give me the words and the music, tell me where to stand and which way to look, and even (sometimes) what to think, and I will do the rest'. The involvement of performers at every stage of the creation is thus of particular value because it leads them to consider – sometimes for the first time – questions of form, and the relationship between form and content; questions of taste, or at least of choice between alternatives; and questions about the difference between intention and fulfilment. This experience does not necessarily turn them into original creators, but it inevitably widens their perspective as interpreters of the work of others. Conversely, composers, writers and designers are in the habit of setting things in motion and then, their job done, watching others carry the work to an audience. Just as the ensemble workshops give every performer the experience of facing that empty space which must be filled, so the small-ness of the group very often obliges designers, composers and writers to appear as characters. Another recipe for mediocrity? Again, it depends what you are looking for. How often have we heard about a brilliant piece badly performed, or a load of rubbish saved by its interpreters? Here, no buck can be passed.

The discussions which follow the presentations begin with questions. Each group in turn is asked to recount the experiences of the day. What happened during the afternoon? How were their decisions made? Who did what, and why? How much time was spent talking, and how much re-hearsing? What problems were encountered? And then, how do they feel the performance came off? Did it happen as they planned? Once this re-port is completed, anyone can ask questions, or make comments, in the light of what has been said. Did the piece communicate what was in-tended? Could the group clarify the reason for this, or that? How did they hit on the idea of that *coup de théâtre*? Pleasure and surprise can ob-viously be expressed, or confusion and doubt, but the focus must always remain fixed on the reporting of experience rather than on bald critical judgements.

At the end of the workshop the group is encouraged to step back from the vagaries of each work and consider them whole, as specimens of Music Theatre. Were they all 'Music Theatre pieces'? What is a Music Theatre piece anyway? And so the whole ensemble is exposed to that question, with the opportunity to fashion its own definition. It is surpris-ing how vivid the relationship between words, music and stage action becomes to people who have just been wrestling in its shadow.

At Banff we found that a series of five workshops, held once a week, brought us close to the limits of their value. During the series we would change the composition of the groups, and also ring the changes in the task itself, sometimes replacing the title with a poem, or a picture, or a melodic line – or once even a page of the telephone directory. If we felt that the pieces were becoming too reliant on familiar crutches, we might request that there be no theatrical costumes or props, that pianos not be used, or even that no orthodox musical instruments of any kind be played. All these variations produced their own surprises.

A game? Or a serious exercise? Nothing in all our activities was liable to invite slicker disdain from the Toscaphiles. And not only from them; one youngish and reasonably well-established British composer pro-fessed genuine revulsion at the way in which these workshops pressured our participant composers to achieve quick results, and put them on an equal level with performers. The remote mystery of composition, it seemed, was at risk.

His opinion was fervently enough felt and expressed to be taken seriously. But there are any number of professional composers, writers, designers and performers who have witnessed these workshops and have come to believe just as fervently in their unusual power and value. Indeed, it is hard to be present in the discussions without sensing the way in which the exercise engages every participant, stretching their minds and imaginations, exposing them actively to the wonder of 'creating something where there was nothing before', and insisting all the time on the full responsibility of each member of each group for whatever result is achieved.

Beyond all the social and creative benefits offered by the ensemble workshops, there is, I believe, one other paramount virtue in the exercise. For students who are embarking on a singing theatre training programme and who arrive imprinted with the opera, operetta or musical comedy tradition, it provides right at the start an alternative 'Idea' for a work of singing theatre; an accessible model in which *cliché* and convention become jaggedly exposed because if they are there it is by your choice. It is a model, in fact, stripped down to those elements which we have signalled as singing theatre's primary act: 'a performer who acts and sings a role, in a dramatic performance, with musical support, in a performance area, in front of an audience'. With this stimulus the central importance of new work is established from the start, and in my experience is embraced by the whole ensemble with confidence and grace.

CODA: THE SECOND YEAR PROGRAMME

Since one of the features of Banff's Winter Cycle was that participants had the possibility of returning for a second year, we began designing a second-year programme even before the first ensemble gathered in 1981.

It made sense to us, as well as to the Banff administration at that time, that some of our second-year activities reach out to the citizens of Alberta whose tax money had made the whole Banff venture possible. We therefore developed plans for the establishment of a small touring company, which would take Music Theatre to the province, and particularly to the small communities that did not have the resources to invite and pay for productions from the professional theatres. We knew that not all first-year performers would be able to extend their stay for a second year. Out of those that could and did wish to do so we would pick half a dozen, the precise amount (and also the ratio of women to men) being dependent on the production we chose or commissioned.

In selecting the touring production we had to bear in mind that our predominantly rural public would not be theatrically or musically sophisticated, so that this was not the ideal forum for our more urbanly venturesome work. What was important was that our second-year performers had an opportunity to practise their singing-acting skills before audiences of many different kinds, and that they gained the valuable lessons that come from performing the same work many times in many different conditions. We planned two three-week tours: one in October-November, and another in the snows of February. Musical support varied from solo keyboards (piano and synthesiser) to a group of four.

It was also planned that the touring troupe – known as 'Siding 29' Music Theatre Company after the original name of the Banff townsite – provide instruction and entertainment in the schools of their various touring venues, and that this be seen as another element of their second-year training.

This concentration on production and the preparation of school presentations and instruction meant that the balance between classroom and performance training tilted heavily towards the latter, a change of emphasis which struck us as appropriate for the second-year performers' programme.

Rehearsals for the tour still gave us the opportunity to provide body-conditioning, speech and singing classes to the second-year performers' group (we even occasionally took these out to them on the tour itself), and, after the first tour returned in early November, to set up a four-week studio workshop for them, to be performed for the ensemble only. The second term began with another three weeks of personal or group production work, before the tour was re-rehearsed and sent out again. And on their return in late February they joined the first-year group in rehearsals for the last production of the year, which was therefore able to muster eighteen performers.

Participant composers and writers were also eligible to apply for a second year, but there seemed little point in asking them to return for what was essentially a repeat of the previous course of work. We therefore accepted only those whom we felt were capable of providing a major piece for the ensemble, or had proposed a Music Theatre project which we liked the look of and felt we should support. We billed returning composers and writers as 'teaching assistants', and expected them to share responsibility for the planning and administration of the initial eight-week training period. It was rare that more than one composer returned in each year. And it was even rarer that any of our writers were invited back: those with major talent usually had to resume other projects, while those with less developed gifts were better off honing them elsewhere.

Similarly, if we invited designers back for a second year, it was because we felt that we could offer them at least one major production. This worked well, and the mix of more and less experienced designers in one studio was always beneficial.

For all participants, but especially for those in their second year who had spent a long period out of the swim of things, we also provided opportunities for pursuing 'professional development' – preparing them for their entry or re-entry into the profession. The school took this part of the Banff experience very seriously, and offered formal talks and classes in such fields as agents and management, income tax, copyright, preparation of résumés and photographs, and the use of computers. Within the ensemble we offered help with the selection and preparation of audition material, contacts, letters of introduction or reference to appropriate people in the profession, and personal guidance and advice.

The strong emphasis on projects and productions for second-year participants made this second-year programme complicated to organise but considerably less complex in structure than the first, and I am therefore devoting less space to it. But this must not suggest that we considered our second-year experience less important. Our productions, splendidly planned and administered by tour manager Jon Bjorgum, were seen throughout Alberta, and taken to the Northwest Territories and over the border to British Columbia. Some 4,000 children, many of them of native origin, witnessed our schools presentations in Yellowknife in 1984 and 1985. Our second-year participants had an opportunity to consolidate their first-year training and both to give and receive enjoyable and valuable experience with their large roster of performances. 'Music Theatre' as a name and a concept may present difficulties. But for many rural communities in Western Canada the name and what it represents was for a few years clear and alive.

Chapter Eight

MUSIC THEATRE AT BANFF:
NEW BOTTLES, NEW WINE

The integrated training programme at Banff was, I believe, unique in its interlocking of composers and writers with designers and performers. But the prime distinguishing feature of the Banff programme lay not so much in its training methods as in our placing of contemporary Music Theatre, and particularly new and original work, at the heart of its activity. At first this decision was simply a statement of priority, an expression of *tendance*. But we soon understood that it had become much more than this; that it was in fact the catalyst, the true agent of change. It gave purpose and motivation not only to the work of our composers, writers and designers, but to the development of every facet of our performance training. Instead of polishing skills that would enable us to do what others had done before, we were collecting them in order to prepare for the unknown, the unpredictable.

'Behold, I make all things new' – most people's blood still runs a touch faster at the old promise. Does 'Behold, I make all things old' cast quite the same spell? Now a more modest, more tempered resolve might be to make some things old and some new. How many times visitors, and the Banff Centre administrators themselves, would ask: 'What have you got against Mozart, or Puccini?' To which the answer of course was: 'Nothing, nothing at all. But there are many places where you can study and perform Mozart. Those of our performers who have the vocal qualities and stylistic skills necessary to sing Mozart or Puccini have spent years working at it already, and have been drawn here by the attraction of something different. If we present ourselves as a place where you can study Mozart, then we will have different kinds of students and they will need different kinds of teachers. Singing Mozart will become the paradigm activity, and doing new work will be the oddity. New work will be measured against Mozart and always be found wanting. Singer-actors who are not trained as singers of Mozart will have no place. And so the climate will turn against creation, and within a year or two we will find ourselves reverting inexorably to the leaden alchemy of traditional operatic training.' All this we could see with icy clarity.

This was by no means to say that we spurned the past and ignored its achievements; simply that we used it in the way that history is always most profitably used – as a source of ideas for our own actions. Monteverdi's search for a way of expressing fear and anger through music, which led to his invention of the *agitato* figure, had a pragmatism about it which helped us consider him less as a master than as a colleague. We enjoyed following Verdi's dialogue with Boito on the structuring of *Othello* as an opera, or the decisions Mozart came to in the making of *The Magic Flute*. And equally interesting were the cul-de-sacs of Music Theatre history: in the words of Carl Dahlhaus, 'More rewarding than a search for precedents of modernity is a study of initiatives and interrupted developments that have been left aside by the history that leads up to us'.[13] Looking at some of the brave failures of seventeenth century English singing theatre as it tried to fight off the 'Italian solution', we gathered resources for our own battles with the same key elements of music, words and stage action.

As the previous chapter makes clear, the Banff Music Theatre Ensemble's commitment to performance as a key element of training opened up a string of production dates to be filled. This was the roster (with approximate dates) after three years of operation:

October 15: Touring Production (6 2nd-year performers) opens at Banff and tours until November 8.

December 15: 'Christmas' Production (12 1st-year performers) opens at Banff and plays four performances.

February 1: Touring Production revived at Banff, coupled with new Schools Production (6 2nd-year performers). Both tour until February 21.

February 21: Minifest. As many as 6 one-act Productions, at least three of them written by participant composers and writers, are presented twice: three one night, three the next, and all six once again on the afternoon and evening of the last day (12 1st-year performers, divided among the productions as required).

April 1: Major Production (18 performers, 1st- and 2nd-year) opens and plays four performances.

This adds up to:

Production	Approx. duration	Cast
1 touring production	(2 hrs)	6
1 schools production	(50 mins)	6
1 'Xmas' production	(2 hrs)	12
6 'Minifest' prods	(av. 20 mins)	each 1 to 6
1 'final' production	(2 hrs)	18

TOTAL: 10 productions

CREATING A REPERTOIRE

It will immediately be apparent that we had a steady need for Music Theatre pieces; works that challenged our ensemble performers both musically and as actors/actresses, and which were at the same time of serious intent. We also (ideally) wanted the pieces to offer a performance opportunity not just to a handful of principal players but to every performer in each cast. Since the casting of our major productions turned out, as can be seen, to be built on a duodecimal structure, requiring either 6, 12 or 18 performers with equal numbers of men and women, there were some very precise specifications to insist upon.

We needed to put together a stable of composers and writers who were educated in Music Theatre as we understood it, but who also knew the parameters of our ensemble well enough to be able to meet our needs and still produce interesting and attractive work. We particularly needed creative people who could respond swiftly to the demands of a project, and be capable of meeting deadlines which were precise and usually sooner rather than later – people, in fact, with the sure-footedness of Mozart, Handel and Gershwin! The creators we called upon first were naturally those who had already been exposed to the ideas of the ensemble in our pilot project, and were led off dutifully by Stephen McNeff and myself. We wrote a short piece, *Peking Dust*, for the first October production in 1981 – in a double bill with the theatre première of Frederic Rzewski's *The Price of Oil,* conducted by the composer. We also enlisted our first writer-in-residence Leofwyn Luke to write the text for our first Christmas production, *The Grimwood Clock*, with music by another pilot project veteran, American composer-lyricist Richard Pearson Thomas. Subsequent commissions developed in almost every case after a period of residency with the ensemble either as participant or resource artist. They included two pieces based on stories of local interest: *Ghost Town* by (and directed by) Jeremy James Taylor, with music by a participant, Stephen Gibson; and *Bible Bill* by Calgary (now London-based) writer Ken Jones, with the music of Stephen McNeff. *St Carmen* was commissioned from Canadian composer (and pilot project veteran) Sydney Hodkinson, with libretto by Lee Devin based on Michel Tremblay's play *St Carmen of the Main*. A revised version of this piece was presented by the Guelph Spring Festival in Ontario in the spring of 1987.

The only exception to the residency rule was librettist-composer Stephen Oliver, to whom audition videotapes of all eighteen performers were sent in September 1982; he watched them with Colin Graham at Canada House in London, and the following January delivered the complete text and piano-vocal score of *Sasha*, a three-hour, through-composed piece based on Ostrovsky's play *Artistes and Admirers*. The piece gave all eighteen performers at least one 'place in the sun': the characters were tailor-made for the ensemble, and the vocal lines were written with each performer's vocal quality and range in mind. It was a *tour de force* – a rather long and complicated *tour de force*, I grant you, even under Colin Graham's expert and loving direction, but a more compact version for twelve is still on the drawing-board and being considered for professional production in Britain.

The ensemble's roster of productions was not limited to new and original works; the energy required to generate a constant flow of such pieces was too much even for us. In the first place, our 'Minifest' – in which priority was given to the works of our participant composers and writers – also had to provide reasonably equal opportunities for our performers. During the development of the participants' pieces we were able to nudge the numbers and voice types towards the requirements of our twelve first-year performers ('Could you make that second tenor a baritone, and expand that rather dreary postman's part – oh, and could it be a postwoman?') and in this way could see that most were given at least one challenge in the new pieces. But some of them found themselves with two challenges, and so in order to balance the opportunities for everyone we had to supplement the (usually three or four) participant works with others. This was sometimes an opportunity for a new kind of creative project: during one year in which Charles Causley was our writer-in-residence we asked nine of the performers each to select one of Causley's poems, *and compose a setting for it*. There were protestations of incompetence, but two weeks later all the settings were submitted, some of them fine, all of them performable. They were vetted, edited as necessary, and lightly orchestrated by our resident composer, and then woven by director Campbell Smith into an attractive thirty-minute piece. But we also looked to already-written works of singing theatre to complete our bill; in this way we were able to enjoy and learn from working with pieces such as Gustav Holst's *Savitri*, Menotti's *The Telephone*, Brecht-Weill's *Little Mahagonny*, Strindberg-Weisgall's *The Stranger*, Britten's *Abraham and Isaac*, Bernstein's *Trouble in Tahiti*, Menotti-Barber's *A Hand of Bridge*, Stephen Oliver's *A Man of Feeling*, and others.

Our major productions also included non-commissioned pieces, including an English-language version of Poulenc's *Les Mamelles de Tirésias* (billed as 'Fit to Bust!') – reorchestrated by Stephen McNeff in a 'cabaret' arrangement for seven players; *The Shivaree* by two Canadians, poet James Reaney and composer John Beckwith – which had been premièred by COMUS Music Theatre earlier in Toronto and revised for our production; and Dylan Thomas' *The Doctor and the Devils*, originally a film script and brilliantly adapted for Music Theatre by Charles Causley, with music by Stephen McNeff (expanded for our production). Touring productions included Roy Hudd's *Beautiful Dreamer* based on the life and songs of Stephen Foster, and the musical *Working* (based on the book by Studs Terkel, with songs by various composers) – as well as commissioned Music Theatre versions of Stewart Walker's Northern Irish play *Spokesong*, and of Gogol's *The Government Inspector*. A piece for schools called *Music Theatre Machine*, with lyrics and music by Richard Pearson Thomas and with my text, has since played in Louisiana and Chautauqua, New York, and is planned for other venues. Only one commissioned work was never performed: a piece called *Crazy Horse Suite*, with libretto by Morgan Nyberg and music superbly composed by Stephen Chatman. The piece was scheduled for Christmas production in 1985, but fell victim to the changing views at Banff about the value of performance training. Buxton Orr and I also wrote a piece, *Ring In the New*, which was never performed, for reasons of time: it subsequently won first prize in the 1988 US National Music Theater Network competition.

Three other production activities deserve to be mentioned. First, we encouraged our second-year participants to develop their own performances, and some of these were effective adjuncts to our production roster. In some cases the performance was a concert or song cycle, sometimes featuring original work, sometimes not, but always presenting twentieth-century material. We used to refer to this material as 'associated repertoire' and encouraged our performers to become literate in it as a sideline for their career. Sometimes the performances were Music Theatre pieces: memorable among them was a startling theatrical realisation of *Pierrot Lunaire*, and also Cocteau's *La Voix Humaine* – performed first in English as a play, and then once again, after an intermission, in the original French and in Poulenc's operatic version (piano only).

Secondly, our actors' workshops, conducted by visiting directors, frequently culminated in workshop performances for the ensemble as audience. Some of these were not singing theatre at all but straight plays chosen as teaching vehicles. I particularly remember an act of *The Cherry Orchard* directed by Helen Burns, Molière's *A Doctor In Spite of Himself* under the direction of Jean Gascon, and a reading of C. Day Lewis' radio play *The Dark Tower* staged by Charles Hamilton. Among the Music Theatre workshop pieces, I will never forget a searing *Little Mahagonny* directed by Richard Jones.

Thirdly, we occasionally staged a concert performance of works or parts of works which interested us, but which we were not able to present in full production. These performances, rehearsed and open to the public, were carefully recorded, so that the composer was able at least to carry away a tape of his/her work to assist in subsequent attempts to land a production. Among these pieces were 'concert version premières' of the Calgary composer Quenten Doolittle's *Silver City* (based on a local story), Chatman's *Crazy Horse Suite*, and a passage from *Inook* by Wolfgang Bottenberg.

The principles on which we determined our repertoire can therefore be summed up thus:

1) to commission new works specifically tailored to the numbers and needs of our ensemble;

2) to produce the work of our own participant writers and composers if at all possible;

3) when producing works which were not new, to restrict our choice to pieces created in the twentieth century, and to try and select either works that were established singing theatre 'classics', or ones that had never (or hardly ever) been performed. Works by Canadian composers were of particular interest.

These principles were adhered to with reasonable strictness throughout the ensemble programme. The only pre-twentieth-century Music Theatre piece which we presented in the six-year period was Monteverdi's *Il Combattimento di Tancredi e Clorinda* (1624).

BACK TO BASICS: QUESTIONS ANSWERED

The challenges involved in making this whole system function are obviously considerable. But are they any more complicated than the eternal problem in all theatre and opera training, in which already-written pieces do not exactly fit the student numbers and voice types? I know of many students who in their opera schools found themselves on the margin of one production after another because their voice or their deportment was not 'right' for the works chosen. We at least had the opportunity to write specifically for each of our performers, and if necessary – since these were new works – to adjust pieces to suit particular needs or limitations.

The stress of preparing new work in the singing theatre is real, but it is no different from the stress of any other genuinely creative enterprise. The oddity is that in the non-commercial singing theatre (e.g. outside Broadway) stress of this kind is so rare an atmosphere to work in. There were times when every available copyist, including participants from the Music Programme, was pressed into service to copy parts not just for one or two new works, but for five or six: in fact our pianist-coach Kerry

McShane with his encyclopedic memory later reminded me that at one time we had eight pieces being copied at the same time – in every available corner pens were scratching, while stage managers' hands twitched waiting for the fresh pages. 'It's like the basement of La Scala in 1864', observed McNeff gleefully, looking in on the scene. Yes, indeed. The pressure of doing original works was very real in 1864, because in the nineteenth century they did nineteenth-century works, just as in the eighteenth century they did eighteenth-century works. Why should the twentieth century be any different?

To complete this sketch of our creative work at Banff, I should answer in detail four more questions that might be asked:

WHAT DID WE DO ABOUT MUSICIANS AND CONDUCTORS?

During our pilot project in 1980 the Banff Music Programme and its participants stayed aloof from our bustle and hustle, and we brought in nine or ten musicians from Calgary for our final presentation, supplementing our coaches and those among our composers who could play instruments. Composers conducted their own pieces if they wished – though they were persuaded to pass the baton if they were likely to be incompetent. McNeff conducted his own pieces and others as necessary, and we continued with the same system throughout the life of the ensemble.[14]

In the following years we worked hard to make an arrangement with the Music Programme, with its sixty or so winter participants – interdisciplinary activity was, after all, supposed to be built into the system. But most of the music participants were either budding – or occasionally blooming – soloists, or were preparing for orchestral auditions. They were at Banff to make the best use of their own time, and quite reasonably were not prepared to spend the necessary hours rehearsing and performing with us. We therefore devised the setting up of a Music Theatre Orchestra Scholarship, that would cover the 20 per cent or so of the Banff fees and accommodation costs not already covered by the Banff Centre's scholarship funds. In return for this extra scholarship the player was to be available during the winter as needed. It was astonishing how interested the solo string and wind and brass and percussion players suddenly became in Music Theatre, and we found ourselves able to hold auditions to select the most suitable players. This system survived until our last years, when a new Head of Music elected to take our scholarship money into his budget and arrange for us to have the players as we needed them – thus dishing out the funds more widely and equitably. There was no problem with this, although we missed the pleasure of having regular colleagues in our orchestra, with our hand-picked concertmaster.

As for orchestral numbers, these varied according to our projects.

For our participant composers writing for the 'Minifest' we established a 'basic' group of instruments which they would have available: usually about ten. Some would choose to make use of only some of these instruments. If they wished to have different ones, or one or two more, we would discuss the possibilities and the cost, and try to be flexible within our over-all orchestral budget. For our larger commissioned pieces we twice reached twenty players, but this was in the early years; subsequently we reduced the group to something between eight and fourteen. The 250-seat theatre in which we preferred to play during the winters had no orchestra pit, thus giving our designers some useful practice in incorporating 'musical support' into the stage design. But wherever the orchestra was placed, there was never need for a larger group to balance a total of twelve or even eighteen voices.

WHAT DID WE DO ABOUT DIRECTORS?

It may have been noticed already that the employment of directors has been mentioned only briefly in this account, although clearly there were many productions to be directed, and thus many requirements for direction. It is important to share the policy that we evolved with regard to guest directors, and to directing in general.

My firm conviction was that we wished to steer clear of directors who desired to exhibit their directorial skills using the ensemble as their vehicle. It must be remembered that one of the principles on which this vision of singing theatre has been constructed is that of shared creative responsibility. The theatre and opera of the twentieth century, while developing opportunities for scores of directors with extraordinary gifts, has allowed many of them to exhibit these gifts through the exercise of almost unlimited personal power in the artistic process, and often in much else besides. This in turn depends on being fed a regular supply of performers and other artists (as well as administrators) who will be in awe of this power, and even positively enjoy submitting to it.

In a training programme there was yet another consideration. If we wished our participants – composers and writers, designers and performers – to take responsibility for their own work, then we wished to avoid at all costs submitting them to a director who would use them as pawns in his/her personal chessgame. What was the alternative? Amateur directors who did not know their business? No, this would be as bad, and was one reason why we did not institute a regular category of participant directors in the ensemble – too little to offer for most of the year, and then too great a chance to do harm when their opportunity to direct finally came.

So did we employ directors at all? Of course we did – directors with authority too, and driving imagination: Jean Gascon, Michael Langham, Richard Jones, Jeremy James Taylor, Colin Graham, Billie Bridgman, Charles Hamilton, Campbell Smith, and others. We also invited some of our teachers to direct, enlarging on the trust that they had built up between themselves and the performers and so able to carry the principles of their teaching through into performance. Our movement director, David McMurray Smith, created that splendid *Pierrot Lunaire*, and Colin Bernhardt the highly imaginative *La Voix Humaine*; and as resident director I was of course responsible for many productions myself. But no director was ever chosen – or ever chosen twice – who was not able to understand his/her role while with the ensemble, as a bringer-on of the talents of the participants, and encourager of their own mature decision-making.

WHAT DID WE DO ABOUT AUDIENCE AT BANFF?

Calgary, Banff's nearest international airport, is one hour by air from Vancouver, four-and-a-half hours from Toronto and New York, and seven-and-a-half hours from London. These distances do not encourage regular cosmopolitan attendance at Banff events, and used to lead city friends, for whom everything outside their city is off the brink of the world, to ask what on earth we did for an audience. There would certainly be little point in long production runs, but the image of us performing to a discerning public of bears and elk was somewhat off the mark. The Bow River valley in which Banff sits contains other communities, and the total population of what is known as the 'Bow Valley Corridor' amounts to about ten thousand. This is augmented by a transient population of nearly twenty-five thousand each day during the summer tourist season, and with the area's rising status as a ski centre the period from December to April is also increasingly busy. Calgary, a city of more than six hundred thousand souls, is just over an hour's drive away and well within striking distance for potential audience, although winter road conditions in the mountains do not always encourage travel.

Within the Banff Centre itself there was a staff of three hundred and fifty, and the Winter Cycle participant and resource artist population averaged perhaps one hundred and sixty.

From this catchment area, even without heavy promotion, it was not difficult to find a healthy-sized audience for four performances of a production in our 250-seat theatre. Heavy promotion was something which in any case we did not wish to embark on, because it is almost impossible to do it without making extravagant claims; these would have been out of place for works that were seeing the light for the first time, and that also were serving as training vehicles for a group of performers. Entrance at our workshops and studio productions was free, and seats for our full productions were very modestly priced; the box office revenue, as at most schools, was not considered a vital part of our budget. What was important was that our participants had the experience of playing to an audience – without which theatre does not exist.

One of the oddities about the Banff Centre, then and now, is the divide between its goals and those of the community in which it sits. Having divested itself of its original role as a kind of arts university for the province of Alberta, and become an international school with international status and pretentions, it has to strive to keep in contact with and be a part of the contemporary urban art scene; but at the same time feels an obligation to express at least some interest in the people of Alberta – whose tax dollars sustain it but whose cultural predilections are a good deal less 'contemporary'. This double act is never so clear as when Judy Chicago pays a visit, or sexually explicit paintings are exhibited in the reception lounge. Those who spend their lives like green peas poised nervously on the knife of fashion will tend to wince when the down-home roots and usually amiable red-neckery of Western Canadian culture begin to assert themselves. 'Come, let us dive into the world of digital computer art, video art, post-serialism, post-modernism, affective post-photochronicism, post-...' – 'Well, the wife and me, we like square-dancing usselves...'

What set the Music Theatre programme apart from one or two colleagues in other disciplines at Banff were two policies. First, we applied no dogmatic rules about musical or verbal or decorative style – participants and commissioned creators were free to create in any way they pleased. Composers offered up all kinds of music from post-Webern complexities to Glassy minimalism, from late-Stravinsky to post-Weill, from sub-Sondheim to super-Lloyd Webber. There was no recognisable 'sound' to the work we produced, and no pecking order of acceptability, provided that an attempt was being made to write for a theatre rather than the concert-hall. We were happy to stage anyone's experiment in any style if we could justify the time spent on it by our students – and if it gave them something to get their teeth into. Secondly, we were theatre people enough, and dare I say socially aware enough, to care about the society we lived in and to want to bring it pleasure and interest through our work. I have already described our touring through the province and beyond, but we were also keen to look for new ways of communicating with our immediate neighbours, down the hill from the centre's eyrie.

One project is worth describing as an instance of our effort to engage the local community. In 1982 we commissioned a text from Jeremy James Taylor about 'Bankhead', Alberta, a coal-mining town a few miles from Banff established by the Canadian Pacific to feed its railway engines at the turn of the century. At its peak the town boasted a population of several hundred, a church, a school, a football team and a brass band; but when the mines were closed after the First World War the town was abandoned. Some of its houses were moved to Banff or another mining town nearby. The rest rotted, and now, in its mountain valley, nothing beside the odd foundation remains to provoke the imagination. Taylor was gripped by the story and proposed a script that would make use not only of our twelve first-year performers but also of a group of local children, and perhaps even one or two of the old-timers who had been born in the defunct town. We saw this as an opportunity to build a link with the community, and fastened on it eagerly. And for the music? We invited a second-year participant, Stephen Gibson, a graduate of the University of Birmingham, to create the score. There were no prescriptions as to style; but I remember suggesting that as many composers living at the time of Bankhead's prosperity had made use of folk-songs as the basis for 'serious' music, so one starting-point might be the folk tunes familiar to the Irish, Scots, Italians and Ukrainians resident in the town. We were imagining, I suppose, something between a musical and a folk-opera – in fact a piece of Music Theatre. I have already made note of its title: *Ghost Town*.

Taylor directed the piece with warmth and energy, handling the work of the children with a skill to be expected from the founder of the London-based Children's Music Theatre (see p. 202). Gibson produced an impeccable score, sturdily 'tonical' and in no way aiming for fashionable modernism, but showing craft, lyricism and drive.

The local interest generated by this work far exceeded our expectations, and its four performances were packed. For a moment the school on its lofty hill above the town meant something to its community.

It was during the buoyant first night reception that one of our colleagues came frowning to McNeff and myself and asked: 'Hey man, why are you doing this crap?'

Was the clash between these two attitudes to creative work a war between clever people and stupid people? Between the courageous and the timid? Between the sentimental and the hard-nosed? Between low and high art? Between humour and seriousness? Between the bourgeois and the radical? Between the avant- and the arrière-garde? Between Apollo and Dionysus? Between the city and the country? Between fashion and datedness? Between anal repression and the free-ranging libido? The answer – if there is a right one – would make many things clear about the practice and goals of art in the twentieth century.

WHERE DO THE STUDENTS GO AFTER TRAINING?

It is never possible, as every Mr Chips knows, to keep up with all the departing students of a school. The Music Theatre Studio Ensemble (MUTSE – pronounced MUTSY – as it was known among us) did manage to create a sense of family. From letters and calls and chance meetings or planned reunions, the news has kept coming in of the 200 or so ex-participants, but like all family news is of strictly family interest. It is enough to say that several have gone on to play leading roles at Stratford, Ontario, and at the Shaw Festival; others to the Vancouver Opera, to the Canadian Opera Company, to Chicago Lyric Opera, to the Welsh National Opera, to Scottish Opera, to St Donat's Music Theatre, to Broadway and to the West End. One sang the role of the Celebrant in Bernstein's *Mass* at the Barbican, and on Bernstein's recommendation repeated it for Sarah Caldwell in Boston. One has sung for Berio all over Europe. One is a Canadian film star. One has written a play and also an opera (text and music) for the Edmonton Fringe Festival and a libretto for the Canadian Opera Company Resident Composer programme, and more than one have performed in the Canadian production of *Phantom of the Opera*. One, whose two 'Minifest' productions went on to win prizes at the US National Opera Association, has been a resident composer at an English public school; another has founded a computerised music-printing company to subsidise his composition. One is a resident playwright for a Toronto theatre, and wrote a libretto for one of COMUS Music Theatre's last productions. One has been through clown school in Florida. One founded an opera company in Ottawa. One offers Music Theatre courses in Devon.

It is an immensely varied picture, as one might expect. But many of them still report that they are not entirely satisfied with what they are doing, and that they are waiting to find, or to found, a genuine Music Theatre company. They seem to know what that is...

POST SCRIPT: the End of the Ensemble

One of the ironies surrounding the Music Theatre Studio Ensemble programme at Banff was that while it was treading out new ground for singing theatre training, and offering a unique opportunity for the creation of new works, it was considered by the opera world to be foolishly radical, and at the same time – as we have seen – viewed by Banff's techno-artists as esthetically conservative. These two opposing forces made a handy pair of nutcrackers, and it was not long after a change in the Centre's leadership in 1983 that we realised how the trust originally placed in what we were trying to do had now to be earned all over again. A review of the programme was called for, and only a late intervention by a still sympathetic director of the School of Fine Arts allowed us to organise the review internally. It was clear to him and to us that the opinions reached by an 'independent' survey would depend entirely on who would be posing as independent. If they were singing theatre experts they would be either sympathetic to the aims of the programme, or not; and we knew precisely who would be of each persuasion. What we were at least shielded from was that familiar corporate technique, an 'objective' review carefully manipulated to give the leadership the justification to do what they may have wanted to do all along.

Through the review year of 1984-5 an exhaustive report on our activities was compiled by a heroic Music Theatre scholar and writer-director named Kerry White, who was with us for most of that tense and important period. National and international visitors of distinction were invited – or their visits to Banff taken advantage of – to spend a day, or two days, or a week with us, and then to write reports. All turned out to be approving, and most of them dazzling in their approval. Former participants and resource artists were sent questionnaires, and their sketchy but supportive responses tabulated. We wrote a long report of our own, listing – Chinese style – sins of omission and commission, and proposing changes for the future. The whole massive review report was finally put on file, and members of the Banff staff invited to read and comment on it. In December, 1985, the review was presented to the Meeting of Heads and Managers of the School of Fine Arts. Few had read it, and fewer still felt competent to comment. Although one unhappy colleague was there with suggestions that the review had been a 'whitewash', the report was accepted.

The review was over. But the stress of that time, piled upon the already strenuous work we had set ourselves, had begun to sap the pioneering energies and idealism that had sustained us. For one reason or another, the Centre still seemed anxious to break up what seemed to some to be a closed circle, a too independent satrap. The ensemble was so closely dovetailed, so interlocking in its activities, that its members were not available for work with tthe Inter Arts activities which were under the control of another department. It was resented that we had our own composers – why did they not reside in the music department? And why were the designers not under the control of the theatre manager? The ensemble seemed to its critics to be altogether too individual in its character and direction. It needed, perhaps, to take the collaborative needs of Music Theatre less seriously.

It was hard not to be aware, too, that the Centre itself was beginning to enter a new phase, undergoing the strain of so many institutions whose life is dependent on promotion. The need for an effective 'image' appeared more and more to drive its activities. In pursuit of the acceptance that was necessary for the attraction of government and corporate sponsorship, the 'no small dreams' grandeur of the Banff School of Fine Arts vision seemed to have lost its force, and corporate systems and procedures bit more and more deeply into our daily lives. Arts programme managers, having their capacity to render 'customer service' put to the test, were asked to study the daily activities of a hamburger stand and then to apply its lessons to their own work. A building, which struck many as being of amazing vulgarity, was thrown up and dedicated to trendy Media Arts. An attempt was made, happily withdrawn under pressure, to place precise numerical values on each element of a faculty member's work in order to arrive at the correct salary to be paid. The corporate metaphor, which had irritated but impressed me when applied to the 'marketing' of education, seemed to many artists who loved Banff to be slowly seeping through the philosophical foundations of the place, and the marked lack of participatory governance suggested that these changes could not be long resisted.

It would be unfair to suggest that Banff in the late 1980s was alone in falling prey to the power of marketing attitudes and strategy. Throughout the cultural scene, more and more often referred to as the cultural 'industry', the job of attracting funds and a public to that intractable thing called 'art' has inexorably moved from its original service function to take a commanding role in the selection of art to be sold, and in its critiquing – indeed, even in its very making. Thus opera companies and symphony orchestras create 'bankable' descriptions and interpretations of the 'Masterworks', simplifying and distorting the musical and dramatic material to give it an image accessible to all: 'no hard work necessary, just sit and receive'. Irrelevant devices (gala openings, guess-the-star's weight, a week in Hawaii for the correctly numbered ticket, etc.) are deployed to attract attention and boost sales. And yet the resulting full houses, the incontestable sign of successful marketing (but not of genuine audience participation) are increasingly being interpreted as a sign of the 'product's' innate artistic value. The truthfulness of art, which is art's eternal and shining quality, is sold by lies and half-lies; and so powerful are these in shaping daily events that artists themselves lose touch with truth.

With galloping consumerism rampant in Big City versions of art, Banff would have had to have held exceptionally strong alternative convictions of its own if it was not to fall in line. After all, it had always been felt that Banff's isolation in the mountains could only be overcome by persuading the Big City to recognise the school's value. If what the Big City now valued was a sleekly huckstering version of art, then Banff must change its ways in order to conform. 'Exceptionally strong alternative convictions' were not in evidence.

The devaluation of truth always compromises education, and it was not surprising that at Banff in the late eighties even the very idea of 'training' seemed to be becoming a burden too ignoble to carry. This was now to be a place for mature artists to work. We would pay them to be here (they would not come otherwise). We would remove the word 'School' from our name. And we would support all this with more conferences and management courses, as well as with our grant from the Alberta government. We would be simply a 'centre': that splendid Newspeak word which draws everything to a vanishing point. It remained to be seen whether the Centre could hold, and how long Alberta's Minister of Advanced Education would accept this bizzare use of his educational funds.

So bleak a view of recent events at this remarkable institution will easily look like personal animus. But I was only one among many who believed there were things at Banff to be held on to at whatever cost: a largeness of spirit, and – yes, a moral vision. Both seemed to be floundering, and the disappearance of such things in any society is too important to be politely and 'loyally' ignored.

The Welsh composer John Metcalf, who had been my associate director for one term, took over the Banff programme on my resignation in January 1987. Within months the name of the ensemble had been dropped and its structure broken into separate elements; it was now simply the Music Theatre programme. As such it continues still, undergoing in 1990 a further change of leadership. Performers were now trained separately from their Music Theatre co-artists; there was no more intricate dovetailing of artistic needs and resources, nor risky performances of work written under pressure. Two productions of Brecht and Weill toured regions of Canada under the name of the Canadian Music Theatre Ensemble, but the ensemble for these was for the most part a cast of paid performers, many of them brought in from Toronto. A three-person Music Theatre piece newly commissioned from Quenten Doolittle and writer Rex Deverell – and billed as an opera – began its performance life at Banff in September 1989, continuing with a small tour of Great Britain. And early in 1990 a workshop preview took place of Metcalf's new piece for the Welsh National Opera *Tornrak* – later to be performed by WNO with a different cast. In 1990 the programme, under mounting economic pressure, was shortened from seven months to three. It underwent a further change of leadership, and began now to offer a group of separate specialised courses, while also inviting composer/librettist teams to submit 'first draft' projects for revision, polishing and production. 'Music Theatre' continues to be the name and the goal, and let us hope that valuable contributions continue to be made.

In September 1989, Banff's long and always uneasy alliance between artistic vision and corporate goals finally fractured; the Banff Centre for Continuing Education was formally trinitised. Its School of Fine Arts was renamed 'The Banff Centre for the Arts': its Conference Division was now the 'Centre for Conferences'. And where its broad amphitheatre of green grass used to look down to the Bow Valley, with the river and railway winding through the wetlands of Vermilion Lake, and the peaks of the Bourgeau Range beyond – the view that for forty years has made every student's and teacher's heart miss a beat when they first come upon it – a new 'pavilion' was to be erected the moment that funds were available, in order to house courses run by 'The Banff Centre for Management'.

It was sad that the integrated ensemble had come to an end. But there was much to rejoice at. We had shown to ourselves and to many others that an ensemble training programme was possible and effective; that it stimulated new work and provided new and important goals for the singing theatre not only in Canada but also in the United States and Europe. The same year that we were reviewed we were showing a film of our work to the Music Theatre Committee of the International Theatre Institute, and it was described as the 'jewel' of the meeting. I was invited the following year to talk about our work in the USA, Finland, Sweden, Britain and the USSR. From the Banff experience we had been able to draw many new perceptions, and above all a profile for a new kind of singing theatre artist.

Banff's early generosity and vision in making the Music Theatre Studio Ensemble possible will not be forgotten. It was now time for the idea to move out into the world.

Chapter Nine

PORTRAIT OF A SINGING THEATRE ARTIST

Among many discoveries made in the training programme at Banff, one was of especial value – the opportunity we had, through the creation of a complete Music Theatre 'world', to develop a portrait, an imaginary profile, of the complete singing theatre artist.

All good teachers reckon they know more or less, most of the time (or at least on a good day) what they are doing. And any teacher hired by an educational institution will bring to his/her work the methods that have been tried and proven in other places, with other students. We learn to rely on a particular workshop structure, or a special way of handling a new student, or even a kind of trickery with which to initiate the new teaching-learning relationship. And anyone who is putting together a group of teachers will naturally be looking for people who have confidence in their own teaching skills, and a record of 'success' – however that may be defined.

In finding teachers for the Banff Ensemble we were on the same quest as anyone else running an educational programme. We needed experience and knowledge, and references from colleagues who had a sense of our needs and a judgement which we could trust; and we needed teachers who had professional experience as artists. At the same time we were aware that most teachers, even if they are teaching in a school alongside others, are working on their own, independently of their colleagues; and that while this freedom was to be respected at Banff, the fact that everyone was working with the same group of participants in several closely overlapping fields meant that we should be clear what each of us was doing, and careful that we were not working at cross-purposes with one another.

We therefore developed the habit of asking our resource artists to come with all their experience and ideas, but also with an open mind and a preparedness to listen and to change. We were not at all keen for them to do for us exactly what they had done elsewhere; in fact people who spoke with breezy confidence about 'doing their thing' we immediately suspected of being too heavily armoured in their relationships with students, using a mechanical method which made it unnecessary to have to 'feel at each thread, and live along the line'. Many teachers after all do work in comparative isolation, and become accustomed to having to serve as a one-man band. It is satisfying, and a solace to the ego, to be the one lifeline for a student, but at Banff this was not necessary.

From the very beginning we encouraged interchange of ideas among the teachers. Classes were always open on principle, but at the start of each term we brought the faculty together two or three days ahead of the participants, not only to organise the teaching schedule and outline the plans for the coming term, but also as an opportunity for teachers to present their thoughts about the goals of our work, and their points of view and approach. Classes would also be arranged in this introductory period in which teachers would give each other lessons (a practice that often continued throughout the term). Then, in the first days of the term, all the resource artists would be asked to give a talk to the whole ensemble about where they came from, what they had done and what they were planning to do while with us. If they wished they could present themselves and their ideas within the context of a master class or group class. Once the regular schedule went into operation the faculty would get together every so often to discuss the individual participants, and to share any information that might be important or useful in working with them. But in the classroom itself teachers would be left on their own.

After a couple of years it occurred to me that while we were developing admirable friendliness and co-operation between faculty members, and were working within a set of general Music Theatre goals to which we all subscribed, we might still have very different ideas about what we were doing with individual participants. This was particularly so with the performers, who were having regular classes with four different performance teachers, as well as with coach-accompanists. What was the movement teacher trying to make out of these students of his? Was it his goal to turn them into ballet dancers, or jazz dancers – or something else? Was the acting teacher, who sometimes had not taught singers before, preparing them for a career in legitimate theatre? Where did speech fit in? Was the singing teacher doing anything fundamentally different from what would be done in any private singing lesson in any context?

As a result of asking these questions, which led to much further intense discussion, we decided to attempt an imaginary picture of 'The Complete Singer-Actor'. What skills, knowledge and abilities would such a creature be able to bring to the new singing theatre? Faculty members dealing directly with performers were asked to make a down-to-earth inventory of these qualities, each concentrating on his/her own area of expertise. The musical staff were also asked to make their contribution. 'Describe the student whom you have nothing left to teach.'

One of the first discoveries was that all four performance teachers that year started out with the same list of fundamental qualities, which in each case formed a basis on which to build the various specialist skills. Relaxation, breathing, sense of rhythm, and posture, for example, were all considered as the foundation of all other qualities. It became more and more important then to ensure that in these areas, at least, there was a common approach.

From the results of this exercise we were able to put together a document to use as a collaborative goal for our training. It was not a method. It was quite simply an inventory of the knowledge and skills that we would expect of an accomplished singer-actor in the new singing theatre. At the beginning of each subsequent year the document would be brought out and reviewed by the teaching staff, some of whom would be new; they would be invited to propose revisions in their own area of expertise, and these would be incorporated into a new edition. So it remained a living and responsive guide, with no mandatory force but providing a direction for all of us. It helped us all understand how the areas of our professional expertise fitted into the whole.

It has to be said that this same document served a remarkable function in stimulating the thoughts of teachers as they arrived for the first time to work with the ensemble. A highly distinguished singing teacher with a lifetime of experience behind her announced after a short time with us that she had 'learned more in the last three weeks than in the previous twenty-five years'. Our inventory helped to expose the fact that she had been teaching in a vacuum.

Having developed this comprehensive guide to our work with performers we set about gathering ideas for a parallel document for the composers and writers of the singing theatre. This was considerably more difficult, and perhaps more presumptuous; and it is only now, with the help of former resource artists, that the material has been assembled into coherent form, to serve perhaps as provocation rather than exemplum.

In the area of stage design we did not feel it necessary to establish a similar inventory. The skills that a designer needs for the singing theatre are obvious extensions of normal design practice: the ability to read a score, to have a developed sense of the relationship between colour, light and sound, to have a working knowledge of acoustic theory, to respond to musical as well as textual clues with reference to atmosphere, characterisation and structure, and to understand and have solutions to the basic problems of configuration (audience, stage, musical support) for the 'primary act' of singing theatre.

The inventory that follows, then, represents the results of six years of experiment in Music Theatre. It makes no claim to be all-inclusive, or even 'correct'. It simply offers a picture that might be of use not only to teachers but to all singing theatre artists. Evidently, the competencies of very few will come up to all these expectations – some very distinguished artists in the past have been noticeably lacking in some of the skills listed. It is after all just an inventory; it makes no attempt to contain or 'box' an artist, let alone to prescribe the passion and the individual vision without which all this knowledge and skill will be so much lost baggage. At the same time, the total document is dedicated to the idea that if the singing theatre is a profession, then we must not continue to produce performers, composers and writers who are professional in some of the necessary areas of expertise, but downright amateurs in the rest.

AN INVENTORY OF KNOWLEDGE AND SKILLS REQUIRED OF SINGER-ACTORS, COMPOSERS AND WRITERS

THE SINGER-ACTOR

I SKILLS COMMON TO ALL PERFORMANCE AREAS

a) RELAXATION: The ability to be in a state of dynamic, concentrated readiness in which the performer is prepared – physically, mentally, emotionally – to act upon and within any given situation with proper economy of effort to achieve a desired result.

b) BREATHING: The physical freedom and ability to breathe from the diaphragm as required, without tension. Effective control of breath: neither too much nor too little.

c) SENSORY AWARENESS: The knowledge of, and sensitivity to, the correct alignment of the body and its weight distribution through the body to the feet. Posture not to be fixed and rigid.

d) RHYTHM: The mental and physical awareness of and sensitivity to internal and external rhythms, their sources and relationships, as well as an ability to create, maintain, and react to the interplay of rhythms, to particular rhythms and to rhythm states.

e) FLEXIBILITY: The ability to respond with alertness and suppleness – physically, vocally and psychologically.

f) ADAPTABILITY: The ability to adapt to the demands of a variety of creative work, within the limits of individual capabilities.

II SKILLS WITHIN SPECIFIC PERFORMANCE AREAS

1 SINGING VOICE

a) TONAL CONSCIOUSNESS: The ability to colour the voice according to musical and poetic demands.

b) AGILITY: The ability to meet the demands of all kinds of music, including twentieth-century music – to pitch clearly and to sustain pitch.

c) DICTION: The ability to form clear vowel sounds and consonants while singing.

d) APPRECIATION OF WORDS: The ability to appreciate the colour and weight of words, and how these may be reflected in or influenced by music.

e) IMPROVISATION: The ability to improvise sounds.

f) INTEGRATION OF SKILLS: The ability to integrate technical, musical, vocal and histrionic skills into a performance that expresses the intrinsic intention and values of the composition.

g) CLASSICAL VOICE TECHNIQUE: A sure grasp of classical voice technique, and ability to extend that technique to cope with today's demands.

2 SPEAKING VOICE

a) ARTICULATION: An ability to articulate clearly, with correct placing of sound, and with no speech impediments.

b) MODULATION: A wide range in both pitch and dynamics, with awareness of tonal colour, enabling the expression of a wide variety of meanings, emotions and emotional nuances.

c) RESONANCE: Awareness of the principal voice resonators, and the ability to employ them, as appropriate, in the production of sound.

d) CHARACTERISATION: The ability to manifest character through the voice.

e) VOCAL AWARENESS: A thorough awareness of one's own voice, and the ability to control it; an awareness of its strengths and weaknesses, and an ability to work on maintaining its condition, and to correct its areas of weakness if any.

f) CENTRED VOCAL EXPRESSION: The ability to connect vocal expression with inner feeling.

g) INTEGRATION OF SKILLS: The ability to translate a text into a carefully thought out and emotionally expressive performance, making use of all the skills developed in articulation, modulation, resonance, vocal awareness and centred vocal expression.

3 MOVEMENT

a) UNDERSTANDING: A knowledge of and sensitivity to the physical nature and biomechanical functioning of the human body, sufficient to ensure ability and confidence in the use of it.

b) PRECISION: The ability to be both technically precise and spontaneously free.

c) CONCENTRATION AND STAMINA: The ability to focus clearly, and act upon, intentions or objectives both mentally and physically for any desired length of time.

d) AWARENESS: A developed awareness of time, dynamics, space and motivation, and their inter-relationship in movement and in theatre generally.

e) PHRASING AND GESTURE: An overall ability in and sensitivity to the phrasing of movement and gesture as appropriate to the particular dramatic situation.

f) CORPORAL EXPRESSION: Familiarity with the different vocabularies and techniques of corporal expression, and their value and use for the singer-actor in helping him/her to perform physical actions that are truthful in relation to the desired intention.

g) CHARACTERISATION: The ability to manifest a character physically.

h) DANCE: Familiarity with the basics of classical ballet vocabulary, and some experience of contemporary, jazz, social and folk forms.

i) TUMBLING AND STAGE COMBAT: Familiarity with the technique of tumbling and other gymnastics, and some acquaintance with the techniques of stage combat, both armed and unarmed.

4 ACTING

a) BELIEF AND BELIEVABILITY: An ability to behave on stage as if the 'given circumstances' are real.

b) EMOTIONAL RANGE: Access to a wide range of emotional states, and the willingness to express them.

c) TEXTWORK: The ability to read and analyse a text, both in song and speech, and to use it as the 'given circumstance' for a class exercise or a theatrical performance.

d) CREATIVE CONFIDENCE: The ability to make theatre out of any material and any situation.

e) ENSEMBLE: The awareness of 'the other' and an ability to meet the demands of ensemble playing.

f) STYLES: Familiarity with the whole spectrum of expressive styles, and the ability to develop an appropriate style for each character and each work, using stylistic elements (e.g. singing, period clothes, verse) as the 'given circumstances'.

g) IMPROVISATION: The ability to improvise character and situation within guidelines, both with and without an audience, and in both solo and ensemble situations.

h) MOVEMENT: The ability to move with grace and economy, in the clothes and activities of any period or culture.

i) CHARACTER: The ability to use the 'given circumstances' provided by text, music, production and audience to build characters who move, speak and sing.

j) MASK: The ability to play different types of mask, and to understand masks as tools in the development of character.

k) VERSE: The ability to speak verse; a familiarity with Shakespearean and other dramatic verse.

5 MUSICIANSHIP

a) ACCURACY: An ability to sing with correct pitch and rhythms, and to project words clearly and with correct or appropriate pronunciation.

b) SIGHT-READING: An ability to read rhythms and intervals; to find pitches in relation to the accompaniment fluently enough to read most music at sight. The ability to imagine accurately the sound, tempo and general feel of a piece, by looking at the score alone. An ability to adapt to non-traditional notation.

c) STYLE: A knowledge of the musical and technical features which are traditionally associated with any style of music which the performer is likely to perform, and the good judgement to know when these traditions are to be followed and when they can be modified.

d) REPERTOIRE: An awareness of which types of roles and which styles of music are appropriate for the vocal quality and the stage of development of the performer.

e) PERFORMANCE: The willingness and the freedom to 'bring to life' any piece of music. The ability to respond appropriately, not only to events on stage, but also to those heard in the accompaniment and to the overall musical/dramatic design.

f) INSTRUMENTAL SKILL: The ability to play one or more musical instruments is always a valuable addition to the skills of the singer-actor.

III RESPONSIBILITIES

1 CREATIVE RESPONSIBILITIES

a) An ability and preparedness to see the needs and scope of the whole production, not only the performer's individual role within it.

b) An ability to work with composer, writer and director as colleagues, offering creative ideas, and working to realise the creators' intentions in all situations however difficult.

c) A clear understanding of the need for each performer to do his/her 'homework', and to bring the results of this work to rehearsal and performance.

d) An understanding of, and enthusiasm for, the process of creating new work.

e) A familiarity with the creative collaboration required between designer and performer; an awareness of the contribution to performance made by costume, set, lighting, props and stage make-up; and an understanding of the responsibility of the performer to become familiar with and practised in the use of same.

f) An awareness that good ensemble work is born out of the generosity, openness and courage of each performer, and his/her ability to work closely with fellow performers; an awareness that all good theatre is ensemble work.

g) A passion for accuracy (without pedantry) in the learning and performance of text and music.

h) An understanding of the particular performance demands of film, radio, recording and television, and familiarity with working with microphones and in front of cameras.

2 PROFESSIONAL RESPONSIBILITIES

a) Punctuality, courtesy to fellow artists, and the ability to maintain a positive attitude and sense of humour under stress.

b) An awareness of the obligations of each performer and what is expected of him/her.

c) An awareness of the various roles of coach, choreographer, conductor, performer, designer and director in the rehearsal process of all kinds of Music Theatre.

d) The maintenance of independent study and training in all performance areas, to ensure that the performer is in optimum condition for every rehearsal and performance.

e) An awareness of the appropriate attire, including clothing, for every kind of rehearsal.

f) An awareness and concern for the safety of all performers, at all times, both in rehearsal and performance.

IV BACKGROUND KNOWLEDGE

a) Awareness of the vocal music of the twentieth century.

b) Awareness of the principal movements and directions of twentieth-century theatre.

c) Knowledge of the history of art from earliest times to today.

d) Familiarity with some of the masterpieces of literature, drama, music, singing theatre, and art.

e) A working knowledge of the traditional categories and esthetic theories of theatre, music, and singing theatre.

f) An interest in the relationship between art, society and politics.

V TOTAL PERFORMANCE

THE ABILITY TO INTEGRATE ALL THESE SKILLS AND AWARENESS AND KNOWLEDGE INTO A PERFORMANCE WHICH COMBINES TECHNICAL VIRTUOSITY WITH 'BELIEVABILITY' – AND DISPLAYING THAT UNPREDICTABLE DANGER WHICH CHARACTERISES THE OUTSTANDING CREATIVE PERFORMER.

AN AWARENESS THAT THE SINGER-ACTOR, LIKE ALL CREATIVE ARTISTS, IS NEVER IN FACT 'COMPLETE', BUT MUST CONTINUE THROUGHOUT HIS/HER CREATIVE LIFE TO DEVELOP KNOWLEDGE AND SKILLS THROUGH STUDY, READING, OBSERVATION AND REFLECTION AS WELL AS THROUGH PRACTICAL EXPERIENCE.

APPENDIX: TOOLS OF THE TRADE

1 A selection of audition pieces appropriate to the individual performer and suitable for different situations, including both musical and dramatic pieces.

2 Well-prepared musical scores, clearly written and in the correct key, to take to auditions.

3 An accurate and well set out résumé and a recent 8 x 10 photograph.

4 A well-recorded performance sound-tape.

5 A carefully thought-out career plan.

6 A clear understanding of the audition process.

THE COMPOSER-WRITER COLLABORATION

We here assume as I have elsewhere in this book that a composer and writer are creating a work in collaboration. Clearly this is not always the case: Wagner is the most obvious example of someone who successfully wrote both words and music for singing theatre. But his ability to do this meant simply that he had the skills listed here for both writer and composer, and did not need – which was just as well – to develop collaborative skills with a writer.

I SHARED KNOWLEDGE AND SKILLS

SINGING THEATRE/WORDS AND MUSIC

1 A familiarity with the history of the singing theatre, and of all writing for the voice.

2 Familiarity with many settings of his/her native language to music, in song, chorus and singing theatre, in all periods and styles; together with an understanding of the particular difficulties posed by the language, and an ability to surmount these difficulties.

3 A detailed familiarity with both the text and the music of many works of singing theatre, historical and contemporary, operatic and otherwise.

4 The ability to analyse the dramaturgy and musical structure of any work.

5 The ability to read a piece of writing (poem, short story, novel, drama) and be able to imagine it as a piece of singing theatre.

THEATRICAL KNOWLEDGE

1 A knowledge of the principal masterpieces of dramatic literature, including the work of Shakespeare and contemporaries, Molière, Ibsen, Chekhov, and contemporary playwrights.

2 A knowledge of the history of the theatre, with its principal developments, its different types of theatrical space and its changing social functions.

3 An understanding of the historical principles of form as discussed in Aristotle's *Poetics*, and an ability to make use of this knowledge as appropriate.

4 A familiarity with the basic language and work habits of the stage, with the protocol and ethics of the theatre, and with the roles played by each member of the collaborative team.

5 A knowledge of stage design, set and costumes, and the part they play in the creation of a stage work.

6 An extensive knowledge and understanding of stage lighting, and its potential as an element of the finished work of singing theatre.

7 A habit of theatre-going, and a lively interest in the stage and all its works.

8. An understanding of and ease with the psychology of performance, of performers' methods of work and needs.

COLLABORATIVE SKILLS

1 An ability to collaborate: in other words a capacity to share the responsibility with other artists for the final result of a collaboration, and not to mistake egotism for divine right.

2 A genuine interest and pleasure in sharing with an equally collaborative writer the responsibility for the development of a work; the ability to collaborate without either taking control or surrendering control.

3 A preparedness to listen to the opinions of all other collaborators, and to make changes to a score if convinced of the necessity; a preparedness to be convinced of the necessity.

4 A capacity for vision, but also for convincing colleagues of the worth and substance of the vision, so that it animates the collaborative work.

II SPECIALIST KNOWLEDGE AND SKILLS: THE COMPOSER

MUSICAL KNOWLEDGE AND SKILLS

1 A sound grasp of harmony and counterpoint.

2 A familiarity with musical styles of all periods, including popular music.

3 An understanding of the principles of 'atonical' music (Peter Schat's term), including twelve-tone and serial music.

4 Familiarity with the demands of vocal writing, for all combinations of voices from solo to full chorus.

5 An ability to write for a particular voice, and/or in a way which reflects the specifics of character.

6 Ability to orchestrate for every size of instrumental and vocal group: implying a knowledge of the ranges, colours, timbres and dynamics of all instruments and of the voice, and a competence and imagination in their use.

7 A basic feeling for drama, and an ability to create dramatic effect through music.

8 An understanding of and feeling for musico-dramatic structure.

9 An imaginative and inventive ability in the setting of words to music in unconventional ways.

10 A familiarity with the masterpieces of Western music in all genres.

11 Some acquaintance with musics of other cultures.

12 Familiarity with esthetics and philosophy, and a knowledge of some of the major modern statements in these fields, especially in the area of music.

13 An ability to play one or more musical instruments, including the piano.

14 An ability to conduct.

15 A curiosity to explore new musical solutions.

16 An inherent desire to create.

KNOWLEDGE OF LITERARY AND VISUAL ARTS

1 An interest in and feeling for words and language, and a respect for their meaning, tone and style.

2 A knowledge of and feeling for poetry and literature of all kinds.

3 A familiarity with some of the great works of world literature.

4 A knowledge of the cultural and social history of art, with particular reference to the twentieth century.

5 An acquaintance with the work of painters and sculptors throughout history, and particularly in recent times.

PROFESSIONAL CRAFT

1 The ability to write musical manuscript in a clear and understandable manner, regardless of the method of notation; and a knowledge of the correct musical format for each situation.

2 Familiarity with the professional requirements and work habits of all professional situations, including the theatre, film, television, publishing, and the recording studio.

3 An ability to work fluently and under pressure.

4 The ability to make musical arrangements of works for all sizes of musical group.

III SPECIALIST KNOWLEDGE AND SKILLS: THE WRITER

If it is hard to attempt an inventory for the singing theatre composer, the task of listing all the skills and knowledge valuable for the singing theatre text-writer is almost impossible. The capacity to express ideas in words is after all one of the distinguishing marks of the human being, and we all know one way or another what it means to do this well or badly. We have therefore avoided all attempts to describe the basic skills a writer needs to be able to write (a capacity for clear thought, imagination, knowledge of grammar and syntax, vocabulary, etc.) and listed simply what he/she will find useful or necessary when applying these basic skills to the writing of text for the singing theatre.

WRITING SKILLS AND APTITUDES

1 An ear for verbal rhythm, colour and vowel-consonant progressions: the ability to 'hear' the words not only for their meaning but for their meaning in relationship to the sounds they make.

2 A capacity to write in a variety of poetic rhythms and metres, and to make inventive and sensitive use of rhyme when appropriate.

3 An extreme sensitivity to differences of style and tone in language, and the capacity to establish appropriate style and tone in the writing of text for singing theatre: a feeling for 'appropriateness'.

4 An ability to imagine words sung, and a sensitivity to the tension between words and music in union.

5 An ability to portray the personality and individuality of a character through what they say and do.

6 An understanding of musico-dramatic structure, and a preparedness to allow dramatic structure to be established by music; an ability to 'make room for the music'.

7 The ability to read a piece of writing (poem, short story, novel, drama) and be able to assess its possibilities as a work of singing theatre.

8 The ability to adapt a work for singing theatre.

9 Ideas and visions which he/she has a compelling need to express, and an inventive approach to the potential of singing theatre as a vehicle for expressing them.

MUSICAL KNOWLEDGE

1 An interest in and feeling for music, and knowledge of music of all styles and periods.

2 A familiarity with the masterpieces of Western music in all genres.

3 Some acquaintance with the music of other cultures.

4 Some acquaintance with musical esthetics and philosophy, and a knowledge of some of the major modern statements in these fields.

PROFESSIONAL CRAFT

1 The ability to write clearly and legibly, or to use a type-writer or word-processor.

2 The knowledge of how to set out a page of text for the singing theatre.

3 An ability to work fluently and under pressure.

4 The ability to rework and rethink passages of text in response to musical needs as expressed by the composer, without losing the integrity of the text as a whole.

5 A desire to create.

A SUMMARY

The principles I have listed and my account of the Banff Music Theatre training programme have made clear, I hope, my convictions that a strong and vital new singing theatre will emerge not from the eventual isolation of a new and specific genre, but from the development of a new 'context', peopled by singing theatre artists who are capable through training or natural aptitude to take advantage of that context. This is why I have repeatedly headed off the question 'What is Music Theatre?' as a delaying tactic, appropriate for a swimmer who prefers to discuss the buoyant properties of water rather than jumping into it.

Without a new context such as I have outlined, new singing theatre will remain marginalised, disembodied. But I have endeavoured to be undogmatic about what kind of Music Theatre can be created within it; what kind of music written, what kind of vocal style employed, what sort of vision transmitted. The only parameters offered for new creation propose a modesty of scale, an interest in communicating with the audience, an all-round professional versatility of performer, and respect for – and understanding of – the principle of collaboration; none of these proposals, I would suggest, being prescriptive enough to be any kind of a straitjacket.

By stripping from the primary act of singing theatre its historical accretions, we have in fact sought to salvage and identify the basic vehicle of expression offered by the singing theatre to composers, writers and performers. It is, after all, simply another medium, this singing theatre; another way of communicating human experience. It has its strengths and weaknesses like any medium: things it does well, and things that are perhaps outside its nature. But limits are only found by seeking to go beyond them, and the socio-political pressures on this particular medium have narrowed the field of exploration. Indeed in our own century, as we have seen, the freight of history has effectively prevented any enduring forward movement in the art.

An art is only alive as long as it is being added to, as long as it attracts the interest of superlative creative artists, giving them opportunities to deploy their talent, vision and energy. If the doors appear to be closed, if restrictions – whether economic, social or formal – seem to discourage freedom of imagination, then the creative artist will search elsewhere for an outlet.

Within the context of new singing theatre the spectrum of creative vision, of technical idiosyncrasy and emphasis, of musical idiom, of vocal style, of content and attitude, can be as wide and various as its equivalent in the world of contemporary dance. What is needed is a form of training which prepares young performers, composers, writers and designers for this whole range of possibility, by breaking down barriers of snobbery and tradition, and in their place encouraging a new openness, a new versatility, a new sense of adventure. What is needed is a new kind of singing theatre space to serve as a home, freed from the hierarchial configuration of another century.

The final part of this book, then, is intended not to prescribe the way new singing theatre should develop, but to share some of the perceptions that have emerged from work in the field, and to suggest avenues of exploration for the composer, the writer, the performer, the designer. It will assume that the context has been identified, the expressive medium dusted off. It will even assume, brashly enough, that some enthusiasm has been generated by the story so far, and that you, patient reader that you are to have reached this point, are now impatient to do something.

Let us then move section by section through some of the major – and overlapping – themes of singing theatre activity; and allow me if you will to play the role of the hoary traveller who can tell you of places you might try and things you might avoid, and what you might want to take with you along the way. Inevitably the journey will pass through many specialist territories, in each of which my commentary will have the limitations of any tourist's guide. Those specialists whose views are already honed and polished will I hope forgive me if, in my enthusiasm to de-mystify this whole complex interplay of themes and to encourage action, I sound once again too simple. As I made clear at the outset of this book, I cannot subscribe to the view apparently held by many professional commentators, that the most important reaction to any situation is merely to develop an opinion about it.

PART 3

THOUGHTS ON THE NEW SINGING THEATRE

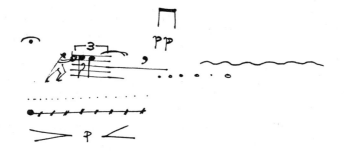

Chapter Ten

FORM AND CONTENT, AND THE QUESTION
OF ADAPTATION

If all the literature about writing libretti for operas and operettas, or books and lyrics for musicals, were stood up cover to cover, it would not fill many shelves. Some of the most valuable material on the subject comes not from books of instruction – it is hard to lay hands on these – but from the correspondence between composers and their librettists, or from accounts of particular collaborations. From these it is interesting to examine the way that singing theatre projects are conceived, discussed, chosen and begun, because it is in these first moments that the whole question arises of what is appropriate subject matter and what is not.

As we have already seen, the lofty social stance of opera from its beginnings determined that certain kinds of story were appropriate for it, and for serious opera these stories were taken – almost exclusively until the nineteenth century – from classical legend or chivalric romance. Comic opera began as an overlarding of spoken comedy with song, and *opera buffa* continued to remain to some extent dependent on the spoken drama for the basis of its plots. In the eighteenth century Metastasio's *Drammi Per Musica* were the first and last word in well-crafted libretti of the old Italian tradition, and were used by scores of composers until Gluck led a return to the purity of classical legend and to a simpler directness of feeling. For his collaborations with Mozart, da Ponte adapted a play (Beaumarchais' *Le Mariage de Figaro*) and an earlier libretto (for *Don Giovanni*) and in the case of *Cosi Fan Tutte* constructed his own plot in a familiar and somewhat old-fashioned style.

The new impetus given to 'serious' opera by the French Revolution (being in fact a new idea of what was serious) opened up the range of possible sources for adaptation to include theatrical dramas and tragedies, narrative poems and soon the historical novel. The romantic historical works of Walter Scott and of his French imitators Victor Hugo and Alexandre Dumas, father and son, were among the major sources; and as soon as Shakespeare became adopted in France and Italy as the ultimate Romantic his plays became prime operatic material: 'Shakespeare is my god,' said Verdi. The prolific playwright Eugène Scribe (known for his *pièces bien faites*) was also the most prolific French librettist – and two of his plays were also adapted for the singing theatre. Later in the century the novels of Zola provided material for the French composer Alfred Bruneau, and fuelled the development of naturalism in opera, with its Italian counterpart the 'verismo' school initiated by Mascagni and carried forward by Leoncavallo and Puccini. Mascagni's masterwork, *Cavalleria Rusticana*, was based on a short story of peasant life. Leoncavallo wrote his own libretto for *I Pagliacci* basing it in part on the familiar situations of *commedia dell'arte*; and Puccini used both novels and plays (including two by American playwright David Belasco, *Madame Butterfly* and *The Girl of the Golden West*) as the sources of his major works. Tchaikovsky's sources included two of Russia's major literary figures, Pushkin and Gogol: Pushkin's narratives were subsequently used by Glinka, Rimsky-Korsakov, Mussorgsky and Stravinsky. Wagner was the only major composer of the last century to resort neither to novels nor to plays, and only once, with *Parsifal*, made some use of the verse of a contemporary poet; like Gluck, his main preoccupation was with the mythic, adapting medieval chivalric romance or constructing his own mythology from Teutonic legend.

In the twentieth century the range of adapted material has widened considerably. *Commedia dell'arte* stories continued to be popular with composers until the twenties, and Shakespeare is still being adapted (*The Tempest, King Lear, A Midsummer Night's Dream*, to name a recent few). But short stories or novellas served as the foundation for several of Britten's operas; a mystery play, a Noh play and a Bible story were the basis of his church parables. Auden's neo-classic *The Rake's Progress* libretto for Stravinsky was based on the famous series of paintings by William Hogarth. The Old Testament, Sophocles and Oscar Wilde provided material for Strauss. Schoenberg also borrowed from the Bible for his *Moses and Aaron*. Tippett's opera librettos have been original creations of the composer; so have Menotti's. Operas have been based on political stories and situations (*Nixon in China, The Consul, The Electrification of the Soviet Union*) and – in the long tradition – on poems (Britten's *Peter Grimes* from George Crabbe) and novels (Prokofiev's *War and Peace* from Tolstoy, Carlisle Floyd's *Of Mice and Men* from Steinbeck). Weill-Brecht adapted *The Threepenny Opera* from *The Beggar's Opera*, but *The Rise and Fall of the City of Mahagonny* appears to have been original. Berg's *Woyzeck* is, of course, based on Georg Büchner's play of the same name; interestingly its episodic nature and anarchic content attracted no composers of his own time.

Lehman Engel, in his studies of the American musical, claimed that historically there have been only one or two exceptions to the rule that a successful musical must be based on an already written story. His view

was that there were so many difficulties in the creation of a piece of singing theatre that the original work was needed to serve as *terra firma* in the
quicksands of the enterprise, the only common ground for the collaborators to meet upon. The history of opera suggests that much the same
rule operates. But as we see from the brief survey we have just made,
there have been some notable exceptions; and I have never been impressed with the idea that new singing theatre must for ever continue to
borrow its content from other genres. It is the film, after all, which has
taken over from opera as the regular dramatiser of successful literary
works, and for the same reason that opera did so in the nineteenth century – hanging on to the shirt-tails of a best-selling play or book is one
way to guarantee interest before the show even opens. With *Gigi* and *42nd
Street* we have even seen the reverse of the usual pattern; they were films
first, and then stage musicals. And nowadays, at least in New York City,
it is increasingly television that makes stars – who are then inveigled into
the theatre to boost the sale of tickets.

The singing theatre is in a sense relieved from a major pressure on
it by not having to supply a mass-market 'version' of popular fiction. On
the other hand it will continue to be dependent on other genres until writers of great skill and musicianship decide that they wish to express
original visions through the medium of singing theatre. And for this to
happen they must have developed the skill of working in collaboration
with a composer – or be themselves poet and composer of equal prowess.

In moving towards this kind of goal we need to consider a re-formu-
lation of what makes 'suitable' material for the singing stage. Do the same
rules apply as they always did? In his introduction to the correspondence
between Strauss and Hofmannsthal, Edward Sackville-West wrote of
Strauss' interest in the libretto for *Die Frau ohne Schatten* in 1914:

> The man of the theatre – the born opera composer – was naturally
> and genuinely inspired by the romantic atmosphere of the poem,
> with its scenes of magic, its dramatic contrasts, and its many oppor-
> tunities for grand stage spectacle...[15]

But is this what the person of the theatre today – the born 'new singing theatre' composer – should also be inspired by? The tradition is
perhaps seeing its rebirth in the brilliant world of effects created by a musical like Lloyd Webber's *The Phantom of the Opera* (adapted from the
thriller by Gaston Leroux); such spectacles will always have their popularity – and win it like any other astutely judged commercial enterprise.
But are we not now in a position to think of other ways of being dramatic,
of sources of inspiration other than romantic atmosphere, magic and
spectacle?

One of the best ways to shake up our preconceptions of what singing theatre is or can be, is in fact to look at some of the ways that opera did *not* finally go: the roads not taken – those 'initiatives and interrupted developments that have been left aside by...history', as Dahlhaus described them.

THE BEGINNINGS OF OPERA

Italian opera developed out of a scholarly attempt to re-create Greek tragedy by restoring to it its 'lost' musical element. Because sophisticated vocal singing at the end of the sixteenth century was polyphonic, the gentlemanly researchers of the Florentine Camerata had to invent a style of music in which the chief melody was emphasised and sung by one voice at a time, in such a way that the words could be heard. Plato, after all, had said 'we shall adapt metre and melody to the words..., not the words to the metre and melody'. The solo voice was therefore isolated, and 'expressed' the poetic text by means of a musical line which carefully followed the rhythms of poetic speech. This faithful aping of poetic speech by music became known as the *stilo rappresentativo* or 'recitative'. Music, in other words, began as a more or less humble handmaiden to words; the early composers were pre-occupied with developing its capacity to match the (readily acknowledged) superior expressive power of language.

The oddity of those first few experimental hearings can be imagined. The poetry of the text was sung with heavily exaggerated stresses, accompanied by lutes, viol da gamba, and harpsichord or organ. We must admire the adventurousness of the singers and the audience; but it was not long before it was decided to relieve the sameness of it all (or did the singers insist?) by interpolating airs ('arias'). Monteverdi is credited with writing the first aria, 'Il Lamento di Ariadne', in 1608 (although his *Orfeo* of 1607, the 'first opera', already foreshadows the aria form). The action stops while a character encapsulates his/her feelings in a melodic song structure – words now being organised by music. Thus music began its ascent in the partnership with words. Monteverdi's inventiveness in creating new kinds of instrumental sound and figure to represent anger and fear, and his adoption of musical 'signatures' – like the chromatic descending scale to represent suffering – armed music's means of expression still further, so that within a hundred years, as I have written elsewhere, 'the emotionally expressive power of music was the marvel, and the composer and his company of technically adept singers and instrumentalists were the new heroes'.[17] It was in the arias that the singer's chance came. Into them composers wrote opportunities for display of voice and feeling, and the end of the aria signalled a time for applause and bows before the less dazzling narrative continuity was returned to.

We had to wait until Wagner before the original idea of *stilo rappresentativo* was broached again; this time with the resources of an enormous orchestra in which the dramatic text was embedded. Verdi carried on the re-discovered style in *Falstaff*. But look again at those small-scale early experiments: is there hidden in them an alternative to what became the 'Italian solution' with continuous music alternating recitative and aria?

Or look at another 'interrupted development' – the attempt in Britain to reach just such an alternative to the Italian solution in the relationship between words and music.

Shakespeare and his contemporaries had in a sense spoiled it for opera in England. Their multiple theatrical achievements, in the control of plot and loose dramatic structure, variation of pace and mood, and the maintenance of dramatic urgency; in delineation of character and in the capacity to reflect nuances of emotion and ethical choice; in the development of a dramatic vernacular language, and a poetry which combined beauty with freedom; and in the building of a popular as well as aristocratic audience – these achievements set a standard which continued to separate the British stage from the rest of Europe for two hundred years.

Ben Jonson had hopes of the Court Masque, which was popular with the Stuart kings a very few years after the first operatic experiments in Italy. He pronounced with somewhat shaky determination that masques 'either have been, or ought to be, the mirror of man's life'. But his stage designer, the ingenious and arrogant Inigo Jones, was rather more ruthlessly determined to stun the audience with visual effects, and considered masques 'nothing else but pictures with light and motion'. If Jones had been less dismissive, could the story have gone another way? Read Jonson's *Neptune's Triumph* and translate it into modern terms. Creaky as its language and style may strike us now, the form could still be, in Eeyore's phrase, a 'useful pot to put things in'.

Later in the century, when theatre was still banned by the Puritans but music was permitted, the playwright d'Avenant rewrote his play *The Siege of Rhodes* in the form of an opera, getting three composers to set his entire text to music (now lost), and presenting it in the autumn of 1656. D'Avenant was clearly using the operatic form as a Trojan horse to reintroduce drama into England; but the adjustments to his play suggests he had some feeling for the variety of line length which music could take advantage of, and the choice of a recent historical event as his subject set the piece apart from contemporary Italian operas. More interesting still perhaps was his very first cautious venture six months earlier, billed as 'The First Dayes Entertainment at Rutland-House by Declamations and

Musick: after the Manner of the Ancients'. Edward Dent's description of the piece is worth quoting in full:

> The Entertainment began with a 'flourish of musick' after which the curtain was drawn and the Prologue entered. He apologises for the discomforts of the room, which was low and narrow, and indicates plainly the future intentions of the author:
>
> Think this your passage, and the narrow way
> To our Elisian field, the Opera:
> Tow'rds which some say we have gone far about,
> Because it seems so long since we set out...
>
> A 'consort of instrumental musick adapted to the sullen disposition of Diogenes' was then performed, after which the curtain was drawn again, and there appeared Diogenes and Aristophanes, sitting in 'rostras' of purple and gold. Diogenes makes a long speech in condemnation of 'publick entertainment by Moral Representations'; another piece of music is played to illustrate the cheerful disposition of Aristophanes, who thereupon argues the case from the other side. The speeches are lengthy and tedious, but were perhaps appreciated by an audience accustomed to Puritan sermons. The curtains close, and a song with chorus and instruments follows. The second part of the entertainment consisted of similar speeches by a Parisian and a Londoner, each abusing the other's city. Each speech was preceded by appropriate music, and the speeches were followed by a song deriding Paris and the French. The Epilogue, despite its apparent regret for the suppression of the drama, alludes ironically to its old-fashioned principles of construction.[18]

In comparison with works of the developed operatic genre, we judge all this now as a pathetically feeble and naive effort. But its very odd and rambling format has always struck me as strangely attractive. Updated to our own time, would we see it simply as a rotten opera, or as something else? There are countless later pieces to look at, some of which must have been desperate afternoons and evenings in the theatre. But many of them found quaint and distinctive ways of entertaining their audiences, and can still be quarried for their gold.

At the same time we should be aware that these expeditions into the past always run the risk of sucking us into a bog of historicism, and for anyone doubtful of his/her ability to prise form away from ancient content they should be avoided. After all, there is territory closer to home.

THE POST-WAR PERIOD

How has the singing theatre been affected, for example, by the radical changes in the theatre of the post-War period? What does Sackville-West's recipe of 'romantic atmosphere'...'scenes of magic' and 'opportunities for grand stage spectacle' have to do with, say, the work of Pinter and Beckett? When their work first appeared on the stage it was deemed at first to be without any dramatic power. That view has changed; and now is it not possible to capture in singing theatre the tone and rhythm, the wit and pathos, of the work of these playwrights, or of a dozen others that have revealed our century to us? Not with the music of Strauss, or even of Berg or Stravinsky or Schoenberg, but with a music that seeks to represent or even to 'imitate' the emotions of the language of these works in the same way that Monteverdi sought to expand music's range and idiom to match the far greater expressive power of poetry? (I believe that Benjamin Britten, whose respect for words and for literature was legendary among his collaborators, was working towards the same goal in his last opera, based on an English translation of Mann's *Death In Venice* – a story larded with ambiguity, full of inner musing rather than external action, and entirely devoid of sharp dramatic confrontations. The text was not adjusted in order to incorporate these traditional operatic requirements. On the contrary, it was the music that pulled back, to reach a different kind of *entente* with the subtleties of the text.)

But since Pinter and Beckett first altered dramatic language in the fifties, the world has been radically changed by the arrival – the arrival to stay – of television; and it is likely that the time for seeking to emulate the work of these playwrights is passed. It seems clear now that any art groping for new forms of expression – and this is the present position of new singing theatre – cannot assert itself without considering the modes of perception which have been engineered by television, and by means of which an increasing number of the world's population view reality. By this I do not mean that we must now write solely for television, only that the forms which television has established as frameworks for information and entertainment have become as much second nature as the forms of fiction were in the nineteenth century, and that at the very least they are worth looking at. Can a television debate (like that strange one between Aristophanes and Diogenes) be a form for a singing theatre piece? Or a television interview or panel show? Or a commercial or rock video? For two hours? – no, I doubt it; but for ten or fifteen minutes, why not? Could a documentary film not be also a Music Theatre piece? Is the environmental movement not an attempt to sing with the planet? Could the struggle of Eritrea to free itself from Ethiopia not be a vehicle for the passion of singing? Must singing characters always be victims either of fate or of the composer's grandeur?

It is in this area, then – the choice of form and subject matter – that the new singing theatre has ahead of it years of stimulating exploration, searching both around and behind us. In fact our venerable art stands in an enviable position. Like the first nations to embrace the Industrial Revolution, which then found themselves encumbered with outworn machinery, the arts which first moved away from academic forms are beginning to exhaust themselves. The singing theatre, only now emerging from the nineteenth century, is an ideal vehicle for fresh thinking and feeling.

So, imagine your television news commentator singing on the evening news. Absurd? Of course. But what does it, could it, mean? Are there any other responses than the conclusion that he/she has flipped his/her lid? We cannot discuss any further questions of form and content without also considering the most troublesome of the singing theatre's basic characteristics: the way it deals with the question of lifelikeness.

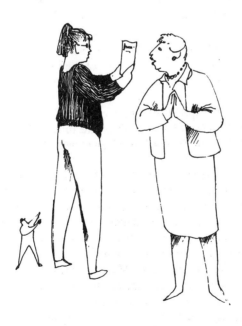

Chapter Eleven

THE QUESTION OF LIFELIKENESS

As in the spoken theatre, the singing theatre can portray human beings (or beings behaving like humans; they can be gods or animals, or machines for that matter) as characters in some kind of dramatic episode. These characters communicate their thoughts, feelings, intentions and reactions to one another and/or to the audience through utterance, gesture and action. The essential characteristic of singing theatre is that part or all of this utterance is sung. Usually this sung utterance will take the form of words placed on specific pitches and within specified musical rhythms, with musical support from on stage or close to it.

If you make the decision that the episode you are going to create will make use of people singing words *without appearing to notice the fact that they are singing*, then this business of tying words to music needs thinking about – because you immediately raise the question of lifelikeness (I use this word in preference to 'naturalism' or 'realism' because of the confusion such concepts kindle). Shakespeare shows us characters who do not know that they are speaking five-foot lines; but if the energy of the meaning is well married to the rhythms of the verse, and if the actor behaves in every other way as if the given circumstances are real, the audience generally responds to the character's utterance as though it is spontaneous. We respond with part of ourselves to the 'music' of the verse, but we are also able to concentrate fully on what the words are saying, and 'believe' that the character is making them up as he goes along.

But music makes this belief (or 'willing suspension of disbelief' to borrow Coleridge's brilliant over-borrowed phrase) more difficult. If you want it to seem as though your characters do not know they are singing (as in nearly all operas and most story musicals), not only must the audience accept that a character is *singing* his thoughts, feelings and intentions – which he would not generally or not ever do in daily life – but the structure of the music will often push the words around in a way that makes it clearly pre-written. Can this still be accepted as spontaneous?

When a good singer in a night-club, cabaret or concert hall sings a song – the song of a lover rejected, for example – we know that we are not listening to an actual rejected lover, and yet we are able to enter into the spirit of the song with the singer, and to experience the emotion of her performance as though it is real and spontaneous. At the end of the song the rejected lover becomes once more the singer that we know, and we applaud her for the technical skill of her performance but also for her emotional commitment to the lover's plight. For the duration of the song we accepted that she was the lover; in fact, the more committed she seemed to be the more difficult we find it to believe that she was not singing about her own real experience – even if the song is one most of us know, like 'Smoke Gets in your Eyes'.

The singing of a single song, then, is a situation in which disbelief is willingly suspended; and the acceptance of the applause by the singer at the song's end is the sign that she is no longer the person in the song. In fact she will soon become another person in another situation in another song, and if she is a skilful artist we will once again accept the new illusion while that song lasts. This short-term acceptance by the audience takes the form almost of a connivance with the performer; as the introductory bars begin to play we find ourselves concentrating, expectant, even smiling in anticipation, as though giving her permission to take charge of the moment. The singer is applauded for her virtuosity and emotional transformation, but also because she is in some sense singing on our behalf, portraying the feelings of a life situation which we may well recognise and even identify with, and which we want her to represent for us.

What is the difference between this night-club performance and the portrayal of a character in a piece of singing theatre? It lies in the fact that in the night-club song the illusion is restricted to the emotional situation, and to a limited range of gestures and facial expressions, which reinforce what the voice is singing about. No attempt is made to suggest that this song is being sung by a character in a real time other than our own, while washing dishes last Wednesday, or driving a cab or ruling an empire or dying. The singer occupies real time.

In a dramatic episode in the singing theatre, on the other hand, the singer would usually have us believe for the length of the episode that she is not the singer but someone else – someone living in a time and place other than this time and this place. Consequently, she and her fellow performers must appear to be living from moment to moment, and not to know what is going to happen next. Decisions, recognitions, emotional states must appear to arise out of the fictive situation. This is what is meant by that fundamental definition of 'believable' acting; the performers 'behave as if the given circumstances are real'.

THE 'ABSURDITY' OF SINGING

Are we willing to suspend our disbelief in this kind of situation? There is a long pedigree attached to the idea that we cannot – especially in England, where Italian opera made its way in the early 1700s against vigorous opposition from the literati. Its 'absurdity...shows itself at the first sight', wrote Addison; 'an exotic and irrational entertainment', said Dr Johnson. Even lovers of opera are prepared to 'subject themselves as willingly to its absurdities as to its compelling expressive powers'.[19] Schmidgall suggests that it is opera's capacity to express passion which forces us to suppress our disbelief: we want to be carried away on a tide of feeling, in which absurdities count for nothing because we are no longer reasoning. W.H. Auden, who wrote several librettos and whose comments on libretto-writing should be read by all text-writers for Music Theatre even though his hand is deeply dyed by the operatic convention, contends that the opera is in fact 'an imitation of human wilfulness'; it is 'rooted in the fact that we not only have feelings but insist on having them at whatever cost to ourselves'.[20] Auden goes on to glory in opera's absurdity:

> the librettist need never bother his head, as the dramatist must, about probability. A credible situation in opera means a situation in which it is credible that someone should sing...it offers as many opportunities as possible for the characters to be swept off their feet by placing them in situations which are too tragic or too fantastic for 'words'. No good opera plot can be sensible for people do not sing when they are feeling sensible.[21]

If you believe that the only counterweight to the 'absurdity' of singing characters is the vastness and inevitability of their passion, and if you plan that your characters should not 'know they are singing', then it follows that your piece of Music Theatre must portray characters in some form of emotional crisis. The climaxes of the piece become extended cries of love, anger, joy, jealousy, fear, despair, pain, or horror.

I happen to believe that this view, in which excess of personal emotion licenses the art form, is what locks opera firmly into the Romantic mould, and is one powerful reason for its unreadiness to change in our own century. We are not necessarily running away from our own primal emotions if we find ourselves reluctant to join the party; we may simply feel that it is the opera's Mediterranean origins which are responsible for the lavish display of raw feeling in opera, and in Romantic music in general; and that other arts in the twentieth century – while still capable of generating powerful emotion – have an infinitely wider set of possibilities in front of them. It is as though melodrama were still the prevailing style in the theatres, and the faint and the swoon, the cry of anguish and the paroxysm of tears, were still normal ways of carrying on, both on the stage and in life.

If your singing theatre piece involves both speech and song, one solution is to follow Brecht's example (in *The Threepenny Opera*) by switching to the cabaret/song recital format when someone is about to sing. This certainly takes the curse off the 'absurdity' of singing, but it is no longer 'lifelike' in the sense we have been discussing – it makes no attempt to pretend that the characters don't know they are singing. And in fact for Brecht it was part of a comprehensive rejection of the illusion of 'lifelikeness', along with announcing scenes, insisting that the source of all dramatic effects be visible, putting the orchestra on stage, and even – as we have seen – attempting to reject emotional commitment and imitation of reality in the style of acting. It is a method that has had major influence on theatrical staging, although less on styles of acting.

But are there other alternatives to justifying the 'absurdity' of singing as though it is a normal method of communication? It is, for example, a commonplace among writers of opera that music cannot be associated with commonplaces; that 'pass the salt, please' cannot be set to music without sounding absurd and making people laugh. Music, we are told, demands elevated language, and a degree of abstraction. In fact Auden observed that 'as an art-form involving words, opera is the last refuge of the High style, the only art to which a poet with a nostalgia for those times past, when poets could write in the grand manner all by themselves, can still contribute...'.[22] But, as I have already suggested, as long as serious singing theatre's texts must be written in the grand manner, it will stay cooling its heels in the past. We no longer feel comfortable with the grand manner, in politics, life or art. If commonplaces sound silly when they are set to music (and of course they often do) then perhaps they are being set to music in the wrong way, or to the wrong music, or sung by a 'tenore' impatient for the next money-note. Perhaps the entire concept of singing theatre dramaturgy is still fumbling around in a daze, searching for the heroic vein.

This whole question, involving the fundamental 'contract' between audience and performer in the singing theatre, is another rich area of exploration. Central to it, because of the fact that we talk rather than sing when we communicate in daily life, is a consideration of the relationship between speech and song.

SPEECH AND SONG

Most of us find ourselves bursting into song on one occasion or another, and the occasion is often a moment of high emotion. We discover that we have got the job, or won the lottery, or been lucky in love; or (perhaps less often) we turn a cry of anguish into song when we are grieving a loss or suffering pain or disappointment. There is an instinctual sense, as Auden suggested, that at these moments speaking is not enough, that it does not release the feeling in the same way. This capacity of song to release emotion in real life is unquestionably at the heart of singing theatre. The desertion of talk for song at moments of high emotion is very similar to what happens in singing theatre forms which mix speaking and singing.

In naturalistic musical comedy, for example, a moment of increased emotion is usually approached in the spoken dialogue, and then, when the temperature reaches a certain point, the introductory music sneaks in under the dialogue, or bursts in stridently – whichever way best represents the feeling that has been engendered by the situation. This introduction builds, picking up the emotion of the moment and along the way giving the performers their starting-note, until speech gives place to song. The end of the song is still usually engineered so as to create a moment for applause, in which the performers sometimes freeze in an embrace, sometimes in an attitude facing the audience. Either way the freeze accompanied by a stop in the music (sometimes a flourish, sometimes a dying fall) signifies a moment for applause. The audience will normally respond as expected of them, while the performers remain frozen. And then, before the applause dies away – but not too soon either, in case the audience feels that the performers resent their intrusion – action begins again, often accompanied by a return to speech.

But there are other kinds of cue for music in musicals. The beginnings of acts or scenes often present a set piece, in which a bustling or driving picture of some general activity is presented, out of which emerges the ensuing action. These scenes often contain spoken dialogue, but within a framework of choral song, song-text divided among different characters, and energetic movement or dance. Here the opportunity to lift and engage the audience by spectacle is clearly a prime motivation for music, but the music is often 'justified' (if we are tiresome enough to need justification) by its capacity to release the sense of excitement or anticipation or other mass emotion being experienced by the total group of characters.

Another motivation for the song in a musical is the request for a character to deliver some kind of set piece: an explanation, a story, an account of some experience, initiated by some version of the 'Sit down and I'll tell you all about it' line. Here the justification is not so much an excess of emotion as the licence given to a character to take the floor: 'This is your moment – we are all going to shut up and listen to you'. The interchange of thoughts and reactions which constitute dialogue is suspended by general agreement. The character takes on the challenge, and the music represents his/her attempt to 'structure' the account, rather in the same way that in real life someone tells a joke or gives a speech; the speaker accepts the role of 'performer'. There is a sense here, in fact, in which the musical form represents the rhetorical structure of oratorical speech or narrative, and is 'justified' by it; it signals the performance aspect of a lifelike situation. But it is often, of course, the kind of opportunity for which a performer hungers, and the licence is to some extent provided by the composer and book-writer as well as by the characters within the situation.

There is no question that all these uses of music in a mixed-speech-and-song singing theatre piece are accepted by a general audience, at least in European culture. There may be a mild sense of phoniness, of *déjà entendu*, when we hear the music pretending not to be there – as when it drifts in under a romantic dialogue and leads us into the duet. But if the dialogue avoids the *clichés* wheeled out for these occasions, most of us will allow it to lead us into the music with no sense of silliness about people suddenly singing. We accept the convention, and even warm to it, as to a liturgy with which we are familiar.

Through-composed classical and Romantic opera has its own versions of these moments, differing in that it is recitative rather than spoken dialogue which gives way to aria at the moment of heightened emotion. And at the end of an aria most conventional through-composed operas become just a little less through-composed, coming to a provocative stop and allowing time for the same freeze familiar in musicals. But in opera the applause and bravos can sometimes (less often than in former times) draw an encore out of the performer(s), who walk back to where they were before and re-run the emotional moment. These are the moments when all lifelikeness breaks down, replaced by time for virtuosity. They are the moments that Wagner rebelled against, and which those who find opera's unreality absurd will be most discomfited by; the parade of stars through the curtain at the end of each scene or act reinforcing the discomfort.

But these moments in which the music stops and starts are worth close examination by anyone wishing to explore the mechanics of lifelikeness in the singing theatre. If such methods must always be followed for joining the drive of the narrative (contained in dialogue or recitative) to the more formal structure of song or aria, then we already find ourselves dependent on a set of conventions – which serve as a framework on which we must hang our story. Though an audience within our European culture will accept these conventions, it is one of the restrictions that hold the singing theatre back from dealing with different kinds of life experience, the kind of life experience, for example, in which our own sense of reality is uncertain.

There are two areas on which exploration in this field might focus: First, the basic proposition (put forward by Auden) that opera is an 'imitation of human wilfulness' depends on the acceptance of a character's music as self-expression. The fact that the music is actually pre-written by someone else, and then learnt and rehearsed, is as it were covered up. This of course is the nature of the dramatic illusion; the whole idea – if we are trying to make the thing lifelike – is to treat musical expression in the same way that we treat spoken expression in the theatre, aiming to get the audience to 'believe' that it is spontaneous, made up as it goes along. With spoken dialogue the illusion of spontaneity is achievable. With poetic spoken dialogue, the illusion is harder to achieve but still achievable because of the wide latitude in the way verse is delivered, and the fact that the timing of delivery is in the performer's own power. But in words pitched within a timed, rhythmic structure and supported by musical accompaniment the illusion of spontaneity can only be sustained by the audience suppressing reason, and 'subjecting themselves willingly to its absurdities'.

Now the role played by the music in an opera – especially in Romantic and post-Romantic opera, including those of Wagner and Strauss and even Berg – is to express the composer's own view of the situation, and to establish this view for the audience. The existential effect of this (if that word is appropriate) is to place the character of a through-composed opera in a meticulously controlled environment, but to require him/her to behave as if free or 'wilful'. The character is in fact a victim of this musical environment, which establishes not only the world and the fate which cannot be escaped, but even the character's own responses to it.

It is this dominating function of the music, and this passivity (masked by passion) in the operatic character, which is the source of much of the 'absurdity' we have been discussing. When, added to this, we have a man or woman waving a stick at the performer/character, the force of the controlling environment becomes even clearer, the absurdity of the character's 'wilfulness' even more patent. (I believe that this is the source, too, of the famously stormy and difficult temperament of the opera singer; he/she must feel powerfully and individually – but to order.)

OTHER WAYS TO GO

What if the music were to play other kinds of roles? What if, for example, this existential fight between the individual will and the controlling forces around it were made the very stuff of the drama, where music was an alien language and symbol of repression, or of the conqueror? Surely this use of the illusion develops commonly enough out of naturalism. It is one of the themes of twentieth-century theatre, as we see in the work of Pirandello and Beckett – indeed it is the story of Shakespeare's last plays, in which he seems to have lost belief in the convention of dramatic illusion and finally (as it were) puts himself on the stage in the form of Prospero, the magician who commands the action.

Or what if we understand sung words as the expression of some higher (or lower) level of consciousness, induced by drugs or meditation or magic or demonic influence? Or as the mark of lying, of hypocrisy – or, alternatively, of truth? Music, after all, has a long history as a bender of the mind and body, for healing or harming purposes. It soothed the rupturing brain of Lear – 'Louder the music there!' – but its insistence has driven men to murder.

Or what if we learn from Schoenberg in the astonishing idea of his *Moses and Aaron*, in which Moses speaks (all but one line) and Aaron sings, the different forms of expression symbolising the philosophical difference between the two brothers as they fight for the souls of the Israelites? Here the tension between words and music is harnessed to astonishing dramatic effect. It is interesting that the libretto of the third act was completed, but that Schoenberg composed no more than eight bars of its music. The opera is therefore usually described quite correctly as unfinished. But it is almost as though Aaron's music had surrendered to the power of the Word; or as though Schoenberg's inability to finish the work was not only because of his poverty and desperation, but also the effect of the piece itself – that dyer's hand again, subdued to what it works in.

Strauss and Hofmannsthal also found themselves compelled to write a piece that was *about* the business of writing for the singing theatre. After Strauss's *Salome*, and the collaborators' *Elektra* and *Der Rosenkavalier* with their full-bodied action and 100-piece orchestras, they had the opportunity to write an opera to substitute for the usual ballet at the end of Molière's play *Le Bourgeois Gentilhomme*. *Ariadne auf Naxos* (1912) was the result. But the expense of hiring a combined company of actors and singers made further productions difficult, and so the opera was separated from the play and given a prologue – a 'backstage' episode featuring the composer, the prima donna, the dancing master and other artists as they prepare the performance – an operatic episode about opera, in fact. Much later, in *Capriccio* (based on an eighteenth-century original), Strauss once again wrote a piece about opera-writing, in which the question of primacy between words and music is played out in human terms; the composer and the poet both love the Countess, and she must choose between them. But both pieces, for all the artistry of Strauss' music, still reflect something of the aridity of all esthetic or philosophical debate when this seems to be substituting for action. Plays about playwriting, novels about novelists, operas about the creation of opera, nearly always suggest a certain wavering of faith about the buoyancy of the medium itself. And, given the status of opera during Strauss' life, and of his own musical style, this can be no surprise. Schoenberg's treatment of the 'words and music' battle in *Moses and Aaron* is much more effectively subsumed within the drama.

Murray Schafer's piece of Music Theatre, *Patria II: Requiems for a Party Girl*, for which he coined the term 'co-opera', uses a device similar to that of Schoenberg but uses it in a very different way. The work features only one singer – also an 'Ariadne' – and twelve or more non-singing actors (as well as a pre-recorded chorus). At the beginning a brain operation on Ariadne is in progress, and we hear her psychiatrists describing the case but using many languages, none of which she can understand. The actors take the roles of doctors, psychiatrists, inmates in the mental hospital, and dark mythological figures that haunt her increasingly schizophrenic and hallucinating mind. At the climax of her final dramatic and painful aria she shoots herself. In this piece, which is part of a much larger work, music takes its place as one of an immense variety of languages, all of which have the effect of alienating Ariadne from her own self. The soundscape of the piece is her confinement and her torture. Schafer suggests in his preface that the composer should stand in the lobby before the show trying to explain to the audience, in a language which he does not speak, what it means!

Schafer's Ariadne also makes use of a vocal effect first introduced by Schoenberg in *Pierrot Lunaire* (1913): 'sprechstimme', or half-speaking, half-singing. Charles Rosen in his study of Schoenberg quotes the composer as saying that 'he intended the voice of the singer/speaker only to touch on the original note and then quickly to leave it, generally by a kind of glissando moving to the next note... a certain improvised freedom of pitch in the vocal part is indeed necessary for a performance of the work'.[23] The result is – not surprisingly – neither like singing nor like speaking. It has subsequently been used by many of Schoenberg's disciples and admirers, and is clearly an interesting and valuable device for some composers for the way it breaks down the prescription of pitch. But the singer/speaker, skating between two conventional modes of expression, projects – as a 'character' – an abnormal, even neurotic state of mind. Schafer's prescription of it for his violently schizophrenic Ariadne was apt for this reason; but the device is not always used so appropriately, and in many 'avant-garde' concerts comes over as a composer's routinely Schoenbergian affectation rather than as a revealing dramatic device.

Frontiers, as Marshall McLuhan observed, are interesting and exciting because they are where the action is: where one ambience changes to another with relief or regret; where the jurisdiction of one power, auth-

ority and language gives way to another; where border skirmishes release
tension; and where manoeuvres can turn suddenly to invasion. The bor-
derline between speech and song in vocal music shares these
characteristics. And yet thought and creative ideas like those of Schoenberg seem to have been surprisingly skimpy. It is one of the prime areas
of future exploration for the united nation of composers, writers and performers in new singing theatre; exploration designed not merely to find
another handful of surprising effects, but to illuminate our humanity.

Perhaps one caution is worth sounding. One of the dreams of the
united art work, as Wagner expressed it, has been to bring back together
again the 'severed sisters' of the arts, so that their forms of expression
become one. But, as Peter Conrad has pointed out:

> Rather than a sedate marriage between text and music, [opera] pro-
> poses a relationship of unremitting, invigorating tension...Words
> and music are united by antagonism. Opera is the continuation of
> their warfare by other means.[24]

Conrad is here opposing not speech and song but sung text and the music
that continually threatens to drown the sense of the text in sound. The
point is well taken, though if we accept that through song we express feeling, we should never allow it to be suggested that through words we
express nothing but sense. Explorations along the borders are not necessarily aimed at abolishing them, but at understanding and exploiting the
differences that put them there in the first place. Schoenberg first realised
that the border was less distinct than we thought. What we might start
mapping now is the whole spectrum of difference that divides and also
unites the two 'sides'. The unifying force, after all, is the human being –
who both speaks and sings.

If these examples and exhortations nudge any preconceptions about
what the singing theatre can do, they will have achieved their purpose.
But we can go no farther without turning closer attention to two of the
primary elements of singing theatre, elements which are closely bound
up with all that we have been discussing: the singing voice, and the question of musical idiom.

Chapter Twelve

THE SINGING VOICE

Nothing more clearly separates the tradition of opera from other kinds of singing theatre than the way the voice is used, and the importance placed on it. Stories are well known of the singers' dominance of the opera in the eighteenth century; of composers' readiness to give them the chance for vocal display which they demanded and which audiences increasingly expected; and of the occasional attempts, particularly by Gluck, to restrain the power of the singers over opera, and 'restore' the concept of a work in which music, plot, scenery and stage action were given equal care and attention.

There is no question that singers could be arrogant and demanding. But it is idle now to try and determine where the blame should lie for the increasing preoccupation with vocal artistry that took possession of the singing theatre. Librettists agreed to write texts that served as mere frameworks for arias. Composers were happy to provide dazzling opportunities, pushing the human voice to the limits of its strength and dexterity without too much regard for the niceties of character or situation. The 'canary fanciers' among the audience were suitably dazzled, learning to give up any expectation of being engaged by the drama and simply emerging from the backs of their boxes to hear the blockbuster aria of their favourite soprano, male or female – before returning to their cards and ices. The castrati in particular were famous for their absurdly exaggerated trills and witlessly triumphal exit-arias, well calculated to bring the audience to its feet.

In the nineteenth century, with the rapid growth in the size of many opera-houses, orchestras and audiences, composers needed even more urgently to attract the finest and most powerful singers to their works by writing parts to suit the range, tessitura and timbre of these distinguished and still demanding performers. In fact the 1820s and 1830s, with the castrato's occupation more or less gone, saw the high point of vocal display in the extraordinary coloratura feats called for by Rossini, Donizetti and Bellini. This was one of the elements of the operatic scene against which Wagner ranted; he saw himself as the heir to Gluck's reforming efforts, fighting the battle again but with more conviction and even some success – at least in the productions he was able to control.

But out of this strange medley of vocal art and carnival emerged a number of techniques for sensitive and powerful voice production that established themselves as the basis of operatic singing. The dominant approach was the Italian 'bel canto', developed to take advantage of the pure vowels and mellifluously soft consonants of the Italian language. It emphasised beauty of tone, consistent purity of texture up and down the range, control of tone colour, ease of vocal production, agility, and lyricism; and the Italian singers who were exported to every major city in Europe ensured the supremacy of their sound. French vocal style eventually developed somewhat differently, preferring a thinner and more nasal tone. German voice production appears more pressured, making use of the language's sometimes harsh consonants. The Russians like to think of their approach as being 'natural', without the extreme liquidity of bel canto. English singers solved the problem of applying 'bel canto' to the singing of English by making their language sound as much like Italian as possible, thereby making it both ugly and unintelligible to both nations.

But these national differences are too subtle to be perceived by the uneducated listener, who will tend to hear in all these vocal styles much the same artificiality of sound: a careful roundness, an apparently manufactured vibrato, a fondness for vowels at the expense of consonants, and in general a studied manner of delivery which, if we heard people speaking in that same tone of voice, would make most of us instantly dislike them ('pear-shaped tones with the large end of the pear coming out first', as Alan Jay Lerner once put it). In describing the sound of the produced operatic voice as 'artificial', I am of course using the word in its pure sense: it is made by art or skill. But the 'art which conceals art' is not generally part of the trained singer's equipment, unless we mean simply that what is difficult is made to sound easy. To the untrusting ear the singer's artifice tends to mask the directness of his/her communication – the artifice does indeed sound 'artificial' in the sense of 'false'.

The fact is that nearly all of us sing, one way or another, and are aware that there are less 'worked' kinds of singing, less forbidding in their virtuosity and so perhaps more open, more accessible. If the sound is 'untrained', it is easier to feel that the singer is using the song to communicate the words and the feeling with – that the music and words are one – rather than as an opportunity to show off beauty of tone. All of us can be struck with wonder at the sheer athleticism and size of an operatic voice, but it takes a certain connoisseurship, genuine or assumed, to move from wonder to pleasure.

To lump together the sounds produced by all opera singers as though they are all the same is of course absurd: they perform now, as they always have, not only with national differences of technique but with an infinite variety of individual tone qualities and stylistic idiosyncrasies, and sometimes with passionate attention to text and character as well as to the music. But no one will deny that just as there is a 'country and western' style of singing, or a Broadway sound, so there is an opera sound, and that this sound is distinguished by the high premium placed on the roundness of tone with raised soft palate, highly conscious style of delivery, subtle dynamics, and changes of tone colour, extraordinary breath control for long melodic lines, and evenness through the range. This vocal artistry has, since the eighteenth century, been capable of inspiring an idolising frenzy among certain aficionados of opera, for whom opera productions are simply opportunities to hear great voices, and who respond to the great divas and primo uomos with a quasi-religious fervour of sometimes almost psychotic dimensions:

> Aspects of Maria Callas refuse to die ['Diva' Opera Journal informed us in 1986]. Stubbornly, divine tentacles reach out of the diva's grave like ghostly holograms to grip the imagination of her fans and to captivate the thoughts of many artists who seek to interpret her immortality...For as Rolf Liebermann put it, 'Goddesses do not die'...Graverobbers stole Callas' ashes from Père Lachaise, a Paris cemetery. They were supposedly recovered and ceremonially scattered in the Aegean Sea. However, some people believe a portion of the ashes were held back, packaged into tiny acrylic capsules, and sold on the black market to fanatics desiring their own equivalent of the 'true cross'.[24]

The campy style of this article and what it reports may not be representative of the staid mass of voice-lovers, but its devotion differs from theirs more in degree than in substance. It is, after all, this same mystique of divinity that is played upon in all mass-marketing of opera in North America, and has successfully achieved television 'superstar' status for a handful of fine opera singers. We are wafted into a trance of adulation, and judgement falls away. It is not an attractive social phenomenon.

The long operatic history of preoccupation with vocal virtuosity, however, offers a special challenge to new singing theatre. Any movement which proposes a greater emphasis on all-round performing versatility is going to be accused of not taking the voice seriously enough. And if the voice is to be put in its place, as it were, then the gods and goddesses of voice are to be toppled off their pedestals too: something that opera fanatics will kill to avoid. It was in considering this state of affairs that I coined the adage that 'the opera lobby is as powerful as the gun lobby, and twice as vicious'.

The obvious answer, of course, is to maintain the voice at its traditional level of importance, and simply bring up the other performing skills to its standard. But I believe something more than this needs to be done. In Chapter Nine I outlined a suggested inventory of knowledge and skills for the singer-actor, which among other things proposed the need not only for 'a sure grasp of classical vocal technique', but also for 'the ability to extend that technique to cope with today's demands'. And central to the demands that a new singing theatre must make on its singer-actors is not merely general versatility, but also versatility in the actual sound that the voice makes – in the styles of singing that it can cope with.

'CROSSOVER'

In recent years there has been an interesting phenomenon which perhaps underlines the need for this versatility. Recordings of American musicals have been made using some of the supreme operatic talents of our time, sometimes taking all the lead roles, sometimes sharing them with 'actors who sing'. In 1981 Leonard Bernstein conducted a recorded *West Side Story* with José Carreras, Kiri Te Kanawa, Marilyn Horne and Tatiana Troyanos, and since that time we have been offered *South Pacific* (Carreras, Te Kanawa – and Sarah Vaughan!), *The Sound of Music* (Frederica von Stade), *Carousel*, *My Fair Lady*, and a 1989 uncut *Showboat* (von Stade, Jerry Hadley, Teresa Stratas and others). An article by Ethan Mordden in the *New Yorker* magazine reviews the series at some length and in admirable detail, commenting on the 'crossover' phenomenon which it represents. While giving first prize to the *Showboat* recording for authenticity and casting, and noting 'flashes of good things' in others, Mordden is frank about some of the problems with such enterprises.

> Opera is a passionate art, but most of the opera singers taking part in today's crossover seem to be wanting in spirit...in *West Side Story* Te Kanawa splits the differences [among earlier portrayals of Maria] for a one-size-fits-all approach...The opera singers couldn't even be trusted to deliver their own dialogue...How strange that Te Kanawa...suddenly grows numb when she is given a character to pursue...How curious that Carreras, a superb musician, is baffled by the syncopations in *Something's Coming*...What is the point of mixed opera-and-theatre casting if the only artists we can count on are the theatre people?...Crossover is letting authenticity down. Every one of these shows has sounded better – not just more nearly correct, *better* – on earlier disks.[25] (Ethan Mordden in the *New Yorker*, 1989)

Everything I have so far said about new singing theatre might imply that this kind of 'crossover' is encouraging as a sign of the breakdown of barriers between opera and other kinds of musical theatre. The initiative suggests that 'serious' singers are now taking the American musical seriously, and even learning something (if not enough) about its different demands. I fear, though, that it signals no major change in the work habits and musical interests of most of these artists. They have been approached by first-class conductors and no doubt offered first-class contracts by major record companies. They are hired above all for their names and their voices – things they are generally happy to provide. The roles are nowhere nearly as demanding as those of the operatic repertoire, and do not need to be memorised. And so the recording companies have successfully married the *éclat* of great names to the universal attraction of these masterpieces of American musical comedy. It is an imaginative piece of commercial programming, but hardly the prelude to an *apertura* in the log-jam of new singing theatre. It was when established stars like Gielgud, Olivier and Ralph Richardson took the brave step of believing in the young British writers of the nineteen fifties, and accepted leading roles in their raw, 'angry' plays, that British theatre began its modern renaissance. How many stars of the post-War opera have lent their names and talents to modest and unproven new enterprises?

THE NEW SINGING VOICE

The new singing theatre must depend on singer-actors who are confident enough in their musicianship, and in their technique, to be able to develop a much wider spectrum of colour, timbre, style and resonance than is now the norm aspired to by the young singer and worked for by most teachers of singing. The demands of sheer muscular stamina may not be so great in more modestly-scaled and less showily bravura work, but this will simply free the singer from the occupational neurosis common to all athletes, and enable him/her to explore the full potential of the voice within the limits of its good health; allowing the words and stage action to share pride of place with the music, and developing qualities like adaptability, creative imagination and a taste for the untried. Olivier spent six months working to lower his speaking voice by a full octave in order to play the role of Othello in the style of an African leader like Nkrumah. For him voice quality was not a first principle but one of many tools put to the service of a characterisation and of a total dramatic concept.

So am I recommending that singer-actors should sound less like Birgit Nilsson and more like Julie Andrews? This would be simply dropping one prescription for another. The undeniable fact is that the creators of American musicals from *Showboat* to *West Side Story*, with some isolated sparkles since, took over from operetta the task of pleasing an audience unconditionally, and they did so – the best of them – not by offering pap but by introducing into musical theatre dramatically powerful plots, clearly etched characterisation, dialogue of wit, humour and lifelikeness, situations with tragic as well as comic overtones, and above all songs that married text to music in an increasingly sensitive and emotionally connected way. None of these advances would have made any sense without the performers to make sense of them; performers with whose characters the American public from the twenties to the fifties could identify. A florid 'operatic' tone, unless justified by the character being portrayed, was gradually discarded during this period in favour of a voice quality with vowels unmodified by 'bel canto' strictures, and of a text that was clearly the reason for the music. When composer Frederick Loewe (*Brigadoon*, *Paint Your Wagon*, *My Fair Lady*, *Camelot*) observed that 'soprano singing is not music, it's a disease', he was exhibiting a common enough reaction to voices that are more sound and temperamental fury than sense and feeling. And it should be added that Loewe was no Tin Pan Alley hack: he had been a pupil of Busoni and a prize-winning concert pianist in Europe. Trained in classical music, he knew his sopranos.

Broadway has of course moved a good deal further away from 'bel canto' in the seventies and eighties than it did in the 'golden' era of the musical. Barbra Streisand introduced a uniquely personal style, together with stylistic licks and tricks, which became a new model for young female performers Broadway-bound – who would come to auditions passing off as their own the Streisand idiosyncrasies learnt off a recording. Hitting notes plumb in the middle and holding them true became a rarity, as personality singing took the place of musical fidelity. And in the eighties, with the increasing power of the British musical peopled by 'actors-with-voices', we have seen another development, in which eccentricities of voice – husky or whining or booming or shrill or stuffed-nose tones – are prized for their surprisingness and their evidence of quirky and therefore theatrical character. One voice coach for a successful British show described her bind when coaxing from a chorus of untrained voices of this kind the raw edge and sheer volume that she knew was unhealthy but which the director required.

The singing voice that can make a contribution to the new singing theatre is surely a voice that can vary in style, colour and tone, even in nasality and guttural qualities, according to the needs of the new work – and, as I have already cautioned, within the limits of vocal good health. 'Bel canto' training is of immense value in developing the legato line, and in inculcating the fundamental techniques of breathing, vocal production and resonance. The old Broadway music is also of value in stressing melody and rhythm, the intelligent combining with words in the expression of character, and the close relationship with an audience unencumbered by cultural inhibition.

But if some singing theatre composers are going to write difficult 'atonical' scores, the aspiring singer-actor must also be enough of a musician to handle them, and to puzzle out and master all kinds of unconventional notation. And he/she should also have the courage to explore the limits of sounds available to the voice. There has been a wide range of experiments in vocal 'extension' in the last thirty years, including the work of Roy Hart (for whom Peter Maxwell Davies wrote *Eight*

Songs for a Mad King) and his present-day followers at the Roy Hart Theatre in France; the Voice Research Institute in Wales; and the explorations of Kathy Berberian, and of Joan la Barbara in California. Some of these experiments have gone no further than the laboratory or the occasional self-consciously avant-garde concert. Others process the voice through synthesiser-computer hook-ups, and need only one note from the performer to start the process. Still others seem dedicated to turning the voice into a human vacuum-cleaner. But the educated singer-actor should be as curious about all these things as about every other branch of the art, and be continually searching for new sound and new ideas, not just busily whittling his/her talent to fit the checkerboard of traditional opportunity.

Finally, of course, all these vocal adventures will lead the singer-actor back to his/her voice itself, to the voice as an expression of the performer's own personality. Because in the end it is this and only this which distinguishes a complete singer-actor; the capacity to make the voice – whatever it is doing – one with the thoughts and feelings of the character portrayed. From the time that we learn to talk we are bombarded with complexes imposed by ourselves or others, about the way we utter. As soon as we discover that our voices reveal ourselves we learn how to disguise them. If we are teased for being shrill we force our voices down. If we live in a family uproar we learn to shout. If we find a wingeing tone gets us our way, we use it and it becomes a habit. We copy our mothers or our fathers, or we move heaven and earth not to copy them. And then when we start to sing we bring all this baggage along with us, only to find ourselves being handed a new set of disguises, a new set of models and avoidances. From all this it can be a long journey back to find the speaking and singing voice that is our own, with no tricks and no masks. But this is the journey that must be taken.

Noelle Barker spoke in an interview in 1985 about her work as a voice teacher, and her comments make a pertinent end to this chapter:

> I feel it's my job to discover the real sound that the singer was meant to make from birth, not the sound they're making by educated noises. Sometimes it's quite upsetting for a singer to have a barricade of artificial sound stripped away...In the end my aim is...to help the student find his voice and through it himself: or vice versa![26]

Chapter Thirteen

THE QUESTION OF MUSICAL IDIOM

Near the conclusion of Ernest Newman's still indispensable study of Richard Wagner, he predicts that Wagner's work 'will flower afresh some day in some great composer who will sum up in himself, as Wagner did, all the finest impulses of the music of his day – who will have absorbed the essential, durable part of the spirit of his predecessors, and who will have at his command an idiom, a vocabulary and a technique competent to express every variety of human emotion.'[27] Newman believed that Richard Strauss, for all his gifts, was not that new genius. In fact he suggested that whoever it was would perhaps not even write music-drama:

> 'there seems to be a law of musical evolution that at the end of a period of crisis the seminal force that has exhausted itself in one genre passes over to, and finds new life in, a wholly different genre.'

Just as Beethoven had 'no real successor' in the classical symphony, but 'fertilised the music-drama', so Wagner had no real successor in the music-drama, but had perhaps 'fertilised poetic instrumental music'.[28] Newman went on to make clear his own preference for music separated from the artificial and even tiresome apparatus of the theatre:

> Is it not possible to construct an art-form in which the mere facts that it is necessary for us to know are either assumed as known or set before us in the briefest possible way, so that the music can take upon itself the whole burden of expression, and the whole work of art be nothing but an outpouring of lofty, quintessential emotion?...cannot we dispense altogether with the stage and the visible actor, such external coherence as the music needs being afforded by impersonal voices floating through a darkened auditorium?[29]

This view of Wagner's work, very similar to the nineteenth-century preference for Shakespeare in the study rather than on the stage, was not uncommon at that period, and stemmed at least in part from the wide discrepancy of style and evocative power between the abstract beauties of the music and the tattily naturalistic scenery and costumes which still prevailed as much at Bayreuth as elsewhere. But Newman was also writing in a Europe still dominated by Wagner's extraordinary achievement – a world in which music had attained a pre-eminence among the arts for its capacity to induce a state of spiritual exaltation, of ecstasy. The desirability of experiencing 'lofty, quintessential emotion' did not have to be argued; no-one would be expected to ask how emotion is judged to be 'lofty', nor how, when dominated by emotion, one's reason can judge that this particular lofty emotion is not second-hand or second-rate but 'quintessential'. Emotional response to 'pure beauty' had been idealised, even spiritualised, as an end in itself; the craft of music, whose devotional expressive power had been borrowed from the cathedral for the first operas, had now become itself the cathedral, the sacred object, the window on divinity, in which (in the words of Oscar Wilde) 'all subject is absorbed in expression'. Wagner, its greatest craftsman, had become an idol, an object of awe and reverence; and his theatre at Bayreuth, tended by his widow and children and by ranks of devoted adherents, had all the atmosphere and attracting power of a medieval shrine.

In imagining Wagner's successors Newman imagines future Wagners: new developments in music will be born 'out of the burning need of some great soul'. But after a hundred years in which, with its best endeavours, Western music has been unable to sanctify a successor, it has to be suspected that this species of seminal cultural hero may be extinct; that the idolisation of an original creative genius in his/her own lifetime is even against the spirit of the age. Strauss, Schoenberg and Stravinsky, while famous and revered (as well as reviled) in their different ways, never attained the supra-musical status of Wagner. And since their deaths the reverence of those who love high culture has been shifted to interpreters: to the singers, pianists, violinists and conductors that can bring the passionate assurance of the past's music back into vibrant life. The music that 'serious' music-lovers love – I mean *love* – is the music that ends with the waning of Wagner's influence in the first decades of this century. And it is this music which is the food of opera-houses as well as the concert hall.

What are the reasons for this? The theories are many; they are the subject of many books and outside the scope of this one. I have already cited the collapse of the noble *ancien régime*, and the way the bourgeois order which replaced it sought to establish its own nobility through institutions like the opera. Burke in 1790 wrote 'The age of chivalry is gone. That of sophisters, economists, and calculators has succeeded; and the glory of Europe is extinguished for ever'.[30] But he was wrong. Even medieval chivalry was an imitation; and in the First World War the entrepreneurial and competitive spirit that had built vast commercial empires and even vaster 'spheres of influence' during the nineteenth century, became transmuted into a final would-be chivalric quest – the supreme ordeal and test of would-be nobility. It was in this sense that Wagner, as I have already observed, provided background music to the war – and not only on the German side. The gay parvenu knight in armour, riding out merrily on a spring day to prove his valour, fell with his comrades and his retinue into a chasm of horror. And with him disappeared all the certainties, all the assurance, all the disembodied beauty and exaltation of the world of *Parsifal*. The glory of Romantic music is no longer ours, but it speaks, to those who are acquainted with the achievements of 'high' culture, of a past many of us hunger for: it 'brings back the golden age'. For most of us the nostalgia remains on the level of dream, though for Adolf Hitler it provided some of the inspiration for yet one more calamitous war and annihilation. Music driven by 'lofty, quintessential emotion' can, after all, be put to the service of any apparently lofty, quintessential cause.

The new singing theatre, or any other art for that matter, will never be able to compete with this, the surging nostalgic power of Romanticism. Contemporary art fails the test by the very fact of being contemporary. New composers might do well therefore to resign from any aspirations to become successors to Wagner, if it means dreaming of the same awesome mastery over massive orchestral forces, the same architectural capacity for both the broad sweep and the infinite detail, the same apparent philosophical and even religiose coherence – and the same deification by humble aspirants of culture. Like many great men, after all, Wagner was served well by historical accident. He was born at a time when it was possible to pull 'tonical' music to the furthest stretch of chromaticism while it still remained distantly attached to its tonic base. Even those without musical education can sense the power generated by such a tension. This was an unrepeatable moment in musical development, and perhaps no-one for centuries will ever be offered an equivalent opportunity.

SCHOENBERG AND STRAVINSKY

In the years just before Newman was writing Schoenberg had already started to snap the string of tonicality, letting musical sequence run free from the singable lines of melody with which modern Western music began. A concert of music by him and his pupil Berg led to a riot in Vienna in March 1913. And two months later Paris saw and heard the manifestation of another and quite different musical development; Stravinsky had emerged from the tutelage of Rimsky-Korsakov, and had begun to combine assertive dissonance with complex and urgent rhythm. The performance of *The Rite of Spring* also provoked its first audience to riot, with its manic dynamism and more or less overt sexual energy – accompanied by Nijinsky's anti-Romantic dance figures. And yet for all these primal responses by people determined to keep the nineteenth century's orthodoxies in place, the two composers were highly disciplined rebels, both applying exacting rigour to their work. Schoenberg went on to forge the principles of serialism, which provided him and his followers with a minutely organised system for establishing and developing musical material independently of tonic melody and its harmonic implications. Stravinsky brought his own fanatical sense of order to the temporal element in music; realising that music consists of the organisation of sound in time, he had to know before he began to compose exactly how long the piece was to be, and would then be joyfully engaged by the task of dividing up the available time into its sections, sub-sections, phrases and bars. If this image is not enough to show the difference in Stravinsky's temperament from that of Wagner, we should remember his contentious observation that 'music is, by its very nature, essentially powerless to express anything at all, whether a feeling, an attitude of mind, a psychological mood, a phenomenon of nature, etc.'[31]

The two lines of 'serious' musical development drawn by Schoenberg and Stravinsky occasionally intersected; late in his life Stravinsky even went through a serialist period (although influenced more by Webern than Schoenberg). A third line, determined like Strauss to draw further strength from 'tonical' music, led to Sibelius in Finland, Mahler in Vienna, and Elgar in Britain, with others absorbing special inspiration from newly collected and slowly disappearing folk-music: Dvorak, Janácek, Vaughan Williams, Bartók and, later still, Benjamin Britten. But while these various movements were thrusting forward – or back – another development exerted a steadily growing influence on the whole world of music.

PLEASING THE PUBLIC

Around the turn of the century the jolly, syncopated rhythms of ragtime began to spread from the American South to New York and Chicago. Jazz was born. And its passage across the Atlantic, along with tuneful, energetic and jazz-influenced songs from the early American musicals, received a significant boost in 1917 from the entry of the United States into the First World War. British music-hall and French variété were both invigorated by the new infusion, and the war itself, which drew millions of men out of civilian life and gathered them together in vast assemblies, had the effect, for the first time in Western civilisation, of making the concept of 'the mass of people' – urban and rural – a visible, tangible thing. Though leaders, at least in Europe, may have been animated by chivalric zeal, their men were surely not. As the glum heroes were sped up the line to death, it was not *Parsifal* but the popular songs of the day that gave them courage and good cheer; sentimentality, comic silliness and stoic irony were all represented, each of them offering a mood to help in the job of coping with a living, dying hell.

The Russian Revolution sprang directly from the convergence of masses brought together by the war, and the Bolsheviks who took over its leadership were soon ensuring that the masses had their forms of expression. The word 'popular' meaning 'of, or designed for, the people' as in Soviet Russia, took a slow leap away from the word 'popular' meaning 'designed for, and enjoyed by, the people' – as in the countries of Western Europe and North America. Designing for the people was for the communist artist something of a theoretic exercise, with the approval of the leadership being a condition of survival and the people's enjoyment being a bonus. We have already touched on the efforts of the Left in between-the-wars Germany to solve the problem of combining socialist principle with 'serious' art, and on the attempts of 'serious' artists in France to absorb the new rhythms, the new light-heartedness and simplicity, into their work as a reaction to the High art of Wagner. Meanwhile, 'designing for the people' in the non-communist West was a calculated gamble, with the people's enjoyment being the *only* condition of a product's survival. In America's depression years only a few performers like Woody Guthrie came at all close to a genuinely non-commercial popular music, drawing on the fast-fading folk, ballad and worksong traditions, and identifying in their song material with the labouring man, with the poor and the oppressed.

The introduction of radio and the growing distribution of recordings in the twenties and thirties ensured that the newly established 'popular' song product had a forum in every home. And with the invention of the talking picture in 1926 a reproduction of the narrative musical show was also put within reach of nearly every pocket. The development of endlessly reproducible music as an industry, first feeding off the popularity of singers and groups made famous in clubs and on the stage, finally reached the point where 'stars' could be made directly by radio and film, and later by television. But the only test of musical popularity in a world of free enterprise, whether on stage or film or on the airwaves, remained commercial success. And the history of commercially popular music since those days has been shaped by the development of increasingly sophisticated methods for getting new products before the public and persuading the public to buy them.

It would be foolish to claim that the commercial success of 'popular' music in the West was always and only the result of clever marketing. But since the early sixties, with the development of advanced multi-track recording techniques and a battery of electronic aids, it has now become possible to manipulate every event on a recording, every note and chord, every breath and word. Everything – personality, looks, voice quality, even sexual relationships – are subjects for management decision. Even the Guthrie tradition, carried on by Pete Seeger and others, has broadened out into just another division of the commercial market, most of its down-home honest-to-God rusticity being about as authentic as Arborite. And almost every home in North America and in Europe receives the music of its choice, for the most part from radio stations that are in the business of selling time, and so use the music as a bait to draw listeners who will then be exposed to commercial advertising. In the thirties 'popular' music became available to ordinary working people; in the sixties an enormous new market was opened up among the newly affluent and independent young. Electronic advances also made it possible to generate a high volume of sound; and so pervasive is music now in the home, in the office, on the telephone, in restaurants and bars, in the car and on the street, that laws have to be passed to protect us from its excesses. There are those who can no longer endure silence; silence is too much like death. Music gives apparent significance to many lives by accompanying them as a sound-track accompanies a film.

Paul Valéry wrote in the 1920s:

> Our fine arts were developed, their types and uses were established, in times very different from the present, by men whose power of action upon things was insignificant in comparison with ours. But the amazing growth of our techniques, the adaptability and precision they have attained, the ideas and habits they are creating, make it a certainty that profound changes are impending in the ancient craft of the Beautiful.[32]

Aldous Huxley writing in the same period noted the same profound change, but concentrated gloomily on the resulting increase in the production of 'trash'. Talent had always been rare in relationship to the total output of art. Since the output had now increased an hundredfold, and talent remains in the same static ratio to output, 'it follows...that in all the arts the output of trash is both absolutely and relatively greater than it was in the past; and that it must remain greater for just so long as the world continues to consume the present inordinate quantities of reading-matter, seeing-matter, and hearing-matter.'[33]

The question is whether what is now produced in vast quantities is trashy art, or whether it is in fact a different kind of thing altogether, a consumer commodity manufactured just like any other (detergent, bread, dress fabric, toys, cars) in order that a living may be made out of its distribution and sale. Like all these other consumer products, music is designed to supply a need or a pleasure. Like these other products, it is the subject of promotion in order to persuade consumers to buy it, and of modification in response to the response of consumers. What has happened, indeed, is that the art of pleasing people has become a science and an industry, employing psychologists, statisticians, sociologists, marketeers, graphic artists, electronic engineers, and countless other experts. The actual product is simply another variable in the complex equation.

A by-product of these technological developments has of course been the production of extraordinarily fine recordings of the classical repertoire of music. Newman has in a sense got his way: we can now listen to the works of Wagner – or of Mozart, Verdi, Berlioz or any other operatic composer – as though 'listening to impersonal voices in a darkened auditorium'; we don't even have to leave home to do it. Sound reproduction (now more and more frequently reinforced by a video image) may have created a mass consumer art, but it has also extended to everyone the power to choose his/her own background or foreground music; to indulge taste and preference without challenge.

A by-product of the new science of pleasing the public has been the adoption of its techniques by non-mass art, especially in North America: by opera companies, classical music organisations, and repertory theatres. The techniques of course have to be adjusted. The art-product commodity cannot be modified in response to consumer reaction – we cannot shorten Beethoven's Ninth because of customer complaints – but we can work hard on the exciting and self-improving aspects of the experience, and on the sense that if we miss it we are missing out on a social occasion; everybody will be there. And by restricting anything too adventurous in our programming we can in fact peddle that very experience of which Newman wrote: we shall be granted, as one of the self-chosen few, an opportunity to experience the 'outpouring of lofty, quintessential emotion'. I recently saw television coverage of an apparently full-size replica of the Egyptian Sphinx arriving by water in Toronto, in preparation for a vast performance of *Aida* planned for the 'sky-dome' arena, to be presented a couple of months later. On the dock in front of the highrise buildings of the city stood lines of operatic soldiers with their fibreglass armour pieces, their vinyl skirts flapping in the offshore breeze, while music from the opera was played. It was a 'photo opportunity', an event designed entirely for its promotional value. The commentator dutifully mouthed lines about 'Verdi's incomparable masterpiece', and the dates of its performance. This is marketing; and for an opera company with its huge costs, the high cost of such events is essential to survival.

It is in this world of art as a commodity, and of art endlessly reproduced, that the new singing theatre must make its way. As theatre it will continue to be a live art played before a live audience, though forms of it are clearly capable of reproduction on film, television and recordings. But is the new singing theatre to be 'popular' in the sense of 'commercial'? Or should we decide, like Schoenberg, that we must not expect to please a mass public? And if we do not please a mass public, are we simply in the business of organising vague emotional experiences for the over-privileged?

THE ARTIST'S DILEMMA

I remember addressing a meeting of a 'serious' composer's association in the early eighties; it was heavily weighted with academic musicians, whose output was for the most part small, worthy and self-effacing, and I decided to use the opportunity to encourage their interest in Music Theatre. 'Come and join us in the theatre, and work with us to restore music as a communicative art. We can promise you an audience, and fine artists to perform your work. All the great composers of the past have written for the singing theatre: why do you hesitate?' There was a grunt of irritation from the back, and a youngish composer called out, 'Are you asking us to prostitute our art?'

Was I? It was a good question. Whether schooled in post-serialism or rejecting it for Cage's explorations of improvisation, chance and audience-startling; whether embracing the opportunities provided by the new array of electronic devices for generating and organising sound, or incorporating non-traditional instruments, or finding new ways of playing old instruments, or incorporating staging devices into music and making pieces of 'concert theatre', these 'serious' composers like many others seemed to regard the promise of a general audience as profoundly compromising. The adoption by universities of composers (and other artists) in the last forty years has not only provided them with a better living than was ever previously available on a wide scale to the profession, but has also enabled them to look on their work as a kind of disinterested research at the frontiers of sound – research uncontaminated by commerce, and whose discoveries could be understood and appreciated only by other researchers. My contention that after eighty years of basic research it was time to apply our findings to the job of communicating with a public, focussed a few dreamy gazes. But there was a distinct feeling there (as elsewhere over the years) that this particular 'job' was neither a pleasure nor an obligation.

Once again, the problem lies in the questionable goal of 'popularity', and whether in our age of consumerism it is possible to be both popular and true. The 'minimal' music of Philip Glass is perhaps the only by-product of the post-War musical avant-garde that has appeared able to draw large numbers of people, including the 'pop'-loving young. Inspired by the repetitions of oriental music, and accompanying dazzling visual effects, Glass's pieces with or without Robert Wilson have each achieved a one-of-a-kind success, and have provided a genuinely original experience to their audience. But most composers trained in contemporary dogma will reject minimal music on the grounds of its monotonous repetitions, its simplistic harmonic progressions, and its generally formulaic, wallpapering approach to the job of filling silence with sound. And there is no question that what it requires of its performers, like it or not, is a numbing attention to the counting of beats and bars.

Walter Benjamin in his seminal essay 'The Work of Art in an Age of Mechanical Reproduction' (from which the quotations from Valéry and Huxley have been re-borrowed) talks of 'the ancient lament that the masses seek distraction whereas art requires concentration from the spectator'. A less elegiac (and less pithy!) version of this distinction might be that art-making as an industry must aim to give the largest possible number of people exactly what they want, and that if they want distraction that is what will be provided for them; whereas art-making which depends on an active dialogue with its receiver will always require concentration as a first principle, and this requirement makes it much harder to sell to a large number of people. But there are and will always be some for whom concentration is a habit and a need: people who in fact find it almost impossible to surrender to carefully calculated distraction, with their desires and wants being second-guessed by experts; like Dostoyevsky, they would rather go mad than be predictable. The determination to separate oneself and one's thoughts and feelings and desires from those of the mass, without at the same time being disdainful of the individuals who make up that mass, is the tightrope from which Huxley with his talk of trash seems to have fallen.

A PERSONAL VIEW

In this swift and gap-toothed summary of our century's changes, I have attempted to remain impartial, because we need above all to isolate a new, moderate-scaled instrument of singing theatre expression, highly versatile, and able to respond to whatever is played upon it; the choices that any particular singing theatre enterprise might make must remain open. I have suggested as a basic principle, however, that the new singing theatre should be interested in communicating with an audience, and this immediately raises all the questions about popularity that we have been considering here. And it would be against the partial spirit of this book for me not to share my own view of the priorities for new singing theatre.

It is my conviction, even my faith, that in a world that is becoming rapidly dominated by images which 'stand in' for reality, art's traditional imitation of reality – mimesis – remains a supreme obligation; and that the mounting difficulty of distinguishing between what is false and what is true needs a correspondingly mounting effort to distinguish them. In a world that concentrates daily on images, real or fictional, of the violent fight between 'good' and 'evil' – between the law and the outlaw – I believe we are remaining parasitic on an old, worn and dangerous version of morality: a morality inherited from the medieval church, and sub-sequently taken by film and then television from the old operatic melodramas of individual passion licensed at any price. The only mor-ality that cuts across ethics and esthetics is concerned with truth. From truth comes trust, from trust comes community, from community comes law. Love, I believe, is part of our nature and cannot be prescribed, but love cannot survive without trust. The difference between truth and false-hood is not part of our nature; it has to be learnt. Without it we find ourselves in a world of reflections, shadows, substitutes, decoys; we are lost and afraid. And fear turns either to withdrawal or to anger and de-struction.

One of the truths or realities we have to hold before us is multiplicity, variety. To simplify life we allow our perceptions to lie, as they select from multiplicity what they find they can deal with. We do so because it is ea-sier to function in a world of opposites, of blacks and whites, than in the actual world of slow gradation, the spectrum of change from black to white. We substitute a lie of simplicity for the truth of complexity. Polar opposites are dramatic and engaging; they are the stuff of hero-worship, of drama – and of persuasion. They engage our perceptions so strongly that it is hard to bring our intelligence to bear on what is before us, and if bombarded by contrast – or by total lack of contrast – we find ourselves abdicating from the process of thought, allowing our senses to cleave to the object in front of them instead of serving as sensors for the mind. It is the supreme form of 'distraction', drawing us away not just from our anxieties but from our very selves.

High-contrast experiences are the stuff of ecstasy. So does the ec-static state still stand as the goal of our artistic experience? Does it even stand, perhaps, as the goal of our lives? Is it what impels us to the disco, or to church, or to drugs? Are we all pursuing what in the bizarre but graphic language of America 'turns our crank'? And is all this perfectly fine? Is the alternative a drab, repressed existence, neutralised by televi-sion techniques, staring down the tube at the ecstasy of others? The yearning for ecstasy, for the experience of 'standing outside' ourselves, is clearly distractive in origin.

But it is in nuances that truth is to be found; in language which is full and subtle enough to express every detail of thought and feeling; in quiet-ness and listening hard; in steadiness of vision; in the humour that can imagine and respond to the other side of the moon; in the even subtler language of touching hands and bodies.

The energy for the superb flood of Romantic music in the nineteenth century was drawn not from notes, not from music, but from a new idea of individual liberty that burst out of Paris in 1789. Beethoven, Wagner, Verdi – all of them at a critical point in their creative lives linked their work to visions of a new humanity, to dreams of national or individual freedom, of community and social justice. For the first time art represented us as human beings under the mirror of eternity. The intoxicating cry of 'freedom' was enough to rouse these men to fervour.

Two centuries of 'freedom' have helped us to understand how different is that reality, too, from the image it evokes: and how the idolisation of the individual 'free' genius – whether railroad baron, composer or dictator – is also a debilitating distraction. The same cry of 'freedom' went up many times in 1989, as one oppressive tyranny after another – all priding themselves on having freed their people from slavery – crumbled into ruin. But there seem to be fewer dreams these days of a new apocalypse. 'Freedom' is not striding into the dawn, but is the simple, almost banal freedom to buy and to sell, to get and to spend, to move around, to read and speak truth and to resist lies. Can our music give artistic form to freedoms like this? Or will this blessedness always be outside the province of the singing theatre?

Composers who wish not to distract but to concentrate their public, and who are attracted to making things with the 'instrument' of the new singing theatre, might change their very conception of the composer's role by joining with other singing theatre artists as members of a collaborative team – with the task of exploring the world of truth and falsehood.

At their disposal is an extraordinary spectrum of musical idiom, developed from commercial imperatives, from the researches of serialists and post-serialists, from electronic experiment, from jazz and cabaret, from the music of other cultures. The test of appropriateness for the idiom to be chosen will be its ability to convey the urgency of a moral vision – and the sometimes painful truth of reality.

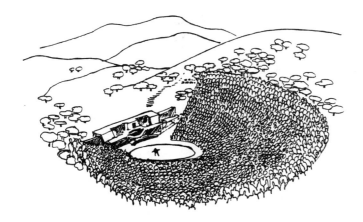

PART 4

WHAT IS TO BE DONE?

Chapter Fourteen

PHASE ONE: DISSEMINATION OF THE IDEA

History, argument, personal experience, and a bunch of more or less contentious ideas have made up the first three parts of this book. This chapter and those following are designed to strike a more practical note, laying out some of the ways in which the context of new singing theatre (from now on let us be dashing and call it NST) is now being developed and can be developed. I will take into account the fact that in spite of the initiatives that have been taken and the scores of new pieces of singing theatre created and presented each year throughout Europe and North America, NST as a movement with an identifiable set of goals, is still beginning almost from zero. It must start not with grand schemes involving large sums of money and many square metres of space, but by connecting together the people who share both a vision of the possibilities, and the talent and energy to realise them. We must be regional, national and international. We must build bridges when possible, linking with existing organisations, spaces and activities; but only if this does not mean compromising our goals. We must disseminate knowledge and ideas by many different means. And we must prefer activity to talk, measuring our progress not by mere busy-ness but by the development and presentation of new works of singing theatre, and the development of a total context for NST, from training to Music Theatre companies and audiences, which is solid and sustainable.

In proposing a collaborative, 'networking' approach to the development of NST, I am conscious that I am flying in the face of the commonly accepted archetype of change in the arts: where an individual of great talent and innovative ideas exerts his/her genius irresistibly on the medium, his/her influence and example finally leading to some kind of permanent shift in the way people experience and practise the art. Every year, almost every month, we read of the glowing new star who has become news, and audiences flock to witness his/her exciting new works. If I have not fallen in with this pattern here, it is in no way to doubt the talents of brilliant opera and musical directors and designers, of superb multi-talented singer-actors, or even of those (perhaps the most startling of all theatre artists today) in the area of multi-media and dance theatre. But – as should be clear by now – I am convinced that deploying these talents in the present world of singing theatre, whether commercial or operatic, is like painting murals on the side of the *Titanic*. What is needed is a new vessel. I also know that the desire for this fundamental change can be found throughout all areas of singing theatre activity, and that the only lack is a catalyst to galvanise, interconnect and focus the movement.

Once the changes begin, it is my conviction that many more talents within the singing theatre will find a means of expression, and that many talents that might have found an outlet elsewhere will be drawn instead to the potential of this revitalised way of making art. The stress I have placed on the importance of collaborative activity is, in fact, one way of trying to avoid the bandwagon being climbed on to by those old-fashioned, Wagnerian 'individual talents' who might see the new activity as an outlet not only for their creative skills but for their need of power and control over others.

Let us see, then, some of the steps that have been taken, and which need to be taken, if we are to realise the possibilities I have outlined.

IDENTIFYING THE CONSTITUENCY OF NEW SINGING THEATRE

Nothing can happen unless the constituency of NST is identified; indeed, there would be little point in pursuing these ideas were it not for the fact that there is already fertile ground for them. In North America, and in every country in Europe, there exist groups of professional singing theatre artists and teachers, isolated often enough in institutions or communities, who believe in the need for NST. They are not necessarily young and ardent; some are elderly and ardent. They are frustrated composers and writers, teachers who wish to change their approach to teaching young professional artists, or singer-actors who wish to be contemporary artists but lack the opportunity. They are people who love the singing theatre, but feel shackled inexorably to the status quo.

These people need only to be exposed to the ideas of singing theatre, and to the possibility that something can be done, in order to be enlisted as potential colleagues. The full list of potentially interested parties could include: young singers and actors, composers, poets and other writers, accompanists and coaches, private voice teachers, teachers in opera departments and music schools, teachers in theatre schools, young designers, producers and directors, conductors and music directors, teachers in design schools, deans of university arts faculties, arts agency personnel, regional and national, private foundations, personal managers and agents, music publishers, cultural civil servants, critics, and any lover of the arts! If this is the extensive potential constituency, how do we get to them? How do they get to us? How do we get to one another?

LECTURES, TALKS

There can be no better first introduction to the principles and potential
of singing theatre than a lively talk about it. I must confess that talking
about NST with enthusiasm and commitment has not been difficult for
me, and I have been fortunate enough to have had the chance to do so in
a number of countries, including Canada and the USA, Great Britain,
Cuba, Sweden, Finland, Norway, the USSR, Czechoslovakia, Holland
and the two Germanies.

The sparks that fly out from these occasions are gratifying. 'I have
been wanting to hear this all my life', said a distinguished British poet and
librettist. 'Wonderful', said the Russian director with shining eyes.'I will
work for it wherever, whenever, whatever', said the Finnish composer.
'A superb attack on all the imitators that fool around in our art, and a
real lesson in what we are all searching for, i.e. a fresh and honest attitude of personal artistic creativeness. Bravo!' said the Swedish conductor
in Prague.

I should stress that it is not I, but the ideas that receive this excited
response. I have found again and again that those singing theatre artists
and teachers who have once come within the orbit of Music Theatre and
committed a little time and thought to the understanding of the principles proposed here have an immediate enthusiasm for it, which they do
not lose.

But talks need to take place within some context. How do we gather
our audience together?

PROFESSIONAL CONFERENCES, MEETINGS

There are several occasions every year in every country when many of the
potential members of the NST constituency can be found in one place.
In North America the most important professional opera conferences
are those organised by the Central Opera Service and the National Opera
Association. Of course the first goal of these organisations is the survival
of the institution of opera, but being acutely aware of opera's problems
they always pay generous lip-service to the need for reform. I have even
known them to break into unruly applause when the ideas of NST are
outlined. Nothing much comes of it, but these gatherings are attended by
a large number of professionals and teachers, some of whom will always

respond – at least initially – to the idea that there might be some other future than *Tosca*.

There are also meetings of professional associations: regional, national and international get-togethers of composers, voice teachers, writers, musicians, arts administrators, and so on. All these – and particularly the first two – will contain likely candidates for NST initiatives.

Though it may not be possible to organise formal addresses to these groups, delegates can often make contributions from the floor, which can begin to focus the attentions of the meeting and attract interest among those who are already disposed to listen.

MUSIC THEATRE MEETINGS, CONFERENCES, SEMINARS

Some countries have already gone so far as to hold conferences and seminars specifically under the banner of Music Theatre. This has usually meant 'singing theatre' in all its diversity, and the meetings have generally attracted a wide spectrum of participant, from those who have come specifically to talk about the future to those who feel obliged to serve as champions for the past.

Those which have taken place since 1985, and of which I have either personal experience or knowledge, include:

MARCH 1986: MOSCOW

'The Training of the Singer-Actor': a week-long seminar/conference organised by the USSR Centre of the International Theatre Institute (ITI), co-sponsored by the Music Theatre Committee of the ITI. Attended by representatives from 22 different countries, including approximately 60 delegates and observers from across the USSR. The participants paid extended visits to the Moscow Conservatory, the Gnessin Institute and to GITIS, and then held seminars on their reactions to what they saw and heard, and on singer-actor training in general. Most evenings spent seeing performances at the Moscow Chamber Music Theatre.

APRIL 1986: STOCKHOLM

'Music Theatre Conference for Nordic Countries': a weekend seminar organised by the Royal Swedish Opera and the Nordic Music Council. Attended by 60 representatives from all five Nordic member states – Iceland, Norway, Denmark, Sweden and Finland. The objective was to develop Nordic initiatives in the area of Music Theatre. From the conference emerged a plan for three Music Theatre training meetings (see below under 'Music Theatre Training Programmes, Workshops'). Evening performance at the Royal Swedish Opera second stage.

DECEMBER 1986: MUNICH

'Music Theatre Video Workshop': a four-day seminar showing videos of an international selection of original singing theatre pieces, all produced in the previous three years. Organised by the FRG Centre of the ITI, co-sponsored by the Music Theatre Committee of the ITI. Attended by approximately 60 participants from 20 countries, including the composers and librettists of the selected works. Activities included showings and presentations by the video creators, and discussions. Evenings at the opera or theatre.

OCTOBER 1987: PHILADELPHIA

'International Music Theatre Colloquium': a four-day colloquium co-sponsored by the American Music Theater Festival, the National Institute for Music Theater (US), and the Philadelphia University of the Arts, with the participation of the ITI Music Theatre Committee. A series of lively panel discussions with names like 'Opera and Musical Comedy are Dead: Long Live Music Theatre!', 'Art and Pop in Music Theater', 'What Stories can Music Theatre Tell?' and 'Extending Vocal Techniques'. Twelve definitions of 'Music Theater' were listed in their report! Evenings spent attending events at the American Music Theater Festival (see below under 'Festivals').

FEBRUARY 1989: PRAGUE

'Meeting of principals/experts responsible for the singer-actor's education': a three-day seminar to exchange and evaluate international experiences in the area of singer-actor training, organised by the Czech ITI Centre, co-sponsored by the Music Theatre Committee of the ITI. Attended by 29 delegates from 20 countries, and many Czech observers. The sessions were mostly discussion, but included a demonstration of singer-actor training by Marie Mrazkova of Brno Conservatory. Evenings at Opera Studio performances, and at the Czech National Opera.

DECEMBER 1989: MUNICH

'Music Theatre Video Workshop': another in the series organised by the FRG Centre of the ITI, with the co-sponsorship of the ITI.

This list makes clear just how much the Music Theatre Committee of the ITI has been involved in advancing the knowledge and idea of NST. The committee has no money of any kind, but it has served as a catalyst

for many of these events, often making major contributions in planning
and organisation, and in the chairing of the meetings. All its members
have done important work in placing the ideals of NST firmly before each
group of participants: particularly Wolf Ebermann of the GDR and Poland's Professor Aleksander Bardini.

MUSIC THEATRE TRAINING PROGRAMMES, WORKSHOPS

The most effective way of giving interested people a firm grasp of the
ideas and principles of NST is for them to participate in a training and
orientation programme.

I have already described the Music Theatre Training Encounters
sponsored by the Music Theatre Committee of the ITI from 1976 to 1982.
Subsequently, at their meeting in 1986 (see above) the Nordic countries
decided to set up three Music Theatre training workshops, to take place
in alternate years: 1987, 1989, 1991. It was also decided to provide a different focus for each workshop. The following programmes were
sponsored by the Nordic Music Council.

JUNE 1987: DENMARK

The first ten-day workshop was designed for the benefit of creators. A
group of three composer-librettist teams was selected, each team providing a work or section of a work for performance. Performers were invited
to come and rehearse the works, and to join in discussions of their me-
rits and needs. The workshop concluded with a studio performance of
the pieces.

JUNE 1989: SWEDEN

The second ten-day workshop was specifically for the singer-actor. Approximately 36 performers enrolled. They were divided into two groups,
one containing 'serious' singer-actors, the other containing 'popular' or
'light' singer-actors. They had acting lessons under distinguished directors, and rehearsed and performed short pieces especially written for the
event.

INTEGRATED PROGRAMMES

WEEKEND MUSIC THEATRE WORKSHOP

Aim: to introduce Music Theatre to a wide spectrum of interested people
– professional and aspiring professional performers, composers, writers,

teachers, critics, and anyone who would like to know more about it.
Total numbers: maximum 36
Workshop leaders: director, composer, acting/speech teacher, voice
teacher
Programme: introductory talk, showings of videos;
                      split into smaller groups for sessions with
                      individual course leaders;
                      Music Theatre workshop;
                      discussion.

A programme on this model was conducted in Bristol, England, in
August 1987, organised and administered by the Department of Extra-
Mural Studies at the University of Bristol. Thirty-five people attended
from all over England and Wales. Workshop leaders were Colin Bern-
hardt, Mollie Petrie, Buxton Orr and myself – all former faculty from the
Banff Music Theatre Studio Ensemble.

TWO-WEEK MUSIC THEATRE TRAINING WORKSHOP

Aim: to provide a short but intense skill-development course for young
singer-actors, with the collaboration of composers, writers, designers.
Participants selected from applicants on basis of appropriate skills and
experience.

An international course on this model has been proposed for Alden
Biesen, Belgium, under the sponsorship of the Belgian Centre of the ITI
and the ITI Music Theatre Committee.

EXTENDED TRAINING COURSES

These are integrated programmes lasting four to eight weeks, providing
intensive training for singer-actors in singing, acting, speaking and movement, and offering opportunities for composers, writers and designers to
create pieces to be performed at the end of the programme. Participants
(total 12 performers, 3 composers, 3 writers, 2 designers) are selected on
the basis of audition and interview, and faculty includes the director,
composer-in-residence, writer-in-residence, designer-in-residence, acting teacher, movement teacher, singing teacher, coach and two
accompanists.

A four-week 'training encounter' on this model was planned for 1988
in Norway, to have been organised and funded by the Norwegian Centre
of the ITI, with the sponsorship of the Music Theatre Committee. This
was to have been the continuation of the committee's first series of training encounters. Unfortunately not enough funds could be raised: the plan
was postponed and finally cancelled.

An eight-week course on a similar model took place in Helsinki, Finland, in May-June 1989. It was organised by the Professional Training Centre of the Theatre Academy of Finland, with some participation also from the equivalent training centre for professional musicians within the Sibelius Academy. The course was superbly supported by the prime sponsor; it broke new ground, and is expected to be repeated at a future date. The Finnish teachers and participants in this first course have since established their own 'Musiikkiteatteri' association in Finland under the leadership of the fine singer and teacher, Pirkkoliisa Tikka, and have begun planning for the future.

There is no precise point at which 'dissemination of the idea' becomes implementation of it: the eight-week course in Finland clearly went further than mere information-sharing, since it also provided an intensive training experience for its participants. But to some extent all the situations listed here have been introductory, serving or capable of serving as the first impulse to a new start. And so it was in Finland in 1989.

Chapter Fifteen

PHASE TWO: BUILDING A NETWORK

As a result of the exposure that people receive in meetings and training programmes, some participants become keenly interested for the first time in the ideas and possibilities of NST, and ask enthusiastically what the next step should be. Others realise, perhaps for the first time, that their own projects and ideas are not as isolated as they had thought. At the end of conferences all these people hurriedly exchange names and addresses while running for planes, and then scatter to their homes in Oslo and Tomsk, Swansea and Arkansaw, Nicosia and Winnipeg. They tell their friends and colleagues about the exciting new ideas that they have been discussing and working with, and what sense they make, and couldn't we do something more here at home?

Unfortunately the lack of communication follow-up means that much of this initial excitement slowly fades, as actors clock back into their theatres for *Kiss Me Kate* or *The Pirates of Penzance*, or as teachers and singers find themselves having to return to their grey trudge around the prisonyard of traditional opera. 'Let's do it' segues into 'Wouldn't it be loverly,' finally transposing into 'Let's call the whole thing off'. *Opera Now* magazine comes through the post with its new glossy number: 'We will profile the singers, the conductors, the producers and the designers who make it happen, and lift the curtain on life backstage. We will usher you through the opera-houses of the world. Not least, we intend to celebrate the visual splendour and theatricality of opera...' Was it no more than a dream, that talk of a new start? Has traditional opera in the West made that quantum leap into the apparently eternal world of industrial megabucks, a line of consumer art to hang prestige advertising on? Ford, Mercedes Benz, Volkswagen, General Motors, Bell's Scotch Whisky, Shell – how can we fight their paunchy espousal of high culture? The obstacles to change seem insuperable, and life is short.

In order to halt this inevitable falling-off of enthusiasm and determination, the proponents of NST need first to take advantage of the new world we live in; making use of computer technology to build a mailing list, which will bring together the scattered constituency of interested people into an international network, and put them in touch with each other.

It has been my conviction for a long time that the Music Theatre

Committee, with its connections through the national ITI Centres to so many countries, and with its long record of service in promoting the goals of NST, should serve as the sponsor for the development of the Music Theatre network. The funds required to do the job would not be enormous, but it would certainly require funding, and it is to be hoped that one of the national centres of the ITI could sponsor the work, soliciting a specific grant for the purpose. If this proves unfeasible, then another group will have to come forward and take on the project.

Once the initial job is done, the task of maintaining, expanding and up-dating the mailing-list is a simple routine.

EXISTING ORGANISATIONS

It would be wrong to overlook the fact that there are already organisations in existence in at least three countries, which have among their objectives the promotion of Music Theatre.

USA: NATIONAL MUSIC THEATRE NETWORK (NMTN)

NMTN, based in New York, has done pioneering work in the solicitation, reading and selection of texts and scores for new Music Theatre works. It has produced a catalogue, and sponsored a competition for the best works, offering cash prizes and a production to the winners. The orientation of the network is very much in line with the NST as described here, and the organisation is run with great commitment to the cause. Unfortunately NMTN suffers from chronic under-financing, and from the familiar difficulty of raising funds for an activity that is only dimly understood. There is the additional difficulty of operating in America where the difference between 'Musical Theatre' and 'Music Theatre' is a prime source of confusion. Lacking an infra-structure of artistic as well as financial support, it operates in something of a vacuum. Nevertheless, the organisation could clearly play a role for the United States in the development of an international network, and also gain considerable benefits from the emergence of a context for its work.

USA: NATIONAL INSTITUTE FOR MUSIC THEATRE (NIMT)

NIMT's name suggests it might be, or might have been, a likely ally in the development of NST (in the autumn of 1989 it was discontinuing operations for lack of funds). It was one of the sponsors of the Philadelphia Colloquium noted above, and its leadership has a genuine interest in the development of NST. Its General Counsel in 1987 boasted an extraordinarily impressive group of names, from Harold Prince and Angela Lansbury, to Leonard Bernstein, Beverly Sills and Marilyn Horne. But its orientation – as these names show – has been dogged by the characteristic American polarisation between opera and musicals – its 'subtitle' reads: 'Advancing Opera and Musical Theatre'. The inevitable result is the marginalisation of NST.

USSR: MUSIC THEATRE ASSOCIATION

This Association was established in 1988 under the chairmanship of Estonian director Arne Mikk. A good deal of enthusiasm for the project was expressed by Soviet delegates at the ITI World Congress at Helsinki in June 1989. Good things may emerge, but I suspect that, like NIMT, it will be herding all forms of singing theatre into its fold – opera, operetta, musical comedy – and will not lay major stress on the particular needs and potential of new singing theatre as we have outlined them. It is still too early to guess what will come of it.

BELGIUM: WALPURGIS

This organisation was originally founded in order to support and to produce 'contemporary music theatre productions'. It has since developed into a somewhat more generalised service centre, programming, co-ordinating and producing projects for other organisations, including the Flanders Festival and the Flemish Theatre Institute. But in January 1990 it instituted a series of 'Contemporary Music Theatre Meetings' for professional singers, actors, dancers, scriptwriters, designers, directors and composers. Walpurgis hopes to hold these meetings every two months, and the series is planned to run to December 1991. They are also planning a series of interesting workshops, with Meredith Monk, Peter Brook, Jacques Lecocq and others. With sufficient funding, Walpurgis seemed well-placed in 1990 to make a valuable contribution to the network of new singing theatre.

Let us suppose, then, that one way or another the international network of NST has been built. What then?

Chapter Sixteen

PHASE THREE: COMMUNICATION

Our network of names, once created, will remain no more than a list until a system is developed for holding the interested group together, informing them of each others' work, and disseminating news of the many developments, happenings and ideas already afoot in the world of new singing theatre. A quarterly newsletter or magazine would be indispensable at this stage, providing a communication tool in which new singing theatre is not marginalised on the edge of opera or music or musical comedy, but becomes the central preoccupation. Computer technology would be invaluable in the preparation and publication of the newsletter.

The language of an international publication always presents difficulties. An obvious choice would be the two official languages of the ITI, English and French – if funds for bilingual production could be found. Countries wishing to translate all or portions of the newsletter into their own tongues would be welcome to do so, but would have to meet the costs. The contents would include: theoretical articles on new singing theatre; re-printing of important articles from other journals; accounts of Music Theatre events, productions, training programmes; notices of Music Theatre meetings, seminars, training sessions; courses, productions, projects; correspondence; and notices of new NST publications.

The newsletter would generate further response to the demand for dialogue and data on NST.

A CONTINUING LITERATURE

If the impetus generated by the process we have described is going to keep moving forward, the NST network needs a steady stream of articles and books to describe the methods, the experiments, the theories, and the activities of new singing theatre. What will be clear immediately to any reader of this book alone is that there are many fields of exploration which have not as yet been covered but which have been pointed *towards*. These include:

PROFESSIONAL TRAINING PUBLICATIONS

1 An Approach to Comprehensive Performance Training for the NST – Although I have outlined some of the basic principles governing the training of singing theatre artists at Banff, it is a complex matter, and needs a manual of its own, if other training programmes want to take full advantage of the experience already gained. Each area of the training also needs to be treated by individual specialists as follows:

2 An Approach to Voice Instruction for the NST – by a professional singing teacher of unimpeachable credentials and experience of new singing theatre.

3 An Approach to Movement Training for the NST – by a movement instructor with experience of working with singer-actors in a singing theatre programme.

4 An Approach to Acting Instruction for the NST – This field has been explored by H. Wesley Balk, with his book *The Complete Singer-Actor* (U. of Minnesota) and its sequels *Performing Power* and *The Radiant Performer* (also U. of Minnesota). There have been many other books designed for the opera-singer, from Stanislavsky and Chaliapin to Boris Goldovsky. For musical comedy performers there are also books that contain a great deal of value for the singer-actor – one of them being *On Singing Onstage* by David Craig (Schirmer, NY, 1978). There is also of course a large selection of books on acting, most of which are of use to the instructor of singer-actors. One of the most important recent contributions has been made by Robert Cohen with his two books *Acting Power* and *Acting One*. But it would also be valuable to see another approach made to the subject by someone with experience of a comprehensive singing theatre training programme.

5 An Approach to Text-writing and Composition for the NST – Although there are many accounts of the collaborative work of some of the most famous operatic and musical comedy creative teams, there exists no major exploratory study of singing theatre collaboration designed as a practical guide to the young composer and writer. Every collaboration has to start from the beginning, and remake the mistakes of the past. Virgil Thomson's last publication *Music with Words* (Yale, 1989) is sagacious, practical and witty about the technique of uniting the two languages. Lehman Engel's book *Words with Music* also contains some valuable material but is primarily directed to the world of the Broadway musical. There is room for an anthology containing selections from everything else that has been written on the subject by composers and writers, and by their collaborators and biographers.

6 An Approach to Design for the NST – This is another area in which there could be a useful study of the specifics of design for the 'primary act' of singing theatre, and for the specific demands of the kind of new singing theatre outlined here.

A COMPUTER LIBRARY OF TEXTS AND SCORES

Nothing is more indicative of the need for a communications network within the world of NST, than the difficulty experienced by people who wish to produce an already written Music Theatre piece. They hear of a new work by chance, and wish to look at it with a view to production; but unless it is one of the rare scores that are published, the problems are frequently insuperable. The original producer will often refer them directly to the text-writer and composer; it then turns out that the composer (who is in New Delhi this month) has not made a final score, and now has no time to complete the work; or the score and parts are in a mess, and need to be properly copied, and the cello part is missing – but no-one has the time or the money to put all this straight without a guarantee of production. In proposing interesting new pieces to producers I have often found myself having to send an untidy pile of third-generation photocopies of scribbled manuscript pages held together by a rubber-band, with a text full of alterations, and an inadequately recorded tape of a live production with more thumps than themes. Small wonder that the proposal is politely rejected – no-one can even muster the energy to wade through the forbidding mass of material. Result? Yet another performance of *The Soldier's Tale* and Walton's *Façade*, or one of the other Music Theatre stand-bys I have already mentioned – or, even more likely, the decision to revert to a tried and true (and elegantly engraved) standard work of opera, operetta or musical comedy.

One of the prime functions of the NST network, preferably in collusion with a music publisher, will be to ensure that new works of value are copied into a computer library, and thus available on demand, on a feepaying basis. News of new acquisitions would be offered in the network newsletter. And an annual catalogue would be an additional service of great value (this is the principal activity of the USA's National Music Theatre Network already referred to).

ACADEMIC STUDIES

Professional artists are not always aware of how much the development of academic study within the field of their art-form helps to sustain and invigorate professional activity. The remarkable growth of theatre in the post-War period, for example, has been backed up by a corresponding growth in the study of theatre history, theatrical theory (including semiotics) and in-depth critical and textual studies. Anyone who has directed a Shakespeare play, for example, will be aware of the immense assistance provided by the work of recent scholars. Meanwhile, others are charting contemporary theatrical developments, editing anthologies of new work, studying trends from every point of view: theoretical, historical, psychological, statistical and sociological.

Opera, and to some extent musical theatre, also have their fields of historical research and critical work. But the silver-polishing ways of the operatic industry have been reflected in the almost unquestioning assumption by students of the art that its form has already been perfected in the past. The form's development is therefore followed as a history of naivety leading finally to perfection and thence to decadence or decay. But the tradition of 'old' singing theatre looked at from the vantage point of a vital interest in NST might well yield new insights and new discoveries, which will in turn be of use and value to practitioners. There are now a growing number of scholars who show interest in Music Theatre, and it will be important that they become active members of the NST network. New singing theatre needs its keen students: theorists and historians.

MUSIC THEATRE IN SCHOOLS

No-one would imagine, I think, that the ideas of NST will transform the profession without a gradual change in commonly held assumptions about it. These assumptions are first inculcated in schools, where music and drama each have their own specialists and their own sometimes stoutly fortified bailiwick. Lone pioneers often succeed in pulling their schools' disparate forces together for a musical or operetta; and sometimes generate extremely imaginative original work, using the creative abilities of both themselves and their students. These ventures create a local stir; but there is a clear need for such initiatives to be known about more widely, and for some kind of informal methodology to serve as a guide and incentive to other teachers. It would also be valuable to start experimenting in new approaches to a more interdisciplinary study of music and drama, and recording their results, as the beginning of a more extensive revision in traditional teaching methods.

In the field of Music Theatre for young people, it is important to mention at this point the unique enterprise of Britain's National Youth Music Theatre, and of its founder Jeremy James Taylor. Taylor began to work in schools in Britain in the late seventies. He would undertake a Music Theatre project with a school, auditioning scores and sometimes hundreds of children, and selecting a company of young singer-actors. The age range would depend on the kind of school he would be working with, but his youngest performers were nine or ten, and his oldest sixteen. Taylor would then write or co-write a Music Theatre piece specifically for that group, and rehearse and present it.

So successful were these productions that in 1979 Taylor formed the 'Children's Music Theatre Company', to serve in the first place as a production agency for taking some of his productions on tour. Over the years these productions have reached more and more audiences, and are now often cast from more than one school – sometimes combining private-school and state-school children. The productions have been highly popular with audiences. They have been featured at the Edinburgh Festival, and have been televised; and tours of the company have been seen in Hong Kong, Australia and Canada. In 1987 the company was taken under the wing of Sadler's Wells, and was given its present name.

I know of no other professional Music Theatre director, writer and *animateur* who has concentrated efforts in this particular field. What Taylor's pioneering work has shown is that young children have a remarkable aptitude for Music Theatre both as singers and as actors, and that the total involvement of these young casts in their work has given many of them a powerful idea of what Music Theatre is and can be. His personality and enthusiasm, and the achievements of his company, already provide a valuable model for education. It should become an item for discussion and emulation at teachers' training colleges and institutes, as should all those pioneering Music Theatre experiments being carried on in schools throughout the world, and seldom heard about beyond the playground walls.

MUSIC THEATRE AT UNIVERSITIES, COLLEGES AND CONSERVATORIES

Those who are involved with full-time professional training programmes in university departments or professional schools, and who are concerned to move their programmes in the direction we have been discussing, are caught in the classic bind of singing theatre education. How do you educate young singer-actors for a contemporary singing theatre that has as yet no solid grounding, no embodiment? Nevertheless, there have been some developments of interest.

USA

In the late eighties a number of university departments in the United States were beginning to set up opera/Music Theater workshops, and even, at Oklahoma City University, 'The Opera/Music Theater Center of Mid-America'! The double-barrelled name generally denotes the fact that there will be some encouragement of original Music Theatre works, and that there is an opportunity for students to participate in these as well as in repertory opera. There is no question that in many cases these activities have been introduced as a result of pressure by teachers genuinely committed to reform in the patterns of singing theatre. But the name also records a certain familiar schizophrenia; the 'Opera/Music Theater Center of Mid-America', for example, is clearly still very much part of the operatic system, declaring that 'close co-operation with Tulsa Opera and other companies will help place the graduate students as apprentices, covers and comprimarios'. Where will the Music Theatre students be going?

STOCKHOLM

One interesting initiative took place a great deal earlier. As long ago as 1968, the National Music Drama School in Stockholm was set up by the Swedish Government under the direction of Lars af Malmborg. In fact the government's first plan was to integrate opera or Music Theatre training as a branch of the Drama School, and this was done in the cities of Göteborg and Malmo; but musical circles in the capital were upset by this idea, convinced that the school's musical standards would deteriorate. Thus a small 'high school' (in the sense of *École Supérieure*) was set up 'to prepare students for different forms of Music Theatre, including opera'.

In its first years the Stockholm school was loyally supported by the reigning intendant of the Royal Swedish Opera, and did some pioneering work not only in its concentration on acting and movement as well as singing, but in the areas of musical improvisation and the generating of original work, with composers working alongside the students and writing directly for them. But in 1971, after a more conservative intendant was appointed at the Opera House, support for the innovative programme began to dwindle, and singing teachers, many of whom had actually forbidden their students to attend the school during its first years, were able to combine with other traditional forces to force a major revision in the school's curriculum. It now offers a successful and entirely orthodox opera training programme, and has been renamed the 'Opera High School'.

LONDON

In the early eighties the Guildhall School of Music and Drama in London permitted a certain amount of Music Theatre experiments to develop, primarily through the enthusiasm and creative work of composer Buxton Orr, and with the support of Noelle Barker as head of the Voice Department. Unfortunately the Opera Department leadership allowed little room for these initiatives, which had to be pursued in the students' scarce free time. Nevertheless some lively pieces were created and presented. Some of this work still continues in the Junior Department of the school, under the direction of Mollie Petrie – who instituted Banff Ensemble-type Music Theatre Workshops there in 1986.

The two older professional schools in London, the Royal Academy and the Royal College were, during this same period, exploring ways of revising their very traditional and voice-focussed opera programmes, and wondering how to deal with the well-established singing teachers who were unkeen for change. The principal of one of these schools, on hearing my description of the Banff programme in 1985, said: 'Everything you are doing at Banff is what we ought to be doing, and we are doing none of it'. Changes may have since been made: I hope so.

But the Stockholm experience tells a cautionary tale. It remains to be seen how well the thrust towards NST in educational programmes can function, how much support it gets from the more traditional faculty within the programme, and how successful it will be in developing a new and different 'profile' for the contemporary singing theatre artist. All these efforts would clearly profit heartily from the establishment of an NST network, and the growth of a more visible and independent NST activity.

FESTIVALS

I have already discussed in Chapter Three the value of festivals in introducing new work and new ideas. Because of their naturally enterprising and festive spirit they can often draw a bow at a venture without falling flat on their faces. We have seen how powerfully Hindemith's festival at Donaueschingen and Baden-Baden influenced new music and new singing theatre in the late twenties, and how – more modestly – Ontario's Stratford Festival in the early 1970s was able to take an initiative apparently closed to the Toscaphiles in neighbouring Toronto.

In 1981 the Music Theatre Committee of the ITI succeeded in mounting its only International Music Theatre Festival in Rennes, France, in association with the French Centre of the ITI and the City of Rennes. The festival brought together productions by five or six companies, most of them small and somewhat under-financed. But the event was stimulating for the participants, and it is to be regretted that here was another Music Theatre initiative which came to a halt for lack of funds.

There are two Music Theatre festivals still in operation:

USA: THE AMERICAN MUSIC THEATER FESTIVAL

This festival was inaugurated in 1984, under the artistic directorship of Eric Saltzman, with Marjorie Samoff as producing manager. Originally taking place in the autumn, it is now a spring event, and instead of being compressed into a few weeks it spreads over two and a half months. This extended period makes it possible to mount a handful of original productions each year without the production staff going crazy. Five or six works of new Music Theatre are presented each year: by 1989 it had produced 25 major productions, including 18 world or American premières. Each production is given a minimum of 14 performances, and often as many as 21, or even more. The festival has also been the major force in the setting up of the American Music Theater Producers' Partnership, whose principal aim is to make the costs of Music Theatre production more feasible by sharing them among a number of production organisations. It also enables new productions to be seen in several cities.

FRG: MUNICH BIENNALE: INTERNATIONAL FESTIVAL FOR NEW MUSIC THEATRE

The Munich Biennale, under the artistic direction of Hans Werner Henze, was first held in May-June 1988. The programme contained no less than eleven works of Music Theatre. They included a *Pop-Oper*, a 'danced melodrama for soprano, bass, narrator and orchestra', '5 Small Operas (waxworks)', a piece entitled *Greek* by Berkoff/Turnage, co-produced with the Edinburgh Festival, and two pieces revived from the 1929 Baden-Baden Festival: Brecht/Weill's *The Ocean Flight* (originally *Lindberghflug*), and Brecht/Hindemith's *Baden-Baden Cantata of Acquiescence*. Both these Brecht pieces are perhaps more usefully classed as Concert Theatre, but then the Biennale's understanding of the term 'Music Theatre' appears to be less rigorous than the one I have been hewing to here. (*Lindberghflug* was originally written as a didactic radio piece for children, and the *Baden-Baden Cantata* was originally performed with a clown interlude and a short film; but both are primarily concert rather than theatre pieces.)

The Munich Biennale's first budget topped US $7 million and was underwritten by the Bavarian Government and the City of Munich. Henze's artistic contribution ensures a high standard in the selection and presentation of the programme, and the future of the festival looks promising.

OTHER FESTIVALS

There are of course many festivals which include Music Theatre pieces in their programmes; among them the Edinburgh Festival, Avignon, Guelph (Ontario), Lake George Opera Festival (New York) and the Holland Festival. There are also festivals which were originally built around the work of one composer or creative team, in the Wagner tradition though usually not with the same rapt concentration on the founder's work. The Aldeburgh Festival (Britten/Peter Pears), and the Spoleto Festivals in Italy and Charleston S. Carolina (Menotti) are in this category, as well as the recently established Peterborough Festival near Toronto, whose main focus is the music and Music Theatre works of its founder and artistic director R. Murray Schafer. It was here in 1988 that the first full production was given of Schafer's *The Greatest Show*, involving forty different pieces performed more or less simultaneously in separate 'booths', in the atmosphere of a medieval fair. Over a hundred participants were involved, and needless to say Schafer made considerable use of amateur resources to stage the massive work.

There is no question that festivals bringing together the productions of different Music Theatre groups, and providing opportunities for singing theatre artists to see each others' work and to discuss their experiences and goals, will be of major importance in the development of the NST network and the growth of production activity. Unfortunately, until NST is more firmly established, large-scale funding (as has so far been available for the Munich Biennale, and to some extent for the American Music Theater Festival) will continue to be difficult to attract. In fact a useful model for NST festivals if we are to see them proliferating is the so-called 'fringe festival' which has become a major event in the cities of Western Canada and is celebrated as a kind of free-and-easy carnival of theatre entertainment. Founded in Edmonton, Alberta, in the mid-1980s, the fringe festivals now operate also in Winnipeg, Vancouver and Victoria. They offer straight plays, dance, dance theatre, multimedia works, performance art works, and musicals, contributed by groups from all over the world, and performed in bewildering profusion, all day and most of the night. Each show generally lasts no more than an hour, and many have small casts. Admission fees are controlled by the festival and in 1989 were set at a maximum of $7 (Canadian). Groups are accepted on a first come first served basis, and pay an initial fee. They are offered locations without charge, and then can take the box office proceeds. The need for swift turn-around between one show and the next at each location means that design elements are light and basic.

These festivals are magnificent opportunities for small groups to present themselves, offering their work to an enthusiastic and interested audience – in which not a single diamond tiara has ever been spotted. One has only to imagine a similar festival devoted to new singing theatre to realise how far away NST still is from the directness, the flexibility, the abundance – and the sheer democracy – of such an event.

Chapter Seventeen

PHASE FOUR: CREATION AND PRODUCTION

There would be little point in suggesting a right way or an only way for NST to be realised as a thrivingly creative activity. Work in the field is continuing all the time with differing originality and success. Conditions vary from country to country and from region to region. All over the Western world NST productions are being created and performed each year, in opera departments, musical theatre departments and opera and theatre companies, in festivals and workshops – and also in 'Music Theatre' companies, although (as we have seen) those two words side by side in the name of a company do not always mean 'new singing theatre' in the sense I have given it in this book. The US Central Opera Service bulletin (a most valuable document, meticulously assembled by its editor Maria Rich) lists 'new operas and premières' both in North America and Europe, and even in Australia, and now includes 'music theater works' in the list. A first glance suggests a healthy state of affairs. But further examination reveals that (for reasons we have already explored) only a very few opera-houses are investing serious effort and funding in new work; that only one, two or three performances are given of most new works; that the scale of financial commitment to new works in comparison with the main programme of grand opera looks in many cases like tokenism; and that even the small companies seriously concerned with new work are limited in numbers of performances. In fact, the Central Opera Service's staunch recognition of Music Theatre activity has the effect of emphasising even more strikingly its marginal nature.

I repeat my refrain: without the 'total context of new singing theatre', these initiatives will continue to lack relevance and sustainable support. What is recognised by the proposal for an NST network is that just as opera is a multinational industry, with four centuries of tradition, a pile of real estate and acres of glossy coverage to prove it, so new singing theatre needs to emphasise its international links, its emerging identity as a 'primary' art-form, its emphasis on collaboration and original creativity, and its opportunity – once separated from the other art forms on which it is now so often parasitic – for an energising integrity and openness, and a voice in society.

So there are countless solutions to the question of how Music Theatre ensembles and enterprises are created. In the professional field the initiative may come from a composer-writer team, from a group of singer-actors who wish to develop a collaborative project, from a theatre company, art gallery or festival, or from a producer or a community interested in offering support for a ground-breaking project. In the educational field the impetus may be provided by a university department or professional training institution, or by a school. The great advantage of NST is that its scale is as flexible as the scale of theatre or dance: one, or two, or three performers may be gathered together in the name of Music Theatre, and still be capable of presenting a coherent work.

I have already described how our NST network could assist in the selection of works by offering a score and text service. But since the prime aim is for the creation of original work, the first priority where possible would be the location of suitable creators, and the provision of an opportunity for them to plan and write new works – either in isolation or in collaboration with a group of singer-actors. Commissioning funds are therefore a necessity, and one of NST's tasks will be to locate or generate sources for this funding. It is worth remembering that the scale of fees offered for the creation of a full-scale opera ($40,000 US is an average figure for a composer of distinction in North America – out of which is paid the librettist's fee: copying costs are often a further charge) bears little relation to a reasonable fee for a short work with a small cast and small orchestra. Any funding agency accustomed to opera fees will therefore look with pleasant surprise at the modest sums involved. And even schools and universities, with their traditional penny-pinching constraints, should find themselves able to allocate funds for the purpose – if indeed they cannot twist a resident composer's arm with no more than the promise of a production.

These individual production projects will be a necessary part of the growth of NST. The process in all its variety will produce works good, bad and indifferent, but quantity as in everything is a necessary prelude to quality: 'experiment' and 'experience' are the same word in French, and for good reasons. The important factor will be the discovery and fostering of talent, the provision of opportunities for it to be shared with an audience, the developing sense of new singing theatre's potential as a vehicle of expression, and experience gained for the future.

THE END OF THE BEGINNING

In Chapter Five I described a concept for a new singing theatre company:

...six or eight singer-actors, a resident composer and writer, and access to others. The company will be housed in a medium-sized theatre building (or will share it with a drama company) and will present a wide range of new work, from accessible pieces to more challenging ones. Its productions will be transportable, and will frequently be exchanged with those of companies in other towns or cities...

It is difficult to see reasons why a community could not sustain a Music Theatre company of this scale and type. Cities which at present support an 'Opera Association', and mount two or three performances of two or three operatic chestnuts each year, could for far less investment support a company that could put the city 'on the map' in a way that 'instant opera' will never manage. Productions with area schools, cabaret, pageants...the resources would all be there.

But the eventual outcome of an independent and sustainable NST will be something even more ambitious: nothing less than the creation and sustaining of a 'national' Music Theatre company, into which the finest resources of talent, energy, and originality are fed, and which could serve as the flag-ship, the beacon of a national 'new singing theatre'. If such a theatre, properly led and funded, became a reality, then 'new singing theatre' itself would become a reality, and the new road I have been marking out and urging us along would have turned a corner into a whole new province of possibility.

Once again, there is no prescription for the form such a company might take. But I have already made reference to the Moscow Chamber Music Theatre Company founded and directed by Boris Pokrovsky, and I would like to leave you with a picture of what I believe to be the most important 'new singing theatre' company in the world today.

A MODEL FOR NEW SINGING THEATRE: THE MOSCOW CHAMBER MUSIC THEATRE COMPANY

Boris Pokrovsky, who made his reputation as Director of Productions at the Bolshoi Opera, has written about some of the reasons for leaving the Bolshoi and founding his company in 1972; and since many of his words strike familiar chords for the Music Theatre movement, it is worth quoting them in full:

Chamber opera is a unique form of art. Its particular qualities have great advantages, its possibilities are limitless.

The nature of opera lies in its combination of two arts, theatre and music: arts which are very different from each other in the way they are formed, the way they are presented, and in the way their special qualities are to be perceived. Music took upon itself the task of throwing light on drama: on the concrete movement of events, on human character – on everything which adds up to the purpose of theatre art, and which had not previously been part of the material of 'free' music. So theatre in its turn agreed to absorb the rules of music into the conventions of the stage. Music became concrete, taking on a material essence so to speak, while theatre took on an intensity of feeling not available to other dramatic arts. The art of opera was born, an amazing synthesis of the particular and the general, of internal and also visual experience, of melody-harmony, of timbre, of rhythmic factors and action.

The birth of opera took place in Florence in the sixteenth century. The circle of people who loved the new art was called *Camerata*, from the word *camera* – meaning the 'chamber' or 'room' where the opera was performed. A small orchestra, and not a great number of performers or audience: these were the conditions in which opera was born.

Of course a narrow circle of spectators can today convert this art into a gourmet's delight, but...how much potential there is here for fruitful creativity, where the conditions allow direct relationship between the music and the audience in the search for truth.

Opera suffered greatly because the singing-actor was forced into big settings with a fixed position for the orchestra, the footlights and the backstage, forcing sound and gesture to develop a pretentious intensity of stage action. In these conditions 'beautiful singing' loses credibility, sacrificing the pursuit of expressive voice colour, and thus compromising the dramatic situation and the portrayal of character.

When there is direct intercourse with the audience we have not only the establishment of genuine feelings and of an aesthetic response to music, singing and action, but also the means of piercing the actual 'mechanics' of human emotions, which are accessible only through music.

None of this, of course, denies the monumental spectacle of 'grand opera': but it opens up yet another possibility in the wonderful effect operatic art can have on an audience.

In Russia chamber opera came to an end, practically speaking, in the nineteenth century. The idea of restoring it to the stage arose out of my attempts to overcome the stereotyped attitude to the nature of opera, an attitude still strongly rooted in the past in spite of the efforts of progressive artists. The essence of opera, its music and singing, has become a fetish activity, which in turn has led to a transformation of the operatic 'synthesis': on the one hand a loss of the theatrical, scenic and referential properties of operatic music, and on the other hand the irresponsible splitting up and destroying of the opera composer's musico-dramatic ideas by the stage director. In short, it became necessary to oppose everything which destroys the miracle-working union of *music* and *theatre*. This is more possible and perhaps easier to achieve in a new theatre space than in theatres of pompous-monumental type, which are tightly hobbled not only by sacred traditions but also by routine.

What future do I see in the theatre of chamber opera? I see the creation of a contemporary repertoire – contemporary both in Music Theatre forms and in content. And the classical? It also is a partner in our purposes, since the geniuses of the past always bring us eternal human feelings. It is important to treat the score in a contemporary way – but with the utmost respect. Freed from *clichés* of stage presentation, the performers' feelings find what is necessary to break the chains for creative work, and the director finds boundless possibilities for making music dramatically effective.[34]

The Moscow Chamber Music Theatre (MCMT) has been housed for most of its existence in a converted cinema. You entered through glass doors at the corner of a large building, and after finding your tickets and going through the Russian cloakroom ritual you walked through the lobby, where refreshments were served at intermissions, and down two flights of stairs to reach the basement auditorium. The room was 20m (65ft) wide and 30m (98ft) long, bare, gently raked towards the stage, and seating between 200 and 250 people – depending on the configuration.

The productions I saw during my visit in 1986 made many different uses of the space. For *The Rostov Incident* (see p. 73) the seats were turned to face in to the centre of the hall, along which a ramp led from below the stage to the back of the auditorium. Much of the action was staged along this ramp, and the good and evil angels often sang from behind the audience on the sides of the hall. The stable was on the stage, and Hell in the orchestra pit: there was no orchestra, the whole piece being sung *a capella*, with pitches occasionally provided by a stringed instrument.

Other pieces were staged more conventionally, but the space taken up by the orchestra pit was often bridged by ramps and stairs, thus bringing the action over the orchestra and close to the audience. Orchestra members, suitably costumed, sometimes entered the action.

Of the many remarkable features of that week of performances, three still stand out in my memory. First was the quality of the singing and acting: these were true singer-actors, with fine vocal instruments but with a commitment to text and character, and to the different energy of each production, that was unique in my experience. The second was the manner of casting; the principals in one production became servants or even stage extras for the next. And the third was the enthusiastic involvement of the orchestra in the stage action; their playing seemed so much

a part of the total effect, so theatrically motivated and so personally committed.

In its first eight years of operation, one brochure told us, MCMT had
given a thousand performances both in Moscow and on tour in other
cities, attended by three quarters of a million people. International tours
had included the GDR and FRG, Finland, Italy, Austria, Greece, Czechoslovakia and Hungary, Bulgaria and Yugoslavia. The wide public
exposure suggested that in spite of its cramped home theatre, this company's work was no 'gourmet's delight', but had played to large and
clearly appreciative houses everywhere. 'Our theatre has been created
by the public, its artistic needs and creative interests', the brochure told
us in meandering English: 'The dialogue between the theatre and public
is the meaning and pledge of successful activity of everyone and all of us
taken together as a collective body of persons holding the same views'.
This statement, stitched together when glasnost and perestroika were no
more than gleams in Gorbachev's eye, conveys more sense of politics than
of art: we could imagine how easily the company's work could be attacked
on the grounds of its small, and therefore élitist, nature. But there was no
question of the public's interest; every performance we attended was full,
and we were told – and saw no reason not to believe – that this was so
wherever they went.

By the time we had seen three productions at MCMT, I had the growing realisation that this was not just another opera house, but that it was
indeed a unique model for an NST company. It was bigger, I felt sure,
than most Western nations would consider affordable for Music Theatre;
there were 98 staff members in the company in 1981, including 29 singer-
actors and 20 orchestra on year-round contract, and these numbers had
grown since. But if we were to compare the costs of such an organisation
in such a theatre in the West, to the costs of an opera company in an
opera-house, I wondered whether the differences would be so great.

I determined to find out as much as I could about the workings of
the company on that first visit, and had an opportunity to talk briefly with
Pokrovsky, sitting over chicken Kiev in the smoky, lively dining-rooms of
the Actor's Union, the day before our departure from Moscow:

MB: Do you like the theatre you are in?

Pokrovsky: It's not satisfactory. We need far more room for rehearsals, good dressing-rooms etc.

MB: But the hall itself, do you like it? It seems to me an interesting
space, and very effective in the ways you use it – even though it's an
improvised theatre.

Pokrovsky: Yes, as I've used it more and more and found ways to solve its problems, I've become more fond of it. I feel young directors should be given this kind of space to work in, to make them ingenious.

MB: Do you use many different designers in your theatre?

Pokrovsky: When I started, I used my friends from the Bolshoi Opera, but they did not have the same kind of vision as I, and did not feel at home in our theatre. So I now use younger designers. The productions you have seen have been mostly designed by the props and costume staff of the theatre.

MB: Is there any formal connection between your training programme at GITIS and the company?

Pokrovsky: No, not at present, though I would like to see it. Sometimes I use final-year students at GITIS to play small roles, and if I know of an exceptionally good performer at GITIS I am obviously in a good position to hire him or her. But there are not enough positions for everybody.

In 1989 in Prague I met with Pokrovsky again, and asked for more time with him. Imagine us, after having seen a performance of quite splendid ghastliness at the Czech National Opera, sitting in a huddle with two interpreters in a dark, cavernous bar off the main lobby of the Hotel International. It is 10.30 on a wet February night, and (this still being communist Prague) the bar is, of course, closed. Imagine Pokrovsky, a tall man of 75 or close to it, hair white and receding, nose as sharp as a pen and almost as long, and eyes so blue and so piercing that his fanatical devotion to theatre seems to look sometimes like a divine madness.

MB: When was MCMT founded, and how many works do you present each year?

Pokrovsky: Moscow Chamber Music Theatre Company has been established 17 years. In that time we have done 32 contemporary works.

MB: How many works are in the MCMT repertoire at any time?

Pokrovsky: Ten, of which two or three are new in any season. At the moment, we operate in poor conditions, and can introduce no more than these two or three into the repertoire each year. When we move into our new house in a year's time, we shall be able to do more.

MB: Do you commission works from composers?

Pokrovsky: Not often. I have had bad experiences with composers. They don't like to change things, and when they do things always turn out worse. I prefer to take a finished work. But just now I have had a meeting with a young composer, Weinberg, about his new opera based on Dostoyevsky's *The Idiot*. He had written it for a big orchestra, but I asked him to reduce it to a string quartet. Weinberg agreed.

I also proposed cutting three scenes, and he agreed. We shall be doing it in the next two years.

MB: Is there any training for composers in the USSR?

Pokrovsky: There is no training for opera composers, and no system of developing their skills. And there are almost no theatres who will take the risk of doing new work. In Leningrad, though, there are many young composers who want to compose operas...

In a big theatre like the Bolshoi, the audience trusts the composer. In a small theatre like ours, the audience trusts the theatre. They believe in it, and they will come even if they don't know the work, or the composer.

At the Bolshoi the audience will know what to expect, even if they are there for the first time. At MCMT, at the beginning they were surprised – they saw something original. But now they come *expecting* something surprising and original; they *expect* it will be always different. Usually I do original works of chamber opera, but occasionally I do something like *Don Giovanni*. And you know, it is a funny thing I have noticed; when I do a work, no one else seems to want to touch it. No one is now doing *Don Giovanni*, and it was the same with Shostakovitch's *The Nose*.

MB: What is the power of critics in Moscow?

Pokrovsky: The critics have a *conjunctura*, a trend, and at the moment the agreement is to say that MCMT is good: we are considered 'modern' and modern is considered good.

But I trust the box office. I always ask which production sold out for the first performance – and which sold out for the last performance.

I know myself which productions should be in the repertory for two or three years, and which should be there for ever. *Don Giovanni*, *The Rake's Progress* – these should be there for ever.

But our audience will always buy tickets for a new production first. If it is sold out, then they will buy the repertory production.

MB: How many singer-actors do you have in the company?

Pokrovsky: Thirty soloists, of which five are on short term contracts of three years; twenty-five are permanent.

MB: Does that mean they can't be fired?

Pokrovsky: Yes.

MB: What if they have a drinking problem, for example?

Pokrovsky: Well yes. But if someone has a drinking problem, there is a long process of inquiry. Everyone wants to know why he is drinking. There are hearings, union problems. And of course there is a camaraderie – the other company members side with him. It's very complicated and difficult.

MB: We have just seen a production in which most of the soloists are over 50. [Smetana's *The Brandenburgers in Bohemia* at the Czech National Opera.] With lifetime contracts at the MCMT, can you see that this will eventually be a problem for you?

Pokrovsky: Possibly. I think about it. And so do the soloists: they know they can age in the company. But it is a different kind of company. There are only thirty of them, and no extras. And the system is that one day a performer plays a principal, next day chorus, next day he may be simply in a dance, and the next day be just a stage hand, helping to move scenery. So when an actor who plays Don Giovanni can no longer play the role, he can still be a servant – not Leporello, but maybe a servant who simply hands a letter to the Don.

MB: Was it hard for the performers to accept the non-star system at first?

Pokrovsky: It was difficult to accept for some, but I just told them how things were going to be.

MB: Do the performers have any say in the creative policies of the company?

Pokrovsky: There is an elected group of ten who represent the company. They serve for two years. The latest group is very active and 'democratic'. This has been the same in all theatres, and it is the reason why some had to close – they were too democratic to accept an artistic director. But then they got a new idea – that theatres need a leader.

MB: What is the basis for salary payments? Is everyone paid the same?

Pokrovsky: There is a seniority system. Those who came more recently to the company are paid less. But now, in the last two years, there has been an experimental system, giving companies more financial freedom to pay people by other methods.

MB: How do you receive your subsidies from the government? Do you have to apply, and submit a written budget?

Pokrovsky: Yes, there is a subsidy each year. The amount you get depends on the manager. Right now I have a good manager, and so they give us a good subsidy. When we did *Don Giovanni* we went a long way over budget. But the manager went to see them and they gave us back all the money we had overspent! They offer us some money, and the manager goes from office to office saying 'Professor Pokrovsky will not be very happy with this' – and they give us more! Just now we have a lot of money. I can't quite understand why. There was a big meeting a year ago which brought together the trade unions, the party, and the city, and since then we have been getting more. Artists are better and better paid. I don't think it's all to the good. Why should they be so rich? Better to use the money on designs, or musical instruments, rather than on salaries. But I was persuaded. Artists are never satisfied. However, one of them said: if it's necessary for the good of the company, he would give all his extra money to the theatre – and they all agreed they would do the same.

MB: What is the size of the orchestra?

Pokrovsky: Twenty-seven permanent members – and for some productions we add others as guests when needed. *The Nose* needs twelve percussion players in some passages, and we couldn't afford this, so the violinists and wind instrument players all put down their instruments during these passages, and come and play alongside the percussionists.

I felt we had gone on long enough, and started to bring the interview to a close, but he said:

'There is one important thing I want to say. We do have problems with the company, which stem from the fact that some performers perform more than others. It is difficult to explain it by saying that some performers are better than others, although this is the truth. And the problem is made worse because every few months, according to the state system established, performers are paid bonuses, and the size of the bonus depends on the number of performances each has given. Of course this leads to bad feeling.

Orchestra members are also unhappy when they do not perform, but of course they are not always needed, and they understand this. They love wearing costumes and make-up, and being part of performances.'

Boris Pokrovsky, although dynamically and sardonically alive, is an old man. There is little doubt that only his high distinction in the USSR saved this highly unconventional enterprise from extinction during the Brezhnev years, and that with his retirement or passing the company would have been summarily dismantled. But in the new Russia, as we learn from these remarks, the attitude to his work is changing. He has as much money as he needs for production, and the company is being moved into more accommodating premises. As Soviet Russia begins its gradual and painful return to the world community, the Chamber Music Theatre Company is one bright spark of modernity and courageous originality in a society long starved of such things.

Could it be, that the extraordinary contribution made by Russia through Diaghilev in the world of dance is going to be finally echoed by Pokrovsky's in the world of new singing theatre?

EPILOGUE

This book, as you see, is open-ended. Our road makes no claim to lead to a new Jerusalem of singing theatre. The aim has been simply to bring us to a vantage point from where we can survey various ways to go forward.

The development of a 'context' for NST will not solve anything of itself. But by separating the primary elements of our art from their crust of tradition, we give ourselves a chance to begin again. And by embracing within our creative processes the principle of collaboration, we have a chance – like scientists – to profit from the work of others, to exchange and improve ideas, and to offer mutual support and encouragement.

Things are moving fast, and I have little doubt that by the time these words appear in print, some of the proposals contained here will have become a reality. Companies and festivals and educational programmes will come and go. New centres of activity will emerge, new and unexpected initiatives will be launched. The changes wrought in Eastern Europe during 1989 have rivalled those of two hundred years earlier, and will affect us all.

Meanwhile, communications technology will continue its resistless changing of the world and of the minds of an increasing majority of the world's population. Live art will become more and more a rehearsal for the electronic immortality of the video-machine, taking its modest place in the vast rush of distractive commercial product.

The primary act of singing theatre contains within it the capacity to express primary human experience, for it takes place on the border between objective and subjective reality. Singing can save it from its attempts to reproduce truth photographically – 'scientifically' – because singing injects imagination and personal 'bias' into truth. And, by the same token, truth will save singing from its evasion of the real, from its capacity to distract us, to blow us away.

Robert Warshow in his classic book of criticism *The Immediate Experience*, talks about the 'problem of communication' in modern life, and suggests that 'the chief function of mass culture is to relieve one of the necessity of experiencing one's life directly.' He goes on to say that it is 'only through an effective vocabulary – that is, through "valid" emotional, moral and intellectual responses expressible in language – that we can truly know what we do and what happens to us'.[35]

The whole spectrum of language combinations that lie between speaking and singing, and the vast potential of different kinds of music linking with the human voice and with human thought and action, are of little value to us, unless they can become a vocabulary for understanding our own experience. Language is not changed by grammarians, but by its resourceful and creative users. New singing theatre needs now to confront the human condition, and to stretch its ways of expression to help us understand and act upon our own times.

NOTES

1. Hauser, Arnold, *The Social History of Art* (Vintage Books, NY), vol. 4, p. 104.

2. ibid., pp. 103-4.

3. *Architectural Design*, vol. 48, nos 11-12, 1978, p. 10.

4. Peter Hemmings, General Director, Los Angeles Music Center Opera, 1987.

5. Table from the Annual Report of the Royal Opera House, Covent Garden, 1987-8.

6. Bruce Crawford, General Manager, Metropolitan Opera, 1987.

7. Ardis Krainik, General Manager, Chicago Lyric Opera, 1987.

8. Willett, John, *The Theatre of Bertolt Brecht*, (Methuen, London, 1967 edition), p. 128. I am indebted to this enormously useful book, and to Willett's indispensable anthology of *Brecht on Theatre*, for much of my information on Donaueschingen and on Brecht's thoughts about Music Theatre.

9. ibid., p. 130.

10. ibid., pp. 130-1.

11. Willett, John, trans., *Brecht on Theatre* (Methuen, London, 1964), pp. 131-2.

12. ibid., p. 34.

13. Austin, W.A., trans., *Esthetics of Music*, (Cambridge, 1982), p. 100.

14. After McNeff left us in 1985 to be the last Artistic Director of COMUS Music Theatre in Toronto, Buxton Orr became my splendid associate director for one winter and took over Steve's duties in conducting as well as composing. Among Buxton's many stimulating contributions to our work was the proposal that our Music Theatre pieces should be composed in such a way that they did not, in fact, need a conductor; that singers – and instrumentalists – should be encouraged to keep in time by ear rather than by eye, and to take responsibility for their own dynamics.

15. *The Correspondence between Richard Strauss and Hugo von Hofmannsthal* (Cambridge, 1980) p. xix.

16. Cornford, trans., *The Republic* (OUP, NY) section 400a.

17. Ricks, C., & Michaels, L., eds, *The State of the Language* (University of California, 1989).

18. Dent, E., *Foundations of English Opera* (Cambridge, 1928; repr. Da Capo, NY, 1965) p. 53.

19. Schmidgall, G., *Literature as Opera* (OUP, 1977), p. 10.

20. Auden, W.H., 'Notes on Music and Opera' in *The Dyer's Hand* (Faber, 1964) p. 470.

21. ibid., pp. 471-2.

22. Auden, W.H., 'The World of Opera' in *Secondary Worlds* (Faber, 1968) p. 102.

23. Rosen, Charles, *Schoenberg* (Collins, 1976) pp. 59-60.

24. Diva, *Summer* 1986, vol. 9, no. 3.

25. *New Yorker*, July 3, 1989, pp. 79-94.

26. *Ensemble Diary No. 7*, Banff, 1985.

27. Newman, Ernest, *Wagner as Man and Artist* (Knopf, NY, 1924) p. 325.

28. ibid., p. 325.

29. ibid., pp. 371-2.

30. Burke, Edward, *Reflections on the Revolution in France* (Everyman, London, 1910) p. 73.

31. Hartog, H., ed., quotation from Stravinsky's *Chronicle* in *European Music in the Twentieth Century* (Routledge, 1957; revised Penguin, 1961), p. 66.

32. Valéry, Paul, trans., *Aesthetics*, 'The Conquest of Ubiquity' (Manheim, New York, 1964) p. 225.

33. Huxley, Aldous, *Beyond the Mexique Bay* (1934, 1949 edn) pp. 275-6.

34. Prospectus on Moscow Chamber Music Theatre, 1975.

35. Warshow, Robert, 'American Popular Culture' in *The Immediate Experience* (Atheneum, NY, 1975) pp. 38-9.

ACKNOWLEDGEMENTS

I wish to express my thanks to the following publishers and authors for permission to use copyright material: Routledge (London) and Alfred A. Knopf Inc. (New York) for two quotations from Arnold Hauser's *A Social History of Art*; The Estate of Ernest Newman (UK) and Alfred A. Knopf Inc. (New York) for permission to quote from Ernest Newman's *Wagner as Man and Artist*; John Willett and Methuen (London) for quotations from John Willett's *Brecht on Theatre* and *The Theatre of Bertolt Brecht*; the University of California Press for a quotation from Peter Conrad's *Romantic Opera and Literary Form* (Copyright © 1977, The Regents of the University of California), and also of material from my essay 'No Opera Please – We're British' in *The State of the Language*, edited Ricks and Michaels (Copyright © 1989, The Regents of the University of California); Faber and Faber (London) and Random House (New York) for quotations from W.H. Auden's *The Dyer's Hand* (copyright © 1962, W.H. Auden) and *Secondary Worlds* (copyright © 1968, W.H. Auden) both reprinted by permission of Random House Inc.; Cambridge University Press for quotations from Carl Dahlhaus' *Esthetics of Music*, from Edward Dent's *Foundations of English Opera*, and from the introduction to *Correspondence between Richard Strauss and Hugo Hofmannsthal*; Oxford University Press for a quotation from Gary Schmidgall's *Literature as Opera*; The *New Yorker* for the excerpt from Ethan Mordden's article ' "Showboat" Crosses Over' (Reprinted by permission; © 1989 Ethan Mordden. Originally in the *New Yorker*).

I would also like to thank a number of friends and colleagues for reading all or part of this book in manuscript, and for their useful comments and corrections. They include Dominick Argento, Noelle Barker, Colin Bernhardt, Wolfgang and Joanna Bottenberg, Bill Clarke, Wolf Ebermann, Joan Lyndon, Patrick Lyndon, Glen Montgomery, Buxton Orr, Yuri and Holley Rubinsky, Florence Staples and Michael Whitfield. Responsibility for the book in its final form is of course mine alone.

I am grateful to The Bristol Press for their initial belief in *The New Singing Theatre*; to Bristol's Jane Rowe for taking on the project midstream and pulling it ashore; and to Jeffrey Bishop and his colleagues at Oxford University Press in New York for their sustained enthusiasm and support.

I must thank my dear friend and colleague of many years, Susan Benson, for undertaking the illustrations.

Finally, in spite of all differences, I owe a debt of deep gratitude to the Banff Centre and to the Ministry of Advanced Education, Alberta, Canada, for the extraordinary opportunities opened for Music Theatre at Banff during the eighties, and for the extended sabbatical leave (1987-8) which enabled me to get this project under way.

M.B.

INDEX

Coq d'Or, Le 56
Cosi Fan Tutte 150
Covent Garden 24, 42, 47
Crabbe, George 151
Craig, David 199
Crawford, Bruce 220n6
Crazy Horse Suite 119, 120
Cuba 189
Czech National Opera 191, 214, 216
Czechoslovakia 189, 191, 213
d'Avenant, Sir William 154
da Ponte, Lorenzo 150
Dahlhaus, Carl 116, 153
Dalcroze, Jacques 54
Dark Tower, The 119
Dartington Hall, Devon, UK 53
Davies, Peter Maxwell 11, 173
Day Lewis, C. 119
Death in Venice 43, 156
Debussy, Claude 25, 51
Delsarte, François 51
Denishawn School of Dance 52
Denmark 190, 192
Dent, Edward 155, 221n18
Derain, André 51
Deutsches Staatsoper, East Berlin 28-9
Deverell, Rex 129
Devin, Lee 88, 117
Devon, UK 126
Diaghilev, Serge 50-1, 55-7, 217
Diogenes 156
Doctor and the Devils, The 118-19
Doctor In Spite of Himself, A 119
Don Giovanni 150, 215, 216
Donaueschingen Festival, Germany 57, 204
Donizetti, Gaetano 168
Doolittle, Quenten 120, 129
Dostoyevsky, Fyodor 183, 214
Dresden 24, 29, 30, 34
Drury Lane 24
Dumas, Alexandre, père 19, 150
Dumas, Alexandre, fils 150
Duncan, Isadora 50, 51
Dvorak, Anton 178
Ebermann, Wolf 192

Edinburgh Festival 47, 202, 206
Edmonton Fringe Festival 126, 206
Edmonton, Alberta 206
Eight Songs for a Mad King 11-12, 173
Einstein on the Beach 8
Elektra 165
Electrification of the Soviet Union, The 8, 151
Elgar, Edward 178
Encompass Music Theatre Company, NY 4, 71
Engel, Lehman 53, 83, 151-2, 199
England 8, 18, 24, 32, 154, 160, 169, 193
English Music Theatre Company 4, 71, 72
English National Opera 43, 45, 88
English Opera Group 4, 47
Enlèvement de l'Europe, L' 59
Eritrea 156
Ernst, Max 51
Essyad, Ahmed 78
Ethiopia 156
Euba, Akim 76
Eugene O'Neill Center, Connecticut 47
European Opera Studio 88
Everyman 48
Exiles 48
Façade 200
Falla, Manuel de 51
Falstaff 154
Felsenstein, Walter 2-3, 6
Ferguson, John 89
Finland 30, 178, 189, 190, 194, 213
Finnish Music Quarterly 30
Finnish Music Theatre Association 194
First Dayes Entertainment, Rutland-House 154-5
Flanders Festival 197
Flemish Theatre Institute 197
Florida 126
Floyd, Carlisle 151
Fokine, Mikhail 50, 52
Forrester, Maureen 48, 83
Forty-second Street 152